Illicit Medicines in the Global South

I0885356

This book investigates pharmaceutical regulation and the public health issue of fake or illicit medicines in developing countries.

The book analyses the evolution of pharmaceutical capitalism, showing how the entanglement of market and health interests has come to shape global regulation. Drawing on extensive fieldwork in India, Kenya, and Europe, it demonstrates how large pharmaceutical companies have used the fight against fake medicines to serve their strategic interests and protect their monopolies, sometimes to the detriment of access to medicines in developing countries. The book investigates how the contemporary dynamics of pharmaceutical power in global markets have gone on to shape societies locally, resulting in more security-oriented policies. These processes highlight the key consequences of contemporary "logistical regimes" for access to health.

Providing important insights on how the flows of commodities, persons, and knowledge shape contemporary access to medicines in the developing countries, this book will be of considerable interest to policy makers and regulators, and to scholars and students across sociology, science and technology studies, global health, and development studies.

Mathieu Quet is a Senior Research Fellow in Sociology at Institut de Recherche pour le Développement, Ceped, Université de Paris, France. His current research focuses on the entanglements of science, technology, and development in postcolonial contexts.

Routledge Global Health Series

Series Editors: Nana K. Poku and Jane Freedman

This timely series provides robust and multi-disciplinary assessments of the actors and dynamics shaping the health of humanity under globalized and still globalizing conditions. Books in the series come from a range of disciplinary perspectives in order to address the complex interactions of human and natural systems and the roles of governments and international organizations in protecting the health of their citizens.

The series welcomes full proposals, outlines and general queries on all themes and issues pertinent to global health. This includes medical, political, sociological and economic perspectives on health, health governance and health finance; poverty and insecurity; the prevention and treatment of important but under-researched diseases; gender and health; the implications of global pandemics; and the varieties and challenges posed by the growing, worldwide expectation of some form/degree of Universal Health Coverage.

The Politics of Surveillance and Response to Disease Outbreaks
The New Frontier for State and Non-State Actors
Edited by Sara E. Davies and Jeremy R. Youde

HIV/Aids and the South African State
Sovereignty and the Responsibility to Respond
Annamarie Bindenagel Šehović

Living with HIV and Dying with Aids
Diversity, Inequality and Human Rights in the Global Pandemic
Lesley Doyal with Len Doyal

Civil Society Organizations and the Global Response to HIV/AIDS
Julia Smith

Illicit Medicines in the Global South
Public Health Access and Pharmaceutical Regulation
Mathieu Quet

For more information about this series, please visit: www.routledge.com/Global-Health/book-series/ASHSER-1232

Illicit Medicines in the Global South

Public Health Access and Pharmaceutical Regulation

Mathieu Quet

Routledge
Taylor & Francis Group
LONDON AND NEW YORK

First published 2022
by Routledge
2 Park Square, Milton Park, Abingdon, Oxon OX14 4RN

and by Routledge
605 Third Avenue, New York, NY 10158

Routledge is an imprint of the Taylor & Francis Group, an informa business

Translation from French Edition: *Impostures pharmaceutiques. Médicaments illicites et luttes pour l'accès à la santé* by © Editions La Découverte, Paris, 2018.

British Library Cataloguing-in-Publication Data
A catalogue record for this book is available from the British Library

Library of Congress Cataloging-in-Publication Data
Names: Quet, Mathieu, author.
Title: Illicit medicines in the Global South : public health access and pharmaceutical regulation / Mathieu Quet.
Other titles: Impostures pharmaceutiques. English.
Description: Abingdon, Oxon ; New York, NY : Routledge, 2022. | "Translation from French Edition: Impostures pharmaceutiques. Médicaments illicites et luttes pour l'accès à la santé by © Editions La Découverte, Paris, 2018." | Includes bibliographical references and index.
Identifiers: LCCN 2021019329 (print) | LCCN 2021019330 (ebook)
Subjects: LCSH: Pharmaceutical industry–Government policy–Developing countries. | Product counterfeiting–Law and legislation–Developing countries. | Drug control–Developing countries. | Drugs–Standards–Developing countries. | Black market–Developing countries. | Drug accessibility–Government policy–Developing countries. | Public health–Developing countries.
Classification: LCC HD9674.D44 Q73 2022 (print) | LCC HD9674.D44 (ebook) | DDC 338.4/76151–dc23
LC record available at https://lccn.loc.gov/2021019329
LC ebook record available at https://lccn.loc.gov/2021019330

ISBN: 978-1-032-04815-4 (hbk)
ISBN: 978-1-032-04814-7 (pbk)
ISBN: 978-1-003-19476-7 (ebk)

DOI: 10.4324/9781003194767

Typeset in Times New Roman
by Newgen Publishing UK

Contents

Illustrations

Figures

Table

Acknowledgements

This book is the English translation of a previously published French manuscript. It goes without saying that it would not exist today without the work of its main translator, Donald Moerdijk, to whom I am grateful. The English version being published a few years after the French one, I took the liberty to add some changes and revisions, which had become necessary in the light of the many discussions I had after the publication of *Impostures pharmaceutiques*. For all their help, their comments (sometimes harsh!) and their generous support, I would like to thank the many people who have taken part in this great journey, before, during, and after.

And to begin with, the wonderful team who reviewed the text when it was still in the making as a "habilitation à diriger des recherches": Maurice Cassier (who was the *garant*) and Christian Bessy, Saradindu Bhaduri, Joëlle Le Marec, Kris Peterson, and Pascale Trompette.

The original manuscript had been read by several colleagues, and in the following years I had received comments from others that helped me in rewriting this version. I want to thank them for their help in putting some order in the *flow* of ideas: Itty Abraham, Dinesh Abrol, Sara Aguiton, Marine Al Dahdah, Carine Baxerres, Valentine Becquet, Rémi de Bercegol, Soraya Boudia, Alila Brossard-Antonielli, Lydie Cabane, Fanny Chabrol, Sudip Chaudhuri, David Demortain, Alice Desclaux, Dominique Dourojeanni, Vincent Duclos, Dimitry Dugeny, Mathieu Ferry, Nicolas Fortané, Jean Foyer, Anne Gosselin, Nils Graber, Sarah Hodges, Rory Horner, Julia Hornberger, Reji K. Joseph, Koichi Kameda de Carvalho, Joan Kariuki Kungu, Nils Kessel, Mina Kleiche, Venni Krishna, Jean-Baptiste Lanne, Chloé Leclère, Ramah McKay, Anne-Marie Moulin, Etienne Nouguez, Kristin Peterson, Anne Pollock, Jessica Pourraz, François Quet, Kaushik Sunder Rajan, Yves-Marie Rault, Emilia Sanabria, Sauman Singh, Jeanne Subtil, Noémi Tousignant, Alain Vaguet, Frédéric Vandenberghe, and Jérémy Ward. Philippe Pignarre who published the French version, and Helena Hurd, Rosie Anderson, Nana K. Poku and Jane Freedman, who published the English one, deserve particular gratitude.

I also presented and put on trial several arguments during events or in academic journals. Some of the exchanges I benefited from were particularly rich and I would like to thank Julia Hornberger, Cori Hayden, and all the participants in the "Good Copy / Bad Copy" workshop held in Konstanz in December 2013; Lydie Cabane and Josiane Tantchou for the session "Sciences, techniques et politiques en Afrique" in July 2014 in Bordeaux; the group Anthropologies of African Biosciences for the conference "Dreaming of Health and Science in Africa" in June 2015 in Cambridge; Carine Baxerres and Fanny Chabrol for the session "Entre abondance et rareté: le rapport ambigu de l'Afrique au medicament" in Paris in July 2016; Parvathi Iyer, Hemant Kumar, and the Centre for Studies and Research in Science, Technology and Innovation Policy for the workshop "Emerging Challenges of Pharmaceutical Manufacturing in India" in March 2017 in Gandhinagar; Carine Baxerres and the participants to the conference "Régulations, Marché, Santé" in Ouidah in March 2018; René Gerrets and Patricia Kingori for the workshop "Genuine Fakes" in May 2018 in Amsterdam. I also owe a particular thanks to Maurice Cassier and the participants of the seminar "Produire et innover au sud" which has been a great source of inspiration. I also thank the following journals for having published some of the ideas that feed this book: *Sciences Sociales et Santé*; *Revue d'Anthropologie des Connaissances*; *Journal of Cultural Economy*; *Sociologie du Travail*; *Theory, Culture and Society*; *Science, Technology and Society*; *International Sociology*; and the *Journal of African Cultural Studies.*

In India and Kenya, I received great help from institutions as well as people, the Centre des Sciences Humaines de Delhi, the Institut Français de Pondichéry, the Institut Français de Recherche en Afrique à Nairobi, Marion Asego, Guy Attewell, Basudeb Chaudhuri, Marie-Aude Fouéré, Marie-Emmanuelle Pommerolle, Christian Thibon, as well as Othmane Chaoui and Caroline Vigot, have been fantastic hosts and have given me great support. From 2015 to 2019, I was a guest faculty member at the Centre for Studies in Science Policy of Jawaharlal Nehru University and the members of the centre helped me feel at home: Saradindu Bhaduri, Madhav Govind, Venni V. Krishna, Anup Kumar Das, as well as Abha Arya and my dear friends of the "Digital Studies in the Global South" group (Rajiv Mishra, Sohan Prasad Sha, Khetrimayum Monish Singh, Vidya Subramanian). Anil, Gopal, and Seema also greatly facilitated my stay in the University.

In France, Ceped and Ifris are my two families. I would like to thank in particular Rigas Arvanitis, Danièle Cavanna, Michelle Coste, and Suzanne Koublanou for their dedication to the collective existence in Ceped, and Marc Barbier and Sandrine Vernhes at Ifris. Several collective projects have also helped me shape my approach: Audrey Bochaton, Laurent Pordié, Fred Bourdier, Jean-Paul Gaudillière, Andrew McDowell, Caroline Meier zu Biesen, David Dumoulin, Mina Kleiche, Marine Al Dahdah, and Aalok Kumar have been particularly great supervisors and collaborators.

My relatives Dominique Dourojeanni, Emmanuelle Quet, François Quet, and Maurice Quet have been fantastic discussants – not always willingly – of this work that kept me busy for quite a while. And at last it must be said that not a line, not an idea that composes this book – and way more than that! – would exist without Marine.

This book is dedicated to all the people I have met during these years, sincerely committed for a better access to health, be they NGO workers, industrialists, traders, and patient activists.

Capitalism has haunted all forms of society, but as a terrifying nightmare, their panic-stricken fear of a flow that might evade their codes.

Gilles Deleuze & Felix Guattari, *L'Anti-Œdipe. Capitalisme et Schizophrénie*, Paris, 1972, p. 164 (my translation)

Introduction

Faith in fakes?

Hunting down fake medicines

To go by the news in the recent years, the hunt is on for "fake medicines" and other "falsified" medical products; developing throughout the world, it is now becoming increasingly organised. In mid-May 2013 French customs in Le Havre seized 1.2 million packets of "counterfeit" aspirin, "*the largest haul of counterfeit medicines ever made by customs in France, and in the European Union*".[1]

On 13 June 2013, the World Customs Organisation and a French anti-counterfeit taskforce, the *Institut de Recherche Anti-Contrefaçon de Médicaments* (IRACM) published the results of Operation Biyela organised in April together with the customs services of 23 African countries. This had led to the seizure of more than a billion items, including 550 million doses of illegal medicines, "*counterfeit antibiotics, anti-malarial remedies, painkillers, anti-inflammatories, counterfeit treatments for high blood-pressure and diabetes, and also illegal nutritional supplements*".[2] The World Customs Organisation underlined the sheer scale of this operation. On 27 June 2013, Interpol in turn announced the seizure of approximately ten million units of "counterfeit" medicines as a result of Operation Pangea 6, carried out in 99 countries, targeting in particular internet sites that sold medicines. According to Aline Plançon, second in command of Interpol's programme on pharmaceutical crime, the quantities impounded were double those seized in 2012 in the previous operation[3].

Apart from these operations, an increasing number of initiatives countered the circulation of illicit medicines[4]. Kenya announced, in 2015, a tripartite partnership between the non-profit *Mission for Essential Drugs and Supplies* (MEDS), the official pharmaceutical regulator, and the *US Pharmacopeial Convention* – an American organisation that sets the pharmaceutical standards that are followed in 140 countries. The aim of this partnership – set up thanks to grants from USAID, the US development body – was to improve the quality of medicines in circulation and to "*help solve the problem of proliferation of counterfeit and sub-standard medicines in Kenya*".[5] In parallel to this partnership, a dynamic technological market promises to keep track of

DOI: 10.4324/9781003194767-1

medicines: increasingly bar codes, identification numbers, and holograms are being printed on the packaging. In 2012, the most powerful economic players were encouraging such a market at the World Economic Forum, by awarding the "Young Global Leader" label to Bright Simons, a Ghanaian entrepreneur, who invented a system that tracked the movement of medicines by means of mobile phones. Yet, another indication of this anti-fake dynamic is the multiplication of legislative measures and legal provisions regulating the circulation of pharmaceutical products on various levels. The European Union devoted a directive to the circulation of falsified medicinal products in 2011[6]; Kenya passed an "anti-counterfeit" law in 2008; and India has continuously reinforced sanctions against spurious medicines providers. These initiatives have gone along a growing production of knowledge of the problem: how many of these medicinal products are currently in circulation? What impact do they have on health? And what impact on the economy? A series of articles published in the *American Journal of Tropical Medicine and Hygiene* in 2015 attracted a lot of attention, denouncing a "global pandemic" of illicit medicinal products and raising concerns on the quality of the medicines in circulation in several countries, on the basis of quality tests. Therefore, organisational, technological, legal and scientific initiatives seem to converge in a combat against the circulation of illicit medicinal products.

Concern is being voiced in various quarters: international organisations such as the World Health Organisation (WHO), Interpol, the World Customs Organisation (WCO); professional bodies (the International Nurses Association); foundations (the Jacques Chirac Foundation); private non-profit bodies financed by pharmaceutical laboratories (the Partnership for Safe Medicines, the Institute of Research Against Counterfeit Medicines); and pharmaceutical laboratories. These groups are all interested in the struggle against illicit medicinal products, although the interests they defend are not necessarily the same; and the solutions that they offer – in order to promote a world market for medicines of quality – are sometimes incompatible with one another. Yet despite their differences, the people and the groups involved, feel the same indignation at the gravity of the problem they are facing. This shows up clearly in their outrage at "affairs". In November 2014, 12 women died in India because the antibiotics they were given after being operated for sterilisation contained toxic ingredients. In 2009, a spurious painkiller contained a solvent which is used to anti-freeze, causing the death of at least 84 small Nigerian children. Not even the better-off are safe – following the death of the singer Prince, investigations revealed that he was in possession of counterfeit Fentanyl that was much stronger than the registered generic drug (he had died of an overdose). The most notorious case came up in 1995, when 50,000 counterfeit vaccines against meningitis – ascribed to the Pasteur-Mérieux laboratories and to SmithKline Beecham, but probably copied in Nigeria – led to some 2500 deaths in the Niger Republic.

Tragic incidents of this sort are by no means rare. The initiatives promoted to prevent them implicitly formulate "fake medicines" as the core problem, and put emphasis on several features. In the first place, people reporting fake medicines feel that, in recent years, the market for these products has grown enormously, both in volume and in value. The "Southern" countries are by far the most gravely affected, though the North is also threatened, due to the increasingly complex nature of distribution networks and the part played by sales on the Internet[7]. Forward estimates are frightening: the market is probably worth somewhere between 75 and 200 billion dollars, with the growth rocketing[8]. The WHO envisages a 10–30% share of the pharmaceutical market in developing countries[9]. Christophe Zimmermann, who coordinates the anti-counterfeit activities of the World Customs Organisation, has said that "*today there are more fakes on the market than real medicines. In 2007–2008 they grew by 596%*".[10] Moreover, a recent study has estimated the number of deaths of children under the age of 5 linked to consumption of sub-standard anti-malarial drugs at 122,350.[11] Anti-counterfeit crusaders tend to see all of this as a plain criminal activity, sometimes linked to older outlaw networks; its *raison d'être* is that it is less risky and more profitable than most. The head of UNODC (the UN Office on Drugs and Crime) explains this:

> *In comparison to other crimes such as drug trafficking, the production and distribution of counterfeit goods present a low-risk/high-profit opportunity for criminals. Counterfeiting feeds money-laundering and encourages corruption. There is also evidence of some involvement or overlap with drug trafficking and other serious crimes.*[12]

If we follow these statements, legislation should be introduced to punish traffic in counterfeit medicines more severely. Furthermore, since the problem is a transnational one, it is also essential to obtain collaboration, not only between the countries involved, but also with the international community in general. This collaboration should be multilateral: between countries, international organisations, the public and private sectors, private charities, and commercial entities. It would involve setting up more centralised data-gathering systems and more transparent forms of reporting – in other words, setting up a surveillance policy better adapted to the global nature of the problem. Any action is welcome, and no effort should be spared, in order to save us from the catastrophe which is threatening us: that of a world in which medicines, rather than curing people, would kill them.

In this bustle of activity one question, however, has been left open. What in fact is a "fake" medicine? There is an element of irony in the agitation surrounding the struggle against counterfeits. The question of what actually constitutes a "fake" has been "quarantined" – as though one had to suggest some lurching monster to succeed in mustering the necessary forces. The fact remains, however, that to be effective one has to understand exactly what one is fighting against. What do the various adjectives used in formulating "fake medicines" as a problem actually imply? How exactly are the surveys and estimates of the quantities of "fakes" in circulation produced? Is the issue of "fake medicines" a problem that can be understood on its own, or is it part and parcel of some broader problem: the problem of pharmaceutical quality? Some anecdotes illustrate the ambiguity of the notions in current use.

On 15 September 2015, Inspector Arun Kumar of the Delhi police was tipped off that an exchange of fake medicines had been planned at the Kanhaiya Nagar station in the urban railway network. He assembled a squad and posted it around the venue. At 19.30, in the usual bustle around the station, a certain Ashok Mittal, who hailed from Haryana, a nearby Indian state, was arrested in possession of a carton of medicines. The questioning that ensued brought to light a well-worn strategy. Ashok, 44, had left school at 16 and had never qualified as a pharmacist. This had not prevented him from putting himself across as a pharmacist and contacting potential customers on Internet. In most cases, the latter lived abroad (in the USA, Britain, or Thailand). He offered to sell them medicines and, when he received orders, passed them on to one of his agents outside Delhi to obtain supplies. The agent then bought generic medicines and put a brand label on the packaging, masking its real identity. The order was then forwarded to Ashok, who sent it to his customer by post. Some of the medicines were banned in the countries to which he sent them. Under interrogation, he revealed that he had a stock of medicines hidden in a rented apartment west of Delhi. Investigators went to check and they discovered goods worth an estimated 60 *lakh* rupees (about 80,000 euros)[13].

A few years earlier, on another continent, nurses in a clinic on the outskirts of Nairobi run by a French NGO, *Médecins sans Frontières* (MSF) – Doctors without Borders, were stupefied to discover (one morning in September 2011) that the anti-retroviral medication they were supposed to give the patients was crumbling. They immediately reported this to the central pharmacy of their organisation. This brought them a further surprise: a well-known distributor had supplied the defective medicines; he was completely in the clear with the local authorities. Shipments of the suspected medicines were immediately "quarantined" and patients were called in for checking. How could these sub-standard medicines have come into the hands of MSF? Investigators first turned to the manufacturer of Zidolam-N, the medicine in question, which was central to the struggle against AIDS. Based in India, the manufacturer was also a recognised producer, who exported throughout the world. At a crisis meeting between MSF, the producer and the distributor, it turned out that batches of medicines coming from the manufacturer and delivered to MSF contained more medicines than usual. They had passed through the hands of an intermediary, a local Kenyan NGO, before being sold to the distributor who had supplied MSF. This raised strong suspicion that the goods had been falsified. Ongoing investigation gradually revealed that the medicines had been bought from their Indian producer quite long beforehand and had passed through the hands of several agents (foundations, NGOs) before being bought by the final distributor. In the course of the process, the medicines had reached their dates of expiry. One of the go-betweens in the chain had simply had them repackaged and, mixing them with more recent batches, assigned new expiry dates.[14] This meant that though the medicines were perfectly genuine, came from the proper producer, and contained the correct quantities of pharmaceutical components, they were out of date and had been registered illegally.

Our third story throws yet another light on the problem. On 10 January 2015, police in the province of Hunan arrested Lu Yong, a Chinese patient with leukaemia. He was accused of selling counterfeit medicines. A 47-year-old entrepreneur in the textile business, between 2006 and 2013, he had bought for himself and for other patients a chemotherapy treatment named Veenat, produced in India. Unregistered in China, it was a generic version of Gleevec produced by Novartis and sold at eight times the price. As it had not been registered with the Chinese authorities, its import was treated as smuggling. After his arrest, Lu Yong's story came to be publicly known and a protest movement ensued. How could one treat as a criminal someone who had merely provided at an affordable price a medication needed for survival? After the media had broadcasted the affair, early in February 2015, the Chinese authorities dropped the case and released Lu Yong. His story remained, however, an illustration of the risks involved in criminalising practices according to rules edicted by governments pressured by pharmaceutical majors.

Notions such as "fake" or "counterfeit" can thus be applied to situations of very different kinds, and to differing kinds of "bad medicines". For instance, the designation "fake" can be applied to imitations of branded products (containing or not containing proper quantities of the active ingredient), to medicines that have deteriorated (having been damaged in transport or affected by climatic conditions), and to medicines that have expired or been repackaged, or in some cases are intentional placebos (without the active ingredient or containing a lighter dosage).

The notion, however, can also be applied to medicines that, though needed for patients' survival, have been banned from a particular territory because of intellectual property rights, defined more restrictively there than elsewhere. Medicines such as these could save many lives, if only commercial negotiations between international organisations, governments, and pharmaceutical companies were not so frequently serving the interest of the most powerful companies. In the stories I have told, the medicines involved share two common traits: (1) they have not been approved by the regulatory bodies of the territories involved; and (2) they have not respected national or international standards. But these features are not enough to characterise the public problem with precision. As a result, the struggle against illicit medicines has raised many debates. Most notably, it has been denounced by various institutions – international NGOs, professional associations, governments, and local groups – as being guided by the commercial strategies of major pharmaceutical companies in the Northern hemisphere. Under the pretext of fighting against "counterfeits" or "fakes", commercial interests might even jeopardise access to medication in Southern countries. Ellen 't Hoen, a former director of the MSF access campaign has objected to the importance attributed to counterfeiting; to her, the issue of ensuring global access to essential treatments is far more serious. She denounces the sheer vagueness of notions such as "falsified" or "counterfeit" – when applied to medicines, they can easily distract attention from the key issue, which is maintaining access to quality pharmaceuticals.[15] According to her, efforts to combat counterfeiting and falsification often play out in favour of the promoters of the most expensive brands and can have an adverse effect on the access of generic medicines of quality to the public.

What is actually a "fake" or "falsified" medicine? What is a "counterfeit" remedy? By virtue of what standards, what laws, what concept of public health are medicines considered illicit? Does combating the use of these medicines actually promote public health or does it merely serve to hide unpresentable commercial strategies? Does it promote the interest of the "Big Pharma" or are genuine medical problems involved?

Unfolding the conflicts

My aim in this book is to answer these questions. I will attempt to clarify the notion of illicit medicine, to show how exactly it is used in the course of public debate, and what is at stake. In order to do this, I have adopted in the first place a strategy that is traditional in the sociology of science and technology; I have started by studying the conflicts surrounding policies, carrying out what is known as controversy analysis. This approach has been applied in many fields and in particular, the anthropology and history of science and the socio-anthropology of health.[16] Initially, it was focused on the systematic analysis of controversies in progress, without attempting to decide who was right and who was wrong. This led to a realisation that it is not possible to separate the procedures of scientific proof from the networks that support particular ideas raised in the course of the debate or values invoked. Controversy analysts were joined by other sociologists interested in situations of conflict and problems of justification; their method revealed broader dynamics of social construction.[17] A conflict always provides an occasion to observe a confrontation between different ways of organising the world and often ends up by stabilising – temporarily – a particular social order. Thus conflicts and controversies frequently act as microscopes focused on social order: they bring out in surprising relief the dynamics at work in the construction of social worlds and the imbrication of science with society.

Policies combating illicit medicines have come up against a good deal of protest, providing researchers with opportunities to improve their understanding of how a society gets built. This is why I have opted to begin my study with an analysis of a controversy. This well-tried technique has provided a convenient starting point. Soon, however, I found myself in unexplored territory. In the first place, the controversies raised by policies combating illicit medicines are by no means easy to describe – being far too "global" and too "transnational".

Former controversy analyses dealt with confrontations between pairs of scientists, for example, Thomas Hobbes and Robert Boyle; Louis Pasteur and Félix Pouchet. These scientists were experts at mobilising social groups to support them and one key of the analysis consisted in describing the networks of people that were constituted around them, together with the concomitant knowledge and techniques.[18] But in these classic cases, the analyst had the advantage of "having at hand" the main characters involved. In today's conflicts – over genetically modified organisms, the nuclear industry, or climate change – the classic approach no longer suffices. It does not adequately take into account the multiple personalities involved, the variations in scale, the various forms of knowledge, and the differences between time frames.[19] Several authors have shown that, today the investigation has to be opened up to transnational and global spaces if a controversy is to be fully understood.[20] This pleads in favour of finding other ways to approach conflicts and other ways of telling stories. In my case, it led me to investigate in India and Kenya, and on the circulations "between" the two countries. Meanwhile, the geographical shift and methodological constraints have become a source of further questioning and suggested more new approaches.

Besides the transnational nature of the conflict, a second reason led me to extend my methodological approach. Using the prism of controversy analysis to view the debate on counterfeit medicines, I was able to tidy up two areas: the interests of the various agents involved and the competing ideas on what a false or illicit pharmaceutical actually is. In the course of my investigation, however, I realised that the controversy analysis could provide only a point of entry. It could show up the stakes that are essential in the eyes of the various agents, who stress, defend, and denounce them, while reformulating and displacing them. But these stakes, if taken seriously, require yet further analyses, opening up fresh fields for research. In that regard, it seems that a controversy should always be "unfolded". Controversies bring out problems and stakes that were not yet visible, showing up counter–narratives that cut across the dominant discourse. However, to understand fully these new problems, stakes, and narratives, it is not enough simply to report the progress of the conflict; one must also take account of its constantly changing horizons and emerging dimensions. New modes of investigation have to be developed.

Focusing attention on a particular controversy, the researcher thus discovers that he has to go into its foundations. One would think that the end was in sight – and that it sufficed to show the agents involved, give their reasons, and clarify their motivation to some extent – but would now find that one has taken on new responsibilities. The controversy has not been confined to the "space" or "arena" in which it initially broke out. One has to now "unfold" new dimensions and explore them, instead of merely narrating a linear progression. The metaphor of "unfolding" enables one to keep one's focus on an essential trait of controversy: it contains within its "folds" the entire social world and its underlying order. Only by unfolding it can the researcher reveal the society that this world envelops.

The demonstration has to proceed in an unconventional way, integrating as far as possible the shifts in perspective brought about by observation and interaction in the field. In my case, this has taken me to a number of fronts of conflict in different spaces or arenas of controversy. I found myself in the company of producers of medicines in India and of pharmacists in Kenya; in offices of copyright consultants, of detectives tracking illicit goods; in laboratories checking the quality of medicines, and of customs officers investigating storage sites. The method could be described as a sort of *gleaning*[21]; it consists in "picking up leftovers": paying attention to problems raised by conflicts as they come up, and generally as they are raised in discourse on the terrain. First and foremost, however, it is driven by a need to locate the investigation in the specific geographical motion to which it has been called by developments that demand closer examination. When one practices this sort of "gleaning", one can never confine oneself to a particular place or approach; on the contrary, one has to remain open to needs that show up from day to day in the course of encounters.

India and Kenya, laboratories of pharmaceutical mutations

This approach led me to pay particular attention to a crucial dimension of the problem of illicit medicines: its diffuse geographical distribution, which can be described as "multi-sited".[22] To document the problem of illicit medicines, one has to leave the "developed" world and go elsewhere. Two countries, India and Kenya, provide a better grasp of the stakes involved. Both have been affected by debates on illicit medicines. When I began my survey, both countries were involved, on different levels, in conflicts linked to policies countering illicit pharmaceuticals. India was involved when European customs officials who suspected counterfeiting seized cargoes of Indian generic medicines; the Indian firms involved denied the allegations. Kenya was involved because legislation on counterfeiting was jeopardising its supply of generic anti-retroviral drugs, and seropositive citizens had applied to Kenyan courts to have the law suspended. This was why I started out with these two countries. Before long, however, their social and economic traits and the history of their mutual relationships gave my fieldwork choice an unexpected complexity, making it more problematic.

India and Kenya provided contrasting examples of what is at stake in pharmaceutical policies. Both countries are key sites from where to observe the emergence of contemporary pharmaceutical practice; at the same time, their respective situations are very different. India has become a global operator in the pharmaceutical field: third-largest producer in the world in terms of both value and volume, and over the recent years, it has recorded a growth of 12–15%. It has more than 2000 pharmaceutical companies on its registers and it is now moving increasingly into high value-added activities such as biotechnology. The industry began to take off in the 1970s and 1980s with financial and legal support from a government that was pursuing a policy of rapid development. The Kenyan pharmaceutical industry, on the other hand, is more recent; it still plays a regional rather than a global role. In Kenya, there are only about forty manufacturers who provide about 30% of the local market; they export to the members of the East African Community, and also to West African countries such as Nigeria and Ghana. Kenyan pharmaceutical manufacturers, however, are still facing many obstacles. There is, for example, no governmental policy of support for local industry; access to raw materials is problematic and manufacturers face harsh competition from foreign firms. India and Kenya offer, therefore, two complementary examples of the stakes involved in pharmaceutical production in the global South. India is promoting a powerful industry, capable of competing with European rivals, armed with innovative intellectual property strategies. Whereas Kenya has an industry that is still vulnerable and, though it does have some export capacity, still has trouble supplying local demand; it is also dependant on imported raw materials.

I have no intention, however, of confining my study to a *comparative* analysis of two pharmaceutical industries and their markets. There is a strong link between the two countries. Over recent years, trade between them has grown significantly, as have Indian investments in Kenya, in telecommunications, petrochemicals, and other chemical products, in flower production in particular; and the two countries have signed engineering contracts and agreements in the field of energy. Since 2008, and in particular since the beginning of the financial crisis, trade between the two counties has expanded rapidly, growing from 1.4 billion USD in 2008 to 3.9 billion in 2012 (according to official Indian trade statistics). India has exported to Kenya pharmaceuticals, steel products, machinery, yarn, and vehicles. Kenya has supplied India with soda ash, vegetables, tea, leather, and scrap metal. It should be pointed out, however, that the balance of trade is amply in India's favour and that Kenya is largely dependant on Indian goods. India is Kenya's sixth most important trade partner and its most important supplier. The Dr. Reddy's, Cadila, and Cipla pharmaceutical companies are well established in Kenya. The relationship, as far as pharmaceuticals are concerned, is one of dependency and emulation. For Kenyan producers, India is both a model and a redoubtable competitor.

The two countries have been in contact for a long time. Relations between East Africa and South Asia date back to at least the 15th and 16th centuries, when the Swahili coast (the present Uganda, Kenya, and Tanzania) began to increase its trade with India. When the British colonised the East African region, tens of thousands of Indian workers were brought across as labourers; many of those who remained after decolonisation are active today in the Kenyan pharmaceutical sector. The situation of Indians in Kenya is symptomatic of the nature of relations between countries in the global South, which are very sensitive. The pharmaceutical industry suggests an overall picture of the development of trade in a post-colonial situation and understanding it requires more than mere comparison; it calls for an investigation of connections and circulations. As readers of this book will find, India, Kenya, and the conflicts involving the two countries, are all bound up with trade. But the very goods that circulate between them are themselves complex objects that can tell us a lot if we take the trouble to examine them. It is this complex relationship between the two countries that will provide us with the elements essential to any formulation of the problem of illicit medicines. And my bet is that understanding global health issues, as well as more general globalisation processes, requires such a kind of "circulatory and yet situated" analysis.

The main issue in my investigation (beyond the analysis of the pharmaceutical controversy) is thus not only the science and technology involved – researchers working in the STS (science, technology, society) fields are used to handling that – but also the multiple economic, geopolitical, and cultural factors that shape S&T issues. Here research objectives are a lot more difficult to attain. My aim should be to include scientific and technological concerns (such as the regulation of pharmaceutical products) in a study that must remain sensitive to technology, to colonial history, to strategies of economic domination, and to monopoly on a global scale; to circulations between countries of the global South; to power relations between governments and industries; and to inter-cultural relations between ethnic and religious minorities, and other social groups. This is the complex, ever-changing challenge to which this book tries to respond.[23] Attempting to deal with it, we will see that illicitness is neither a simple technical problem, nor the result of some smugglers' deeds. It enlights the transformations of global capitalism and the way in which the latter entangles healthcare with commodity flows, biomedical standards, and strategies of control.

Outline of the book

With regards to the composition of this book, it can be put in the following terms. The enquiry of the combined transformations of public health, technological development, and market regimes, takes illicit medicines as a starting point. The opening chapter of this book puts the issues raised by illicit medicines (also known as "fake medicines") as a public problem in perspective, studying transnational conflicts caused by the fight against these medicines. In this regard, Chapter 1 sets out the stakes and the methodology for the analyses developed in the following chapters. The investigation of conflicts raised by anti-counterfeiting struggles allows to unpack the object defined as an "illicit medicine", and it leads to explore three main features of this problem in the rest of the book. I will formulate these features as a series of hypotheses, each of them offering a counter-narrative to the dominant interpretation of illicit medicines as a problem of criminal activity.

The first hypothesis to investigate (explored in Chapters 2 and 3) is that the problem of illicit medicines is linked to global changes in industrial geography and in practices of drug distribution. Illicit medicines are an outcome of reconfigurations of production and distribution and of the new balances that this implies. Strictly speaking, it is not so much the public problem of illicit medicines that is "new", as the way we think about it. Illicit medicines, as a problem, take place in a world market – a market in which the capture of value is being shifted to the distribution sector and to the intermediary operations involved in the circulation of pharmaceuticals.

The second hypothesis (explored in Chapters 4 and 5) is that the public problem of illicit medicines is part of a larger public health history, involving particular ways of framing transnational public health issues in a context of reconfiguration of public health. I highlight the different phases of this formulation and I describe how the problem of illicit medicines has been gradually put into shape by interventions of various sorts. Market strategies, concerns over the management of "global health", concerns created by statistics and sharpened by various incidents, all combine to build the problem as one of "security" – health security as well as trade security. This shift, however, not only entails a change of discourse; it is also embodied in actual practices of supervision, management, and control of the circulation of medicines. The problem of "illicit medicines" is therefore shaped by a combination of discursive practices and surveillance interventions supposed to bring "security" through the integration of policing, marketing, and technological activities to those of health governance, all within an overall context of anxiety concerning global health.

The third hypothesis (explored in Chapters 6 and 7) is that the public problem of illicit medicines is a symptom of tensions lying at the heart of the current *pharmaceutical logistic regime*. Whereas on the one hand this regime contributes to the expansion, multiplication, and diversification of flows of pharmaceuticals; but on the other hand, it maintains a very tight control of these flows, their trajectories, and their classification – a trend that can be described as a colonisation of the trajectories involved. Groups and individuals challenge this colonisation by diverting flows, challenging the coding imposed on them, reconnecting flows that have been separated, and connecting flows that have not been unauthorised, or simply stopping them. In cases like these, the existence of illicit medicines reflects deep-seated tensions in the logistics regime between the release and the control of flows, and between the imposition of trajectories and the ways people and things appropriate or inhabit them.

But let me start by setting out the facts.

Notes

1 AFP Rennes. (2013). Plus d'un million de sachets d'aspirine de contrefaçon saisis au Havre, un record. *La voix du Nord*, 25 May.

2 Berber, M. (2013). Faux médicaments: L'opération Biyela révèle l'ampleur de la fraude sur le continent. *rfi.fr*, 13 June. Retrieved from www.rfi.fr/afrique/20130613-faux-medicaments-operation-biyela-revele-ampleur-fraude-le-continent/.

3 AFP & Lefigaro.fr. (2013). Millions de médicaments contrefaits saisis. *Lefigaro.fr*, 27 June, disponible. Retrieved from www.lefigaro.fr/flash-eco/2013/06/27/97002-20130627FILWWW00452-millions-de-medicaments-contrefaits-saisis.php.

4 As we shall presently see, naming the problem is itself problematic. Following discussions with my colleagues Laurent Pordié and Audrey Bochaton, I am using the notion "illicit" to cover all issues concerning unauthorised circulation of medicines, and also to highlight both the legal and moral aspects of the overall problem. When it is necessary to designate the type of irregularity involved with more precision (e.g., expiry, substandard quality, etc.), I will use more specific terms.

5 Dr. Jane Masiga. Head of operations, MEDS, quoted in The Standard Reporter (2015). Alliance to fight counterfeit malaria drugs in Kenya. *The Standard*, 3 May.

6 Directive 2011/62/EU of the European parliament and of the council of 8 June 2011. *Official Journal of the European Union*, 1 July 2011. Retrieved from http://ec.europa.eu/health/files/eudralex/vol-1/dir_2011_62/dir_2011_62_en.pdf.

7 I often use the terms *North* and *South*, despite their vagueness and the fact that they can mask internal differences and tensions, e.g., between India and Kenya, both countries that are part of an overall "South". The terms should be read as default expressions. My intention is to highlight the contrast between the highly industrialised countries, most of which are in the Northern hemisphere and those in the Southern hemisphere that are still emerging and developing their industries.

8 Mackey T. K., & Liang B. A. (2013). Improving global health governance to combat counterfeit medicines: A proposal for a UNODC-WHO-Interpol trilateral mechanism, *BMC.*

9 WHO. (2006). *Counterfeit medicines, fact sheet revised.* 14 November. Retrieved from www.who.int/medicines/services/counterfeit/impact/ImpactF_S/en/.

10 Christophe Zimmermann cited in John Irish. (2010). Customs group to fight $200 bln bogus drug industry. *Reuters*, 10 June.

11 Renschler J. P., Walters, K. M., Newton, P. N., & Laxminarayan, R. (2015). Estimated under-five deaths associated with poor-quality antimalarials in sub-Saharan Africa. *The American Journal of Tropical Medicine and Hygiene*, 92/6_Suppl, June, pp. 119–126.

12 UNODC. (2014). New UNODC campaign raises consumer awareness of links between organized crime and 250 billion a year counterfeit business. *Press Release*, 14 January 2014. Retrieved from www.unodc.org/unodc/en/press/releases/2014/Januaryl/new-unodc-campaign-raises-consumer-awareness-of-links-between-organized-crime-and-250-billion-a-year-counterfeit-business.html.

13 Deputy-Commissioner of Police, District of North-West Delhi. (2015). Big racket of fake medicines busted by AATS/NWD. *Press Release*, 21 September. Retrieved from http://59.180.234.21:8787/Press_Release_Details_iframe.aspx?cid=UhmuTuGOAXU=.

14 Cohn, J., von Schoen-Angerer, T., Jambert, E., Arreghini, G., & Childs, M. (2013). When falsified medicines enter the supply chain: Description of an incident in Kenya and lessons learned for rapid response. *Journal of Public Health Policy*, 34, pp. 22–30, January.

15 't Hoen, E., & Pascual, F. (2015). Counterfeit medicines and substandard medicines: Different problems requiring different solutions, *Journal of Public Health Policy,* Advance online publication, 16 July.

16 Bloor, D. (1976). *Knowledge and social imagery*. London: Routledge; Collins, H. M. (1985). *Changing order: Replication and induction in scientific practice*. Londres: Sage; Shapin, S., & Schaffer, S. (1993). *Léviathan et la pompe à air*, Paris: La Découverte [1985]; Callon, M., & Latour, B. (dir.). (1982). *La science telle qu'elle se fait*. Paris: Pandore; See also: Pestre, D. (2007). L'analyse de controverses dans l'étude des sciences depuis trente ans. Entre outil méthodologique, garantie de neutralité axiologique et politique. *Mil Neuf Cent. Revue D'Histoire Intellectuelle*, 25, pp. 29–43; Fassin, D. (2006). Quand les corps se souviennent. Expériences et politiques du sida en Afrique du Sud. Paris: La Découverte.

17 Boltanski, L., & Thévenot, L. (1991). *De la justification. Les économies de la grandeur*. Paris: Gallimard.

18 Latour, B. (1984). *Les microbes, guerre et paix*. Paris : Métailié; Shapin, S., & Schaffer, S. (1993). *Léviathan et la pompe à air*. Paris: La Découverte [1985].

19 Foyer, J. (2010). Il était une fois la bio-révolution: Nature et savoirs dans la modernité globale. Paris: Presses Universitaires de France.

20 Aykut, S., & Dahan, A. (2015). *Gouverner le climat? 20 ans de négociations internationales*. Paris: Presses de Sciences Po; Latour, B. (2015). *Face à Gaïa. Huit conférences sur le nouveau régime climatique*. Paris: La Découverte; Aykut, S. C., Foyer, J. (2017). In E. Morena (Ed.), *Globalising the Climate. COP21 and the climatisation of global debates*. Londres: Routledge.

21 On rereading the first version of this work, I discovered that Luc Boltanski and Arnaud Esquerre also used the metaphor of *gleaning* to describe their method. I happily join their parade of gleaners! Boltanski, L., & Esquerre, A. (2017). *Enrichissement. Une critique de la marchandise*. Paris: Gallimard.

22 Marcus, G. E. (1995). Ethnography in/of the world system: The emergence of multi-sited ethnography, *Annual Review of Anthropology*, 24, pp. 95–117.

23 Dumoulin Kervran, D., Kleiche-Dray, M., & Quet, M. (2017). Les sts ont-elles un sud? Penser les sciences dans/avec les suds. *Revue d'Anthropologie des Connaissances*, 11/3, pp. 423–454; translated in English: Dumoulin Kervran, D., Kleiche-Dray, M., Quet, M. (2019). Going south. How STS could think science in and with the south? *Tapuya, Latin American Science, Technology and Society*, 1/1, pp. 280–305.

1 In the beginning, a conflict

December 2009, Nairobi, Kenya: Groups of seropositive patients and activists advocating better access to medication are demonstrating angrily in the city. Armed with loudhailers and whistles, brandishing banderols and shouting slogans, they took to the streets in order to defend their right to life, a fundamental and inalienable right enshrined in the Kenyan constitution. They protest against a recent law passed by the Kenyan government and destined to organise the fight against counterfeit products in order to enhance consumers' safety. The protesters' determination, the strength of their opposition to the law intrigue the passers-by, some of whom, more curious or daring than the others come closer to the group and ask, part sceptical, part hesitant: "Excuse me … what is the meaning of this?"

The way Kenyans know it, that is through newspapers and radio, personal experience or listening to friends and family members, counterfeiting is today plaguing Kenya. "Fake" and "counterfeit" products, smuggled goods are everywhere and continuously interfere with markets that most citizens would like to see less hostile. When your consumption world is populated with fake mobile phones, fake solar batteries, spurious automobile spare parts, together with adulterated alcohol, substandard fertilizers, trafficked milk, and ATMs that deliver fake banknotes, even the simplest purchase is rarely harmless. Consuming gets risky. You learn how to become constantly suspicious, noticing the markers of copy, smelling of fraud; but you also wait for tranquility to come, sometimes even impatiently. And when one promises it to you, you already breathe more easily. How then a law supposed to get rid of such a scourge as counterfeiting could be more dangerous than the evil it is fighting against? The question sums up, in essence, the embarrassment of by-standers.

As if the situation was not complicated enough the demonstrators are not protesting only against the Kenyan government. Carrying banderols reading "*Europe! Hands off our medicines!*", they march from the Ministry of Health to the offices of the European Union (EU).[1] They also protest against some rich countries' negotiations over counterfeiting, and against a free trade agreement between India and the EU. The situation certainly gets hard to understand, even with all the will in the world. Not only do these activists

DOI: 10.4324/9781003194767-2

oppose a law that most Kenyans would see favourably, but their claims place under the same umbrella local laws and agreements no one has heard of and negotiated in remote areas. How could one take their side and stand up with them, whereas one does not get the reasons of their movement and gets the impression not to agree?

What most people coming across the protestors ignore is that the demonstrations are actually part of an international campaign against negotiations on the Anti-Counterfeiting Trade Agreement (ACTA) by the EU, the United States of America (USA), and Japan, but also against the EU–India Free Trade Agreement (FTA). Kenyan activists added their own claims to this campaign, for the anti-counterfeiting fight directly involves them, endangering their access to health. In order to understand their anger, one needs to tell how anti-counterfeit policies have raised international opposition instead of being praised by everyone; one also needs to show how this movement has brought to light the similarities between policies that first seemed to differ. Anti-counterfeit policies are neither neutral nor unequivocal. They mobilise conceptions of science and market that the activists are contesting. It is therefore crucial to clarify these conceptions, but also the alternatives that have been built by protestors. Once this done, one might better understand the reasons why activists took to the streets and even share some of their indignation.

The multiplication of anti-counterfeit policies

To a large extent, it is mainly a single word that has led to recent conflicts over policies of struggle against illicit medicines: the word is "*counterfeit*". Counterfeiting consists in reproducing a copyrighted object without the agreement of the holder of the rights, for example, the unauthorised reproduction of a logo. The swoosh used by a famous sports brand, the green crocodile that gives so much value to tee-shirts, the apple that one would see on prohibitively expensive mobile phones or computers: their unauthorized copy can be severely punished. In day-to-day usage, however, the term designates a product considered to be false, illicit, or of poor quality. From the outset, the term is therefore ambiguous. Technically, it refers to intellectual property and copyright disputes, but in general it is used to qualify a wide array of illicit practices.[2] In the case of pharmaceuticals, this makes the regulator's task particularly difficult. On the one side, it is necessary to assess pharmaceutical quality and to point to objects which are not respecting standards; on the other side, resorting to the notion of counterfeiting might lead one to reduce the problem to an intellectual property concern, thus raising hurdles for the circulation of legitimate medicines. The connected issues of counterfeiting as a practice and of abusive use of this term have therefore been discussed for long by the health authorities of various countries.[3]

Although public health institutions had managed to keep a certain distance with "counterfeiting", at the turn of the 21st century the notion had taken on a new importance. During those years, an increasing number of international organisations and of governments have resorted to the notion of "counterfeiting" to characterize the fight against illicit medicines. The public health concern for medicines that do not conform to specifications gradually became an "*anti-counterfeit*" battle. The notion spread through international institutions and the media under the pressure of lobbying groups. The fight against counterfeiting allows large firms to promote their intellectual property interests and they have been involved for a long time in this activity. The global anti-counterfeiting Group was created in 1998 with the aim of promoting the interests of its members at the international scale and it gathers multiple anti-counterfeiting institutions.

Such lobbying eventually showed some results. In the field of public health, one of its consequences was the creation of a working group, the *International Medical Products Anti-Counterfeiting Taskforce* (IMPACT), under the aegis of the World Health Organization (WHO) – even though it had not been ratified by the assembly of member countries. This was announced in Rome in February 2006. The WHO "Rome declaration" and the acronym IMPACT explicitly endorsed the formulation of the problem of illicit medicines in terms of counterfeiting, underscoring the importance attached to intellectual property. The focus was on counterfeiting, rather than on other non-standard forms of production or circulation (such as quality defects, expiry, or non-registration). The objectives assigned to the IMPACT group were to improve cooperation in the battle against counterfeit medicines, to organise the exchange of information, to propose technical and administrative tools, and to encourage coordination of various initiatives.[4] In setting up IMPACT, the WHO took a strong stance on counterfeit pharmaceuticals. During this period, other international organisations also set up study groups on counterfeiting: in June 2006, for example, the World Customs Organization (WCO) approved the launch of a standards project, SECURE, to bolster protection of intellectual property. Various other initiatives also marked the gradual imposition of an anti-counterfeit terminology on the battle against the illicit circulation of medicines.

These policies prolonged initiatives on intellectual property dating from the 1980s, and in a way, the word "counterfeiting" only manifested the renewal of monopoly strategies led by multinational firms. For the past three decades, pharmaceutical issues have given rise to virulent conflicts on the international stage. The Uruguay Round negotiations that ended in 1994 produced the Agreement on Trade-Related aspects of Intellectual Property Rights (TRIPS), with the central objective of setting up an international regime of intellectual property. These negotiations formed one of the main treaties that set up the World Trade Organization (WTO). The application of the TRIPS was controversial. Under certain conditions, the clauses opened up a possibility for countries to produce or import copies of medicines irrespectively of patents or licensing. These "flexibilities" (the term used in the agreement) gave governments, especially those of the least developed countries, the option to adapt the agreement in the interest of public health. Until 2001, however, it proved difficult to have these flexibilities accepted. An important episode was a case brought at the turn of the century by 39 pharmaceutical firms against the South African government, which had legislated in favour of the use of flexibilities in 1997. This was no doubt only a momentary development, but an important one, at a time – between 1995 and 2001 – when there were repeated disputes between governments, firms, international organisations, and non-governmental organisations (NGOs) over intellectual property in the context of a dramatic AIDS epidemic[5]. In April 2001, the firms dropped their case and in November the Doha declaration reasserted the importance of protecting public health from interference by copyright holders; it also confirmed the right of governments to avail themselves of TRIPS flexibilities.

Whereas the Doha declaration can be seen as a defeat for the Northern industry in the battle for flexibilities, the anti-counterfeiting fight has emerged as another strategy to gain ground on the battlefield. Nevertheless, anti-counterfeit policies took some time to get in place and health access activists did not oppose them right away. Until 2008, anti-counterfeit policies were rarely questioned in civil society. Activist groups were more concerned with other aspects of access to medicines. This lack of interest explains partly how the anti-counterfeit discourse made its way through policies as illustrated by the Kenyan case. In 2006, an activist for the right to health working in Nairobi for an NGO, Health Action International, gained access, through one of her contacts, to a bill drafted by the Kenyan government on the fight against counterfeiting. She found the text intriguing but, lacking legal expertise, sent it to a lawyer in her network. The lawyer was worried about the possible consequences of the proposed legislation on copyrights. At about the same time, a series of discussions started involving the Kenyan parliamentary committee on health, civil society organisations, and representatives of private firms.[6] The bill, however, was not strongly opposed by access advocacy groups.

> *We had the draft in our hands, and there were several indications of its dangers. We discussed this, and met with the government; it was clear that the industrialists were better informed than we were – they arrived with more recent versions of the draft! Despite this, however, it didn't worry the organisations all that much at the time.*[7]

It should be mentioned that in the period following Doha, Kenyan groups working on access to medicines were already being mobilised to oppose attempts to amend the law on industrial property that had been adopted in 2001 despite pressure from proponents of strong protective legislation. The 2001 Act, passed with the support of the Minister for Commerce and Industry at the time, Nicholas Biwott, favoured a flexible interpretation of copyright law and use of the TRIPS flexibilities.[8] Subsequently, there were several other attempts to amend the law to suit Northern firms. Amendments were proposed in 2002, concerning parallel imports, and also in 2006, but were not adopted. Activists' attention during this period was therefore focused less on the counterfeit issue than on parallel imports, copyright law, and flexibilities.

This situation made it possible for the industry to take the initiative. At the end of 2008, after two years of discussions, the anti-counterfeiting act was adopted by a parliament that was under the influence of a trade association, the Kenya Association of Manufacturers (KAM), of which a major European pharmaceutical group was a member.[9] Discussions with civil society brought about no change and the activists for access to medicines were unable to impose a satisfactory reformulation. The Act in question was intended to deal with a serious problem involving copied products and smuggling that affected many domains: not only medicines, but also mobile telephones, printer cartridges, and automobile equipments. The law defined counterfeit products, laying down principles to guide the struggle against counterfeiting and the impounding of counterfeits, and set up an Anti-Counterfeit Agency to take charge of repression of this form of crime. In the case of medicines, the law raised a technical problem. It treated as a counterfeit any medicine that had been manufactured with a view to deceit or that copied a product over which a person or enterprise already held copyrights, irrespective of where the person or enterprise in question might be. Formulated in this way, the clause could also apply to generics. Generics copy a formula over which the rights have expired. However, since the Doha declaration in 2001, it was possible for countries facing grave situations such as health crises or widespread epidemics to produce or have produced by other parties, generic versions of medicines that are still covered by patents. The Kenyan anti-counterfeit law threatened this right by considering that as long as a patent is still in force anywhere in the world, any "copy" of the patented product should be considered as counterfeit. Health access activists were then taken by surprise: under the guise of protecting public health and fighting against dangerous medicines, the industry was back in control of intellectual property.

However, criticism of anti-counterfeit policy kept coming sporadically from various quarters without anti-counterfeit policy being massively contested. In 2006, two intellectual property experts, Kevin Outterson and Ryan Smith, published an important article on anti-counterfeit policy.[10] Entitled *The Good, the Bad, and the Ugly*, it showed that the notion of counterfeit was being applied indifferently to three completely different types of medicinal products. Some of these, the "good", were recognised as being of good quality, but were barred by restrictive interpretations of copyright law. The mechanism of compulsory licensing, for example, meant that medicine produced by a firm recognised by the authorities, but not licensed by the copyright holder, would be considered a counterfeit in some geographical and juridical areas, while it remained perfectly legitimate in others. The "bad" medicines were those that counterfeited a brand and those produced by criminals. The "ugly" medicines were those that were possibly of proper quality and were usually legitimate, but were brought to the consumer through dubious or sometimes risky distribution channels. In some cases, for example, these medicines were not quite up to normal packaging standards. In these authors' view, "Ugly drugs" resulted from a circulation regime in which outsourcing is frequent whereas trade licences segment territories. For that reason, a better integration of international trade should lead to acknowledge the legitimacy of such medicines, whereas anti-counterfeit promoters tried to dismiss them. The most important factor was Intellectual Property (IP); by creating huge price differences between medicines sold in different places, IP was the main cause of the spread of counterfeit products.

Academic circles were not alone in formulating criticism. On 7 June 2007, during the G8 meeting, the international NGO Médecins sans Frontières (MSF) complained that the debate on access to medicines was being reduced systematically to the issue of counterfeiting; it called for this to be stopped.[11] MSF's argumentation was similar to that of Outterson and Smith, but laid greater stress on the occasional use of the issue of counterfeiting to distract attention from a more important issue: that of access to generics of proper quality at reasonable prices. In January 2008, the think tank South Centre, dedicated to the promotion of the interests of the global South countries, published a research paper on transformations of the law on intellectual property that questioned existing anti-counterfeit policy.[12] "Counterfeit", the authors argued, should not be confused with "generic". All of this goes to show that prior to 2008, the issue of counterfeiting was already being debated, though discussions were still sporadic, were not always relayed, and had not led to an organised protest movement. These were still "weak signals" of an impending conflict, "reverse-engineered", so to speak, after the conflict had been established in public space.[13]

Rising tensions

In the course of the year 2008, anti-counterfeit policies became the subject of a more intense debate. In Kenya, civil society groups, initially taken aback by the adoption of the law, now reacted without further delay. As of October 2008, MSF denounced a "fatal confusion" introduced by the new law and demanded its amendment, the definition of counterfeiting being far too broad and creating a risk of its application to generic medicines:

> *By erroneously extending the definition of counterfeit products to potentially include legally-manufactured generics, the 2008 Anti-Counterfeit Bill risks banning the importation of and hindering access to life-saving essential medicines, such as those used by Médecins Sans Frontières to treat people living with HIV/AIDS.*[14]

After several months of debate among the organisations about the answer to give to this law, three seropositive patients lodged a complaint in July 2009, asking for the law to be declared unconstitutional as it endangered their right to life.[15]

Anti-counterfeit policies raised oppositions within international organisations as well. In August 2008, discussion of the struggle against counterfeiting started in the WCO, also focusing on SECURE, which was denounced by certain WCO members as a means of strengthening copyright holders' position and jeopardising the circulation of generic medicines.[16] During the same period, on the occasion of the World Health Assembly held by the WHO, several speakers criticised IMPACT, pointing out a risk of conflicts of interest within the group and objecting to the policing approach that seemed implicitly to be promoted. This matter, however, was deferred to the following year.[17] As of mid-2008, the issue of the struggle against counterfeiting and its "TRIPS+" approach – going further than TRIPS in matters of intellectual property[18] – were more frequently a cause of dissentions in international organisations.

When the first protests were voiced against ACTA, EU bodies and in particular the Commission became a third site of conflict. ACTA had been negotiated on the initiative of several major powers, in particular Japan, the USA, and the EU. The aim of the agreement was to work out a legal framework and set up a governing body for the struggle against violations of intellectual property rights. The notion of counterfeiting covered a variety of cases, ranging from pharmaceutical patents to digital assets. The draft agreement came in for the first criticisms levelled by civil society in 2007 and 2008.

Last but not least, it was in India that a fourth conflict broke out, albeit initially, over a different matter. In August 2006, an announcement was made that a free trade agreement (FTA) was being mooted between India and Europe; a roadmap for the procedure was published in October 2006.[19] As of 2007/2008, desultory protests against the FTA converged at national level, bringing together a variety of groups – fishermen of the *National Fishworkers Forum*, farmers of the *Bhartiya Kisan Union*, and the *National Working Group on Patent Law,* an inter-sector think tank. These groups pointed out a number of dangers to which the negotiations exposed local populations, starting with the reduction or abolition of customs duties, which would make local farming and fishing vulnerable to foreign competition.[20] This conflict is initially unrelated to anti-counterfeit policies and is more focused upon fishery and farming than on access to medicines. However, it will play a pivotal role in the articulation of claims.

Between 2006 and 2008, several sites of conflict appeared, linked directly or indirectly to the question of counterfeiting and the combat against it: in Kenya, in international organisations such as the WHO, in the EU, and in India. These conflicts were still only loosely linked; in some cases, they were not linked at all. However, soon they would merge into a common dispute. This first phase in the swell of protest against anti-counterfeit measures culminated in December 2008 with a declaration by Pascal Lamy, Secretary-General of the WTO, explaining, in an attempt to calm the threatening storm, that *counterfeit* should not be confused with *generic.*[21] The declaration did not have a lot of effect on the controversy, which was just starting.

Seizures of medicines and firing of the conflict

Early in 2009, protests broke out when news came that European customs had seized legitimate goods. As of October 2008, several cargoes of Indian generic medicines were seized by the Dutch customs. One of these consignments consisted of 500 kg of losartan potassium bound for Brazil. Produced by Dr. Reddy's Laboratories in India, this product was covered by patents neither in India nor in Brazil. The cargo was seized at the request of an anonymous company and retained for more than a month on the grounds that it might be diverted to the European market, contravening patent law in the Union. The DuPont Company in the Netherlands held the patent for the original medicine, Cozaar. When it was proved that the goods were merely in transit, the cargo was released, but the product was sent back to India.[22] In May 2009, another cargo, in this case from India and bound for Vanuatu was seized in transit at Frankfurt, Germany. The cargo of amoxicillin was seized because a customs official suspected that it might counterfeit the brand. It was released later when the owner of the Amoxil brand admitted that there had been no violation. Eventually the goods were sent forward to Vanuatu.

Various actors, NGOs, and representatives of the Indian government denounced these seizures as abusive. As of February 2009, India and Brazil denounced the seizures to the executive committee of the WHO, to the World Forum in Davos, and to the general council of the WTO. Ensuing discussions challenged anti-counterfeit policies: the initiatives taken by WHO (IMPACT) and the World Customs Organization (WCO) (SECURE) were criticised, for example, by the Brazilian representative in a speech at the WTO on the issue of seizures, as were the TRIPS+ policies and the "*IP maximalist*" agendas.[23] The seizures had a noteworthy influence on the controversy, in making the fear of anti-counterfeit policies' consequences concrete. The EU's action depriving patients in Brazil and Vanuatu of medication on the pretext of strengthening policies of regulation showed clearly what was at stake in such policies. This was to feature in criticisms throughout the year and give a new thrust to contestation: it was in fact a turning point.[24] In the media, there was now talk of a "global controversy" a propos of the upheaval caused by the seizures.[25]

The seizures marked the point at which the various conflicts began to merge. Initially the merger was thematic. Certain actors used the seizures to show: (1) that apparently separate policies were in reality part of an overall "enforcement agenda" that was motivated more by a concern for security and policing than for public health; and (2) that these policies had directly observable effects on the circulation of medicines. As a result, as of this period the civil society actors now confronted the various anti-counterfeit narratives bluntly, seeing in them a common logic and effects. For instance, on 17 March 2009, an anti-FTA demonstration was organised in Delhi, claiming that the FTA entailed a risk of restricting access to vital medication. In a subsequent communiqué, the Forum On FTA (FOFTA) mentioned the seizures, linking them to issues raised by anti-counterfeit policies.[26] Different conflicts thus intersected in public space, linked by actors in the social movement.

The mixing was not confined to theme, however. In the *scales* of protest and on *sites* of debate, mixing also took place. International institutions such as WHO and WCO, governments, NGOs and industrial groupings also interacted, their boundaries overlapping; sites of debate multiplied, interfering with one another. The case brought before the WCO at the beginning of February, for example, triggered off a whole series of discussions on the legality of the seizures; the atmosphere was tense as further seizures had taken place.[27] New stakeholders entered the arena, such as the association of European producers of generics, who sent a letter to the European Commissioner in charge of customs.[28] This particular intervention shows up the heterogeneous nature of forms of interlocution, which now involve firms, NGOs, governments, and transnational administrations. The NGO HAI, for example, called on the EU to explain its legislation.[29] This first phase of globalisation of the controversy culminated in December 2009 with the Kenyan demonstration mentioned in the Introduction of this chapter. The demonstration mainly concerned the impact of the FTA negotiated between Europe and India. But we can now understand the meaning that it took on, in Nairobi, after the adoption of the Kenyan law and after the seizure in Europe of cargoes bound for countries of the South. Carried out by European customs authorities, these seizures made it possible for disparate conflicts to converge. They made fears tangible – the very fears expressed by NGOs such as MSF: the seizures showed the risks entailed by anti-counterfeit legislation. This was to lead to a re-composition of the whole field of contested legislation. Between 2008 and 2010, controversies on the struggle against counterfeiting gradually merged into a single stream, mixing themes of contestation, scales of action, and activist interventions. Subsequently, the controversy was to produce a firmer structuring of the movements involved.

The globalisation work

Seizures do not suffice, however, to account for the convergence of different conflicts and for the globalising of the controversy. As we have already pointed out, medicines and copyright are not really central to the conflicts taking place in India, Kenya, and the EU. In India, the issue of copyrights to medicines raised by the FTA is only one element among others: there are also protests on the fishing, the automobile, the textile, and the dairy industries. In the EU, much the same can be said of ACTA, the anti-counterfeiting trade agreement: although this agreement also covers the pharmaceutical field, the main issues involved are linked to the digital economy. In Kenya, the law on counterfeiting covers all domains and associations feel that it is not only the pharmaceutical industry that is affected by the changes proposed in the law. If we are to gain a better grasp of the globalising dynamics that are driving these conflicts, we will have to examine the work accomplished by activists in order to articulate the disputes with one another.

This work first consisted in focusing the conflict on the pharmaceutical topic. The reason for this focus is strategic in both India and Kenya. The theme of the "vital nature of medicine" is clearly more relevant internationally than fishing or than car parts. Strategic options were made by activists in order to highlight this and to use it. As a specialist of public health issues working with trade unions explains, in the case of India, the initial contestation of the FTA was not linked to medicine, but to dairy products and fisheries. The decision to orient contestation towards pharmaceutical issues was taken deliberately: as a theme, medicine and health could bring out the worldwide importance of India in the field:

> *It was an important decision for us, as we clearly saw that the protest wouldn't work well if we simply stuck to our initial themes. The world at large isn't particularly sensitive to the fate of the fishermen of Kerala. We had to come up with something better at federating opinions – and medicine was an important aspect of the negotiations.*[30]

This controversy shows that thematic choices can help to internationalise a conflict, globalising it by extending it geographically and reformulating it so as to bring in stakeholders and themes that are considered "global". The social movement aligned its demands with the political interests that were relevant on an international level[31] – in this case, the interests of public health on a worldwide scale rather than those of the Indian fishing industry. The result was a redefinition of the conflict in terms of access to medicines, India being represented as the "pharmacy of the Third World", bringing medicines to the poor, in contrast to the EU that was blocking access for purely economic reasons.[32]

These actions of redefinition cannot be understood out of their socio-historical context: that of activism in India, Kenya, and the EU. Medications are not by nature an obviously international theme any more than fishery or car parts. The special part played in the process described here can only be explained by the robust structuring, as of the 1990s, of the problem of access to medication as an outstanding international theme. The history of conflicts over access to anti-retroviral medicines ever since the end of the 20th century was an essential factor in the emergence and organisation of transnational activism.[33] Collaboration between activists had a long history, which we have already described. The work of globalisation is not merely thematic, but also organisational: organisation over time. An example: when an activist in Indian seropositive patients' movements was questioned on the subject of his organising an international demonstration in Delhi, he immediately replied that contacts had existed for a long time with Nepal, South Africa, and Korea, particularly since the rise of movements on access to generic anti-retrovirals:

> *It's easy, for years I've known ... not everyone, but lots of people in these networks in lots of different countries. Above all in Asia: Nepal, Korea, Thailand ... but also in other countries. And anyway with Internet as soon as one decides to organise something I sent out a message to everyone.*[34]

These long-standing arrangements are maintained by background work, in particular during the international conferences at which activists meet – opportunities for members of a global network to interact; by putting their local themes into the international dynamics, they keep up a common agenda. Because of this, globalisation and the convergence of conflicts should be analysed via a third mechanism: task-specialisation. This division of labour is set up between groups with different types of expertise – for example, technical, legal, communicational, and logistic.[35]

In Spring 2010, the counterfeit conflict reached another turning point. It started in April, in Kenya, when Judge Roselyne Wendoh suspended the Kenyan law. The next development came at the WHO in May, when member states took back control of anti-counterfeit policy and a new working group was set up to deal with issues concerning medicines and labelled SSFFC: "*Substandard, Spurious, Falsified, Falsely labelled, Counterfeit*" to distinguish this new approach from the previous one that was centred solely on anti-counterfeiting.[36] As of September 2010, the IMPACT group was "exiled" to Italy, where it was accommodated by the AIFA, the Italian medicinal agency.

The lull, however, was to be brief; soon a protest movement was organised to re-launch contestation. At Nairobi, Health Action International organised a meeting, inviting several Indian activists, and in particular the Lawyers' Collective, a group of legal specialists led by Anand Grover, who was also involved in the Glivec case and was special rapporteur to the UN on the right to health.[37] The objective was for the Indian activists to help the Kenyans write up their brief for the impending court case. A series of demonstrations followed coinciding with new negotiations on the FTA. In July 2010, at the International AIDS Conference in Vienna, activists "called out" Europe vociferously leading a protest action against seizures of medicines. In September, a group of seropositive patients in Delhi, the Delhi Network of Positive People (DNP+) called for signatures to a letter to the Prime Minister of India that was being sent in collaboration with MSF. Some 240 organisations soon responded to their call.[38] From 4 to 9 October 2010, an action week was organised to protest against the FTA[39]: on October 4, a demonstration in Brussels in front of the European Commission[40]; on October 6 a "Die-In" in front of the Indian Ministry of Trade[41], and an international demonstration in Delhi on October 13.[42] A second wave of demonstrations followed early in 2011.[43] It was during this period that the global dimension of the controversy reached its peak. Some stakeholders, such as the Indian authorities, were involved simultaneously in several different conflicts: negotiations on the FTA, the seizures conflict at the WTO, and criticism of IMPACT at the WHO.

These events depend on collaborations set up between organisations with different competencies, each originally relevant to a particular country or field of action; the conflict was generalised and spread. In India, for example, MSF collaborated with DNP+ and the Lawyers Collective, and in Kenya with Health Action International, Nephak (the National Empowerment Network of People living with HIV/AIDS in Kenya), and KELIN, an organisation of legal experts. What we find here can be described as a cognitive association. Its function is epistemic: the triad consisting of international NGOs, groups of lawyers, and associations of patients "on the terrain" produces original knowledge of a new type. This is a recurrent phenomenon. In India, for example, the distribution of roles is undertaken by local movements of seropositive patients, who organise demonstrations and coverage in the media, while international NGOs take charge of media campaigning producing press communiqués and web publications, and lawyers analyse legal documents. Similar forms of collaboration were set up in different countries, for example, regarding the FTA, an activist involved in the case says that a European organisation initially arranged to have documents "leaked" by a sympathiser working in Geneva, who sent the documents to Delhi, where work on analysis began using the experience of another Free trade agreement involving Korean activists:

> *We are in contact with an organisation in Europe that passes on documents to us regularly. I think it was they who sent us this document the first time. Usually, as soon as we have begun to discuss it collectively in our distribution lists, we try to suggest interpretations.*[44]

In situations like this, with specialisation and division of labour, interviewees all recognised the dynamism of the representatives of Third World Network and MSF Access Campaign, for instance, at the time they were sharing an office.[45] The Indians' competence in copyright issues was no doubt a result of the whole history of pharmaceutical development in India; and also of the early establishment of think tanks – in particular, the National Working Group on Patent Law, set up in 1988 on the initiative of B. K. Keayla, at the time a senior executive of Ranbaxy, a pharmaceutical group.[46] Some actors played several parts simultaneously. Anand Grover, for example, took part in the controversy not only as a member of the Lawyers' Collective (a group of Indian legal specialists involved in access to medicines), but also as UN special rapporteur on the right to health. It was as UN rapporteur that he played a part in the Kenyan court case having already supported the Kenyan groups involved as a health activist.

Collaboration of this sort was both transnational (North–South, South–South) and inter-professional (collaboration mainly between patients' movements, international NGOs, and lawyers' groups). The existence of this type of collaboration is no doubt due to the sheer difficulty of the legal work involved: the law raised particularly technical issues, its complexity and rapid evolution made it necessary to set up collaboration between experts in different fields and from different countries. These forms of organisation, cutting across disciplinary and national boundaries, reveal the importance of the technical dimension in current action on pharmaceutical questions.[47] There is also the increasing standardisation since the 1980s of the modes of operation and intervention of NGOs that work internationally.[48] Collaboration and task specialisation in activist groups are an essential factor that promote the globalisation of this controversy by facilitating, on an international scale, the convergence of conflicts and a unification of themes through "globalisation work".

The opponents' victory … and after?

In Spring 2012, the development of the controversy gave the impression that the opponents of anti-counterfeit policies had gained the upper hand. On 12 April 2012, socialists and democrats in the EU Parliament announced that they would vote against ACTA, and though on April 13 Marielle Gallo (rapporteur of the committee on legal affairs) proposed that the agreement be accepted, in parliament, the criticism increased. On June 9, there were demonstrations against the agreement in Japan, the EU, the USA and Canada; on June 21, the Committee on international trade decided against the agreement. On July 4, the European parliament rejected the agreement once and for all. During this same period, on 20 April 2012, the Kenyan high court, after numerous adjournments rejected the Anti-Counterfeit Act. On May 25, the World Health Assembly decided to promote a new policy against bad medicines at the WHO recommending that the focus be changed from intellectual property to public health issues. The FTA remained undecided and final negotiations were being adjourned time after time. The lack of success of anti-counterfeit policies and the greater tension between India and the EU on other trade issues left the negotiations on medicines at an impasse. In the summer of 2012, after several years of conflict and negotiation, the controversy seemed to have been suspended. Yet, having emerged on several different sites, it had also been globalised. Activists' perception of these events, their strategies of framing, their construction of a transnational public, and the division of activist labour on an international scale had all led (initially separate) conflicts into convergence, criss-crossing spaces, stakeholders, thematics, and temporalities. All of this corresponded to the definition proposed by Jean Foyer of the global controversy as something trans-local, "trans-agency", trans-thematic, and trans-temporal.[49]

But that is not all. Through their critiques, opponents to the anti-counterfeit policies have highlighted several dimensions of the problem, otherwise neglected or deliberately silenced. They modified the common perception of illicit medicines and offered an alternative definition. Confronted to their critiques, the anti-counterfeit discourse appeared less coherent and more fragile. At the same time, they left several questions unanswered. And above all, the one that, if the illicit medicines issue does not stem only from criminal activity, how can one account for it? We now know that it is not only about the unlawful activity of some criminals. By contrast, the richest firms' greediness would offer a weak counter-explanation. In order to escape this alternative, it is therefore necessary to investigate, to unfold the issues raised by the controversies in order to confront them to see what happens on pharmaceutical markets.

For that purpose, one has to follow those, sometimes too silent during the conflict, who have not been heard yet – although they might have a lot to say: manufacturers, distributors, regulatory actors, users, and consumers. I investigated with them from 2012 to 2016 in India and in Kenya. From MNCs to small local firms, as well as drug inspectors, custom officers, importers, and patients, I moved in the maze of issues raised by the pharmaceutical globalisation, paying particular attention to South–South circulations and through trans-continental flow of medicines. How, in the global South, the public problem of "illicit medicines" is raised?

Notes

1 HAI Africa. (2009). Keep your hands off our medicines; health activists in Kenya tell the European Union, *Press Release.*

2 Cloatre, E. (2016). Fluid legal labels and the circulation of socio-technical objects: The multiple lives of 'fake' medicines. In David Cowan & Daniel Wincott (dir.), *Exploring the legal in socio-legal studies*. Londres: Palgrave MacMillan.

3 Chauveau, S. (2006). Contrefaçons et fraudes sur les médicaments (19e-20e siècles). In G. Béaur, H. Bonin, & C. Lemercier, *Fraude, contrefaçon et contrebande de l'antiquité à nos jours*, Genève: Droz. pp. 711–728; Greene, J. (2014). *Generic. The unbranding of modern medicine*. Baltimore: John Hopkins University Press.

4 Participants at the WHO International Conference. (2006). Combating counterfeit drugs: Building effective international collaboration. *Declaration de Rome. Conclusions and Recommendations of the WHO International Conference on Combating Counterfeit Medicines*, 18 February. Retrieved from www.who.int/medicines/services/counterfeit/RomeDeclaration.pdf?ua=1.

5 Dixneuf, M. (2003). Au-delà de la santé publique: Les médicaments génériques entre perturbation et contrôle de la politique mondiale, *Revue Française de Science Politique*, 53/2, Avril, pp. 277–304; Eboko, F. (2005). Le droit contre la morale? L'accès aux médicaments contre le sida en Afrique, *Revue Internationale Des Sciences Sociales*, 4, 186, pp. 789–798.

6 Interview of an activist working with Health Action International, 5 April 2012, Nairobi. I made the choice of anonymising all the interview participants, except when they were making public declarations.

7 Interview of an activist working with Health Action International, 5 April 2012, Nairobi.

8 Harrington, J. (2014). Access to essential medicines in Kenya intellectual property, anti-counterfeiting and the right to health. In M. Freeman & S. Hawkes (Eds.), *Law and global health. Current legal issues*, vol. 16. Oxford: Oxford University Press.

9 Harrington, J. (2014). Access to essential medicines in Kenya intellectual property, anti-counterfeiting and the right to health. In M. Freeman & S. Hawkes (Eds.), *Law and Global Health. Current Legal Issues*, vol. 16, Oxford: Oxford University Press.
10 Outterson, K., & Smith, R. (2006). Counterfeit drugs: The good, the bad, and the ugly. *Albany Law Journal of Science and Technology*, 15.
11 MSF. (2007). G8 declaration on innovation and intellectual property will directly harm access to medicines across the developing world, *Press Release*, 7 June. Retrieved from www.msf.org/article/g8-declaration-innovation-and-intellectual-property-will-directly-harm-access-medicines.
12 Biadgleng, E. T., & Munoz Tellez, V. (2008). The changing structure and governance of intellectual property enforcement, Research Paper 15, South Centre.
13 Chateauraynaud, F. (2007). Visionnaires à rebours. Des signaux faibles à la convergence de séries invisibles, GSPR.
14 Médecins Sans Frontières. (2008). Fatal confusion. How Kenya's 2008 anti-counterfeit bill endangers access to medicines, Briefing Document, October.
15 Ochieng, P. A., Atieno, M., & Munyi, J. Petition No. 409 of 2009. Republic of Kenya in the High Court of Kenya at Nairobi.
16 Third World Network. (2008). Controversy on proposed IP rules at World Customs Organisation. *SUNS*, 6535, 11 August.
17 Third World Network. (2008). IP: Counterfeit issue stirs debate among WHO member states, *SUNS*, 6536, 12 August; South Centre – CIEL. (2008). The international medical products anti-counterfeiting taskforce (impact): Is the WHO on the right track? *Intellectual Property Quartely Update*, Third Quarter.
18 Orsi, F., Camara, M., & Coriat, B. (2006). AIDS, TRIPS and "TRIPS Plus": The case for developing and less developed countries. In Brigitte Andersen (Ed.), *Intellectual Property Rights, Innovation, Governance and the Institutional Environment*, Cheltenham: Edward Elgar Publishing; Susan, K. S. (2007). Trips-plus free trade agreements and access to medicines, *Liverpool Law Review*, 28/1, pp. 41–75.
19 Report of the EU-India High Level Trade Group (HTLG) to the EU-India Summit, 13 October 2006. Retrieved from http://trade.ec.europa.eu/doclib/docs/2006/september/tradoc_130306.pdf.
20 Forum on FTA. (2008). EU-India Free Trade Agreement: For Whom?, 21 November.
21 New, W. (2008). Generic Drugmakers, Activists Praise Lamy; Gurry Defends 'Respect' For IP, *Ip Watch*, 11 December.
22 Third World Network. (2009). Developing countries attack Dutch seizure of generic medicines, *SUNS*, 6633, 5 February.
23 Third World Network. (2009). Developing countries attack Dutch seizure of generic medicines. *SUNS*, 6633, 5 February.
24 Abbott, A. (2009). A propos du concept de turning point. In M. Bessin, C. Bidart, & M. Grossetti (dir.), *Bifurcations. Les Sciences Sociales Face aux Ruptures et a L'Evenement*. pp. 187–211. Paris: La Découverte.
25 Khor, M. (2009). Row over seizure of low-cost drugs. *The Star Online*, 10 August.
26 FOFTA. (2009). EU-India FTA: Public interest groups detained during protest, *Press Release*, 17 March.
27 New, W. (2009). Concern erupts over WTO system and medicines shipments. *IpWatch*, 3 February.

28 European Generic Association. (2009). Letter to Mr. Laszlo Kovacs, 20 February.
29 Health Action International. (2009). Protect legitimate trade in essential medicines. *Press Release*, 11 August.
30 Interview of a member of the New Trade Union Initiative. New Delhi, 7 October 2011.
31 Tarrow, S. (2005). *The new transnational activism*. Cambridge: Cambridge University Press, pp. 62.
32 Participants in the controversy knowingly produce framing suited to the themes that lend support to their claims, despite the risk of rendering some claims "invisible".
33 Dixneuf, M. (2003). Au-delà de la santé publique: Les médicaments génériques entre perturbation et contrôle de la politique mondiale. *Revue Française de Science Politique*, 53/2, April, pp. 277–304; Anita, H. Biomedical hype and hopes: AIDS medicines for Africa. In P. W. Geissler, R. Rottenburg, & J. Zenker (Eds.), *Rethinking biomedicine and governance in Africa: Contributions from anthropology*. Transcript Verlag: Bielefeld. 2012, pp. 77–96.
34 Interview of a member of the Delhi Network of Positive People, New Delhi, 23 September 2011.
35 Siméant, J. (2005). What is going global. The internationalization of French NGOs 'without borders'. *Review of International Political Economy* 12/5, December, pp. 851–883; Siméant, J. (2012). Localiser le terrain de l'international. *Politix*, 4, 100, pp. 129–147.
36 Shankar, R. (2010). WHO echoes Indian view of anti-counterfeit laws in Africa hit accessibility of generics. *Pharmabiz*, 2 August.
37 Interview of a member of Health Action International, Nairobi, 10 mai 2012.
38 Ahuja, V. (Delhi Network of Positive People) *et al.* (2010). Don't trade away our lives! *Letter to Prime Minister Manmohan Singh,* 28 September.
39 Delhi Network of Positive People. (2010). Call for international week of action against EU-INDIA FTA, 4 October.
40 Intal. (2010). Protest action against the EU-India FTA – Brussels, 4 October.
41 PLHIVs lathi charged during protest against FTA negotiations. *Express Pharma on Line*, 16 October 2010.
42 National Association of People Living with HIV in Nepal. (2010). Join the protest in front of EU and Indian mission at 13th Oct 2010, 13 October.
43 Médecins Sans Frontières. (2011). Thousands of HIV+ people march in Delhi with plea to Indian government, 2 March.
44 Interview of an activist in access to healthcare, New Delhi, 8 November 2011.
45 Interview of a member of Act Up Paris, Paris, 19 April 2013.
46 Sen Gupta, A. (2010). B.K. Keayla, A personal reminiscence. *Economic and Political Weekly*, 18 December, pp. 25–26.
47 Krikorian, G. (2014). Un activisme savant. De la lutte contre le sida aux mobilisations contre les accords de libre-échange, *La Vie des Idées*, 20 November, en ligne: www.laviedesidees.fr/Un-activisme-savant.html.
48 Siméant, J. (2005). What is going global. The internationalization of French NGOs 'without borders'. *Review of International Political Economy*, 12/5, December, pp. 851–883.
49 Foyer, J. (2010). *Il était une fois la bio-révolution: Nature et savoirs dans la modernité globale*. Paris: Presses Universitaires de France.

Part 1

Pharmaceutical geographies

The mutations of an industry

During the second half of the 20th century, pharmaceutical industries were profitable and prosperous. Profitable: investment in research was admittedly costly, but returns on investment were higher than in any other sector. Prosperous: health "paid" and the sector recorded constant growth, its consumer base broadening. In the countries of the global North, spending on medicines was growing. New products such as treatments for cancer had come onto the market; the transformation of living conditions (less physical activity, development of multiple pollutions)[1] favoured the development of disease, despite closer medical monitoring. Lobbying by pharmaceutical firms was redefining thresholds and extending consumption (as in the case of cholesterol,[2] health risks were now being seen as chronic); and, belying hopes nurtured during the 1980s, illnesses such as tuberculosis had not disappeared,[3] and in some cases (e.g., whooping cough[4]) had even gained strength or reappeared. In the countries of the South, international policies on public health,[5] the progressive extension of health coverage,[6] the formation of social classes with growing buying power, the transformation of lifestyles and the growth of chronic diseases,[7] the persistence of infectious diseases: all of these factors led to an increase in consumption of medicines, opening up new markets. For all these reasons, pharmaceutical markets were recording brisk growth on an international scale.

Inevitably, this boom brought about important changes. Thanks to the emergence of pharmaceutical poles on all continents, the production and distribution of pharmaceuticals was being globalised – a major aspect of the change. Asia, Latin America, and (more recently) Africa were becoming sites of production and distribution. This trend has had many consequences. It is changing the logistics of the sector. New routes are appearing, and relationships of inter-dependence are being modified as new poles of production of active ingredients are established. Rules of competition change as pressure builds up on the prices of medicines that enter the public domain. Representations of the "innovative" nature of the pharmaceutical industry are also changing, impacted by the rise of generics. The changing geography of the sector is transforming domination relationships on a worldwide scale. South–South streams of finance and of commodities are developing, production sites are

DOI: 10.4324/9781003194767-3

multiplying, forms of financial and industrial inter-dependence are changing, and firms of the North are obliged to revise their strategies if they are to retain their hegemony. New conflicts are emerging as a result of these far-reaching changes. What is now the relationship between the expansion of the overall market, the new geographies of industry, and the power balance(s) that determine the rules governing the circulation of goods? Illicit medicines act as a (photographic) "developer", revealing it.

To analyse these transformations, I have mainly used tools developed for the socio-anthropology of the pharmaceutical worlds, sometimes designated as "pharmaceutical studies",[8] combining them with various socio-economic approaches. Medicines have for quite some time been included in the field of the history and sociology of technology, innovation, and economics. Monographies on innovation have gradually diversified: medicines are now being studied as technical objects,[9] as objects for personal consumption,[10] as legally regulated objects of innovation,[11] or simply as so much merchandise.[12] Approaches have also been developed for a more detailed analysis of the modes of regulation applicable to the marketing and circulation of medicines.[13] The socio-anthropology of science has taken a particular interest in the social issues involved in pharmaceutical research, examining the role played by medicines in epidemics,[14] the role played by social movements in access to medicines,[15] issues raised by the consumption of medicines and by pharmaceutical marketing,[16] clinical testing,[17] and regulation[18]. In a parallel development, research in pharmaceutical anthropology conducted in developing countries has in many cases studied sales and consumption,[19] while the economists and geographers of development have devised tools for the study of the emergence of the pharmaceutical industry.[20] The sociology of industry has shown that it is not enough to study processes of innovation and the use of medicines; to really understand, one needs to grasp the entire pharmaceutical chain, including production and wholesale distribution.[21]

At the confluence of these various currents, research has raised in a new guise the question of the formation of markets in the South[22] and their organisation.[23] Among the more interesting studies, some focus on the intersection between studies of science and the anthropology of health, observing pharmaceutical issues in the global South, and in particular clinical testing,[24] the formation of pharmaceutical markets,[25] medicines conceived of as branded, or generics, or "similar products",[26] and the overall development of pharmaceutical research and innovation.[27]

Most of these surveys have been carried out in the process either upstream – in pharmaceutical innovation, clinical testing and marketing authorisation – or downstream – in consumption and retail sales. Between upstream and downstream, however, relatively little interest has been shown either in production itself and its routines or in distribution; nor has the monitoring of the circulation of health products already on the market attracted the attention it deserves. Pierre Fournier and Cédric Lomba note that investigations have "concentrated on research, on the regulation and the profitability of the sector, and on the consumption of medicines",[28] recalling that several years previously, Busfield had already deplored this lack of interest in production.[29] This was all the more true of the global South. At the time, it was felt that there could be no such thing as a pharmaceutical industry there – apart, of course, from clinical trials in some emerging countries. Little at all has been written about the "dimension of production" and "its routines".[30] In the recent years, however, some research has been emerging. In France, the sociological work of a group led by Pierre Fournier and Cédric Lomba has examined activity in production and distribution in a high-value-added sector such as medicines. In developing and emerging countries, publications on production are burgeoning, though somewhat less than those on distribution. In general, the approaches are economical and developmental, authors being interested mainly in the success of industries in emerging countries[31] and on conditions affecting production capacities in developing countries.[32] Authors have called for a more globalised knowledge of pharmaceutical geographies,[33] and some, such as Cori Hayden in Mexico, and Roger Jeffery and his colleagues in their analysis of pharmaceutical circulations in Southern Asia,[34] have provided insight into some aspects of the medicinal industries in Latin America and India.

The next two chapters will pursue this investigation, concentrating on the question of the internationalisation of industrial production (Chapter 2) and the fight over access to distribution channels that it fosters (Chapter 3). The aim is to link a socio-anthropological approach to an effort to grasp the "global geopolitical configurations" whose role has been studied by Kaushik Sunder Rajan.[35] I will pay particular attention to the type of South–South relationship resulting from this situation, starting with the example provided by pharmaceutical circulations between India and Kenya. In reporting my conversations and the information I have gathered, I will try to show that current debates on issues concerning illicit medicines are symptoms of a new disturbance in the geography of pharmaceutical production. A disruption has tended to depreciate productive activity and to shift the focus of value creation to intermediate activities – distribution and transportation. Practices of regulation and the strategies of firms and governments have now set their sights first and foremost on *forms of circulation* in order to legitimate or discredit them. Mutations of the industrial geography of the world of pharmaceuticals are seen as part of an explanation of the renewal of discourse on illicit medicines.[36]

Notes

1 Austin, M. (2012). *Licensing, selling and finance in the pharmaceutical and healthcare industries. The commercialization of intellectual property*. Farnham: Gower. p. 14.

2 Dumit, J. (2012). *Drugs for life: How pharmaceutical companies define our health*. Durham: Duke University Press.

3 Dye, C. (2006). Global epidemiology of tuberculosis. *The Lancet*, 367, 9514, pp. 938–940, 18 March.

4 Mooi, F. R. Vand Der Maas, N. A. T., & De Melker H. E. (2014). Pertussis resurgence: Waning immunity and pathogen adaptation – two sides of the same coin. *Epidemiology and Infection*, 142, 04, April, pp. 685–694.

5 Brown, T. M., Cueto, M., & Fee, E. (2006). The World Health Organization and the transition from "international" to "global" public health, *American Journal of Public Health*, 96/1, pp. 62–72.

6 Ahlin, T., Nichter, M., & Pillai, G. (2016). Health insurance in India: What do we know and why is ethnographic research needed? *Anthropology & Medicine*, 23/1, pp. 102–124.

7 Farmer, P., *et al.* (2010). Expansion of cancer care and control in countries of low and middle income: A call to action, *The Lancet*, 376, 9747, pp. 1186–1193.

8 Sismondo, S., & Greene, J. (2015). *The pharmaceutical studies reader*. Hoboken: Wiley Blackwell.

9 Akrich, M. (1996). Le médicament comme objet technique, *Revue Internationale de Psychopathologie*, 21, pp. 135–158.

10 Fainzang, S. (2001). *Médicaments et société. Le patient, le médecin et l'ordonnance*. Paris: PUF.

11 Cassier, M. (2004). Brevets pharmaceutiques et santé publique en France entre 1791 et 2004: Opposition et dispositions spécifiques d'appropriation des médicaments, *Revue Entreprises et Histoire*, pp. 29–47.

12 Chauveau, S. (2005). Marché et publicité de médicaments. In C. Bonah, A. Rasmussen (Eds.), *Histoire et Medicament aux 19e et 20e Siecles*. Glyphe. pp. 189–214; Gaudillière, J.-P. (2010). Une marchandise scientifique? Savoirs, industrie et régulation du médicament dans l'Allemagne des années trente. *Annales – Histoire, Sciences Sociales*, 65/1, pp. 89–120.

13 Bergeron, H. (2005). Europeanization of drug policies: From objective convergence to mutual agreement. In M. Steffen (ed.), *Health Governance in Europe. Issues, Challenges and Theories*, London::Routledge. pp. 174–187; Hauray, B. (2006). *L'Europe du médicament. Politique, expertise, intérêts privés*, Presses de Sciences Po; Abraham, J., Davis, C. (2007). Deficits, expectations and paradigms in British and American drug safety assessments. Prising open the black box of regulatory science. *Science, Technology and Human Values*, 32/4, pp. 399–431; Demortain, D. (2007). European agencies. The European medicines agency and the European food safety authority. In D. Benamouzig, O. Borraz (dir.), *Food and pharmaceutical agencies in Europe. Between bureaucracy and democracy. Cross-national perspectives. A commented bibliography*. Grenoble, Publications de la MSH Alpes, Collection Risques collectifs et situations de crise, 7. pp. 15–100.

14 Dodier, N. (2003). *Leçons politiques de l'épidémie de sida*. Editions de l'EHESS; Dalgalarrondo, S. (2004). *Sida: La course aux molécules*. Editions de l'EHESS.

15 Epstein, S. (1992). Une science démocratique? Le mouvement AIDS et la construction contestée du savoir, *Futur Antérieur*, pp. 12–13, pp. 4–5, pp. 245–273; Barbot, J. (2002). *Les malades en mouvements. La médecine et la science à l'épreuve du sida*. Paris: Editions Balland.

16 Lakoff, A. (2008). *La raison pharmaceutique*. Paris : Les Empêcheurs de Penser en Rond/Le Seuil [2005]; Greene, J. (2008). *Prescribing by numbers: Drugs and the definition of disease*. Baltimore: Johns Hopkins University Press.

17 Fisher, J. (2008). *Medical research for hire: The political economy of pharmaceutical clinical trials*. Rutgers University Press; Abadie, R. (2010). *The professional guinea pig: Big pharma and the risky world of human subjects*. Durham: Duke University Press.

18 Greene, J. (2014). *Generic. The unbranding of modern medicine*. John Hopkins University Press; Carpenter, D. (2010). *Reputation and power, organizational image and pharmaceutical regulation at the FDA*. Princeton: Princeton University Press.

19 Van der Geest, S (1982). The illegal distribution of western medicines in developing countries: Pharmacists, drug pedlars, injection doctors and others. A bibliographic exploration. *Medical anthropology*, 6/4; S. Van Der Geest, & S. Reynolds Whyte (Eds.) (1988). The context of medicines in developing countries. *Studies in Pharmaceutical Anthropology*, Amsterdam: Kluwer Academic Publishing; Fassin, D. (1986). La vente illicite de médicaments au Sénégal. *Politique Africaine*, 23, pp. 123–130.

20 Lofgren, H. & Williams, O.D. (Eds.) (2013). *The new political economy of pharmaceuticals: production, innovation and TRIPs in the global South*. Palgrave Macmillan; M. Mackintosh, G. Banda, P. Tibandebage, & W. Wamae (Eds.) (2015). *Making medicines in Africa: The political economy of industrializing for local health*. London: Palgrave Macmillan.

21 Fournier, P., Lomba, C., & Muller, S. (Dir.) (2014). *Les travailleurs du médicament. L'industrie pharmaceutique sous observation*, Erès; Ravelli, Q. (2015). *La Stratégie de la bactérie. Une enquête au coeur de l'industrie pharmaceutique.* Seuil.

22 Baxerres, C. (2011). Pourquoi un marché informel du médicament dans les pays francophones d'Afrique? *Politique Africaine*, 123, pp. 17–136.

23 P. W. Geissler, R. Rottenburg, & J. Zenker (Eds.) (2012). *Rethinking biomedicine and governance in Africa. Contributions from anthropology*. Bielefeld: Transcript-Verlag.

24 Petryna, A. (2009). *When experiments travel. Clinical trials and the global search for human subjects*. Princeton: Princeton University Press.

25 Peterson, K. (2014). *Speculative markets: Drug circuits and derivative life in Nigeria*. Durham: Duke University Press.

26 Hayden, C. (2007). A generic solution? Pharmaceuticals and the politics of the similar in Mexico. *Current Anthropology*, 48, 4, pp. 475–495.

27 Pollock, A. (2014). Places of pharmaceutical knowledge-making: Global health, postcolonial science, and hope in South African drug discovery. *Social Studies of Science*, 44/6, pp. 848–873.

28 Fournier, P., Lomba, C., & Muller, S. (dir.) (2014) *Les travailleurs du médicament. L'industrie pharmaceutique sous observation*, Erès, pp. 10–11.

29 Busfield, J. (2006) Pills, Power, People: Sociological Understandings of the Pharmaceutical Industry, *Sociology*, 40; 297.

30 Fournier, P., Lomba, C., & Muller, S. (Dir.) (2014). *Les travailleurs du médicament. L'industrie pharmaceutique sous observation*, Erès, p. 13.

31 Chaudhuri, S. (2005). *The WTO and India's pharmaceuticals industry: Patent protection, trips, and developing countries*. New Delhi: Oxford University Press; Joseph, R. K. (2016). *Pharmaceutical industry and public policy in post-reform India*. London: Routledge.

32 M. Mackintosh, G. Banda, P. Tibandebage, & W. Wamae (Eds.) (2015). *Making medicines in Africa: The political economy of industrializing for local health*. London: Palgrave Macmillan.

33 Greene, J. (2016). Pharmaceutical geographies: Mapping the boundaries of the therapeutic revolution. In J. A. Greene, F. Condrau, E. S. Watkins (Eds.), *Therapeutic revolutions: Pharmaceuticals and social change in the twentieth century*. Chicago: University of Chicago Press.

34 Jeffery, R., & Santhosh M. R. (2009). The architecture of drug regulation in India: can it be reformed? *Journal of Health Studies*, 2, pp. 1–3, pp. 13–32; Brhlikova, P. *et al.* (2011). Trust and the regulation of pharmaceuticals: South Asia in a globalized world. *Globalization and Health*, 7, 10.
35 Rajan, K. S. (2017). *Pharmocracy. value, politics, and knowledge in global biomedicine*. Durham, NC: Duke University Press, p. 194.
36 This section is based on a survey of manufacturers, distributors, and wholesalers of medicines, and also of regulatory authorities, in India and in Kenya, between 2011 and 2016. In the course of the survey, I made 97 interviews: of which 47 of Indian and Kenyan regulatory authorities, (medicinal authorities, laboratories supervising quality, and customs authorities); 30 of Indian and Kenyan manufacturers, mainly *Managing Directors*, marketing officers, and production managers (in 4 Indian and 5 Kenyan firms); 20 of distributors and wholesalers (based for the most part in Kenya). I also took part as an observer in about ten workshops and professional conferences on the pharmaceutical trade in India and Kenya.

2 The pharmaceutical globalisation

The illicit explained by the market

Nandini Bhattacharya explains that in British India, at the turn of the 20th century, pharmaceutical adulteration was considered a major issue and provided one of the main discussion topics regarding local pharmaceutical markets.[1] Multiple products were targeted and the list included imported brand products such as soap, powders, patented medicines, or bulk products such as olive and almond oils. At that time, the nascent Indian pharmaceutical industry was not the main suspect. The weakness of controls and a trade culture not very concerned with efficiency were incriminated by the authorities, but the harsh competition of foreign firms on the territory was also considered to play an important part. In 1889, an agent working for several British companies accused the German, French, and American firms of weakening the market in bringing all sorts of adulterated products – with the complicity of Indian wholesalers:

> *calomel containing 50% of chalk, santonin half boracic acid, sent here from France and Germany carriage paid and sold in the currency of the country, I fail to see how honest British competition can stand.*[2]

And if, for the British traders, foreign competition and local importers were to blame, not everyone was thinking alike. After World War I, the issue was seized by the Indian nationalist movement; the media attacked the collusion of British manufacturers and importers and accused them of pouring bad quality products into India. During the 1930s, a committee tasked with the evaluation of the Indian market pointed at the aggressive and deceiving marketing that allowed the firms, mostly foreign ones, to supply patented medicines to patients and doctors. The issue ran through the years of colonial domination; its importance explains the pharmacy act of 1944 partly.

This story shows that the emergence of the problem of pharmaceutical illiceity is by no means recent. It also hints at some of its causes. According to Bhattacharya, the importance given to the issue during these years is less related to weak controls – a frequently mentioned cause at that time – than

DOI: 10.4324/9781003194767-4

to the structuration of the market itself. The coexistence of heterogeneous sales practices, following different norms, the competition between foreign and national actors, the diversity of medical practices, and of the expectations of consumers were at the heart of the illicit issue. Saying so, Bhattacharya diverts us from superficial explanations – most of them in terms of State dysfunction. She brings our attention towards some of the structural roots of the illicit. Adulterated medicines have never been a market anomaly: they were one of its pillars.

If we follow this explanation, it is therefore essential to represent the market organisation in order to get a better understanding of the illicit medicines issue. However, it is doubtful that such an organisation has remained the same since the early 20th century. From the colonial market of British India, dominated by England, to the current market, the world of industrial pharmacy has changed a lot, and the contemporary reasons for the illicit are quite far from those given by Bhattacharya. Quite far? Nothing is less certain. In order to determine it, the two next chapters present the characteristics of the contemporary pharmaceutical market, keeping one question in mind: to what extent does the market structure bring an explanation to the contemporary illicit medicines issue?

The internationalisation of production

One of the main characteristics of the contemporary pharmaceutical market has been its globalisation and, in particular, the emergence of an industrial production capacity in most countries of the world. The pharmaceutical market has long been transnational, as N. Bhattacharya reminded us; the global development of the industry is, however, more recent. A first understanding of the pharmaceutical market needs to take this phenomenon into account.

The first driving force of this transformation has been the industry itself and in particular in the richest countries. The pharmaceutical industry in the North, whose leading firms (Pfizer, Roche, Sanofi, Novartis) dominate the international markets, have gone through a long period of changes since the 1990s. The major economic model in this sector, during the 1980s and 1990s, relied upon innovation and research. Pharmaceutical activity was then associated with high research-development costs, low production costs, and the securitisation of profit through intellectual property and patents.[3] During these years, the pharmaceutical profit depended upon the development of complex molecules through clusters associating universities and industries, regulation allowing for large-scale clinical trials, the globalisation of the intellectual property infrastructure, and last but not least, upon the success of some blockbuster medicines, bringing at least one billion a year to the owner company (e.g., Lipitor, a preventive medicine against cardiovascular diseases, or Vioxx, an anti-arthritis medicine, before it was withdrawn from the market).[4]

Some observers consider that this profit model has gone into crisis since the turn of the 21st century.[5] They notice the stagnation of research and the constant elevation of innovation costs. The number of products receiving market authorisations is still growing on European and US markets[6]; but their shelf life is short, in spite of any major discovery, and between 1991 and 2009, the return on investment tended to diminish.[7] In parallel, the patents, which protected the 1990s blockbusters, progressively come to an end, which cuts important incomes for firms that have built their commercial success on intellectual property. Analysts use the evocative expression of a "patent cliff". The industry would be on the cliff's edge! In such a context, the industry experiments with new organisation models such as open innovation platforms, consolidate its intellectual property rights, gets involved in research fields such as personalised medicine, cuts expenses in order to let startups taking risks for bigger companies.[8] Furthermore, the industry increasingly turns towards the global South in order to find trade partners there, to develop new markets and to ensure the protection of its interests. It has outsourced clinical trials and part of its production in the South. The mutation of the industry in the richest countries is therefore directly connected to the growth of industrial pharmacy in developing countries. But these countries have also set up their own strategies in order to develop national industries, as is the case for emerging countries.

Although there have been firms producing medicines industrially in India ever since the early 20th century, the sector really gets underway only after Independence. It is closely linked to support from and management by the Indian State, particularly as of the 1970s.[9] That way, Indian manufacturing illustrates the evolution of the pharmaceutical industry in emerging countries. In the Resolution on Industrial Policy adopted in 1948, the pharmaceutical sector was designated as a priority sector in which India should rely on support from foreign firms and countries in matters of investment and skill transfers. However, the desired investment and transfers failed to accompany the arrival of foreign firms and the government stepped in, defining pharmaceuticals as a field in which the public sector should be preponderant (Resolution on Industrial Policy, 1956). To strengthen this dynamic, in 1970, the government passed an Indian Patent Act that recognised no patent on pharmaceutical products and on processes granted patents that were valid only for limited periods. This enabled local firms to develop copies of medicines by means of reverse engineering. Two measures completed this policy: increased flexibility in licensing and strict control of foreign firms, which were now obliged to link up with the local economy.[10] Lastly, as of 1962, the price of medicines was regulated by the Drug Prices Control Order and increasingly regulated during the1970s, in particular, following the recommendations of the Hathi Committee Report, published in 1978.[11]

In this regulatory context, the Indian government set up five State-run enterprises, two of which – Hindustan Antibiotics Limited (1954) and Indian Drugs and Pharmaceuticals (1961) – were to assert Indian know-how in pharmaceutical production.[12] The government received aid from countries such as Russia and from international organisations such as the WHO and the UNICEF. Playing on ideological competition, it was also able to obtain the cooperation of a pharmaceutical major, Merck.[13] Furthermore, the circulation of knowledge and of competencies between enterprises, and between the private and public sectors were promoted, playing a crucial part in building up Indian know-how.[14] Publicly owned research laboratories were brought in and collaborated with private firms on problems of research and development. By the end of this phase of construction, India had become one of the countries where the price of medicines was the lowest in the world. Yet India was still not considered an actor in innovation; it was seen, rather, as a mainstay of the production of low-cost medicines. The main factors accounting for the Indian success were investments by the State, the regulatory framework, and the construction of local competencies, thanks to a collaboration between the world of research on the one hand, and public and private industry on the other.

During the 1990s, this evolved. First, the orientation of Indian policy changed, turning away from a State-run economy; firms were privatised and the private sector gained importance.[15] Next, India joined the World Trade Organisation, committing itself to respect international intellectual property rights (patents on products and on processes). Gradually the market was liberalised, undoing the bonds between the State and Indian pharmaceutical firms, and in particular relaxing restrictions on foreign firms and moderating price controls.[16] These changes – particularly those in IP law that took effect in 2005 – brought about a change in Indian firms' strategies.[17] The most robust among them, strengthening their positions in the more prosperous countries, applied international standards to themselves and began to invest part of their revenue in research – a share that reached 5% of their budgets in 2005, but however remained low compared to leading Euro-American firms, which allocated about 15% of their own budgets to this post.[18] Other firms – a large majority – confined themselves to local and to less developed markets. This brought about a cleft. On the one hand were a small number of enterprises operating on highly developed markets: of the 15 most profitable generics manufacturers in 2016, 5 were Indian.[19] On the other hand, innumerable small and medium enterprises drew their profits from the business in India and in low- or middle-income countries, using marketing strategies that were very different.[20]

On the international level, Indian industry has thus been caught between two opposite movements. It has been recognised as one of the most inexpensive in the world and is often presented by civil society organisations such as MSF as "the pharmacy of the Third World". One reason for this is its success in sales of anti-retroviral generics that at the beginning of the 21st century were a hundred times cheaper than the original products – the result of a Cipla laboratories' initiative. In addition, the occasional disagreements and disputes between India and Northern countries upon industrial policies and matters of copyright tend to consolidate this reputation.[21] At the same time, the industry is highly dependent on exports to foreign countries; this gives the Northern governments a lot of bargaining power in negotiations, enabling them to weigh on the direction taken by Indian development. The evolution of the Indian industry is, therefore, the result of both national and international policies of access to health, but also that of the renewed interest of leading multinational companies for the Global South as a market – that is, as a site of consumption, experimentation, and outsourcing. The subsequent interactions between the Indian industry and foreign firms are mixed, between collaboration and attempts to take control.

But the pharmaceutical industry went global not only with the emerging countries. Indeed, it is customary to quote India as an eminent example; China, Brazil, South Africa, Egypt, and Turkey are also seen as rising players in the pharmaceutical industry. But it less easy to come across any mention of other developing countries in this respect – in particular African countries south of the Sahara, where nonetheless a local industry is currently getting underway. Ten years ago, the mere possibility of this would have been seen as fanciful. Yet today, it is actually taking place. In 2005, the conference of ministers of health of the African Union asserted the need to "pursue with the support of local partners local production of generic medicines on the African continent".[22] This was linked in the first place to the national policy of boosting consumption. According to World Bank figures, between 2000 and 2013, health expenditure – measured in constant dollars – practically doubled in Africa south of the Sahara.[23] Other arguments were also used to promote the local production of medicines in Africa: an industry of this sort would have a notable impact on job creation, and even more so on the transfer of skills and knowledge; on the availability of affordable medicines; on lessening dependency on currency exchange rates. All of these considerations pleaded in favour of an African pharmaceutical industry.[24] We should not overlook, however, an historical fact: the local manufacture of medicines in Africa is not really a novelty. During the colonial period, and in particular, during World War II, production units were set up in several African countries linked to firms based in Europe.[25] This process went on after decolonisation; in the later 1970s, it was encouraged by the WHO to accompany its policy based on "essential medicines", and also by organisations such as UNIDO and UNDP, and by the non-aligned movement.[26] During the 1980s, however, the period of crises and structural adjustment weakened local capacities, for example, in Nigeria.[27] It was only in the mid-1990s that production in Africa picked up again. By 2005, pharmaceutical production units were operating in 37 of the 46 African countries.[28]

Kenyan industry, a regional locomotive, is an interesting example of the processes we have just described. Illustrating the vigorous dynamics of the sub-Saharan region, it shows how global market reconfigurations have affected regional development. According to Maureen Mackintosh and her colleagues, the first production units were set up before World War II as subsidiaries of European firms: Glaxo is an example.[29] The first steps towards the institutionalisation of the industry, however, date from the 1950s and 1960s. The Pharmaceutical Society of East Africa was established in 1950, becoming the Pharmaceutical Society of Kenya in 1964, after Independence. This institution was to play a central part in formulating the Pharmacy and Poisons Act passed in 1957, laying the foundations for the Kenyan pharmaceutical industry. The Act also set up a regulatory authority, the Pharmacy and Poisons Board (PPB), and laid down the rules applying to the production and distribution of medicines. In 1974, a Department of Pharmacy was set up in the Faculty of Medicine at the University of Nairobi and a course in pharmacy was started. Previously pharmacists had had to qualify outside Kenya.

In the late 1970s and early 1980s, local firms began to appear. The manager of one of them explained that:

> *… in the beginning there was nothing at all. To make medicines, we had to do everything. We had to have contacts, laws, materials. We had to do it all. We were in a country, as it were, where everything had to be built up, it was pretty exciting, but also exhausting, as we'd got nothing at all.*[30]

The biggest firm at the time, Dawa, was launched in 1974 as a joint venture involving the State-run Industrial and Commercial Development Corporation, KRKO Pharma (a Yugoslav firm), and some Kenyan entrepreneurs. Production started up in 1977, and by mid-1980, the company was employing 200 people and producing some 70 different preparations, including anti-malarial medicines. Dawa received government support, but its know-how came from KRKO Pharma, from Beecham in the UK, Abbott in the USA, and Biochemie in Austria.

Dawa had State support and became the government's main partner in pharmaceutical matters. The firm's development was promoted in the 1980s by Kenyan participation in a WHO programme: the New Management System of Drug Supplies to Rural Health Facilities. Also known as the Ration Kits system, it involved supplying large quantities of medicine locally.[31] This had a multiplying effect on local industry. The ministry of industry also encouraged the drive for self-sufficiency in medicines, one of the main objectives of industrialisation[32]. "Buy drugs from local firms", declared the Kenyan President, Daniel Arap Moi, speaking in September 1981.[33] The industry also got organised, the *Federation of Kenyan Pharmaceutical Manufacturers* (FKPM) having been set up in the early 1980s.[34] The structural adjustment and subsequently sectoral programmes in which Kenya had been involved as of 1980 had less obvious effects on the pharmaceutical industry in Kenya than those pointed out in Nigeria by Kristin Peterson, where the industry was swept away by market liberalisation. In Kenya, the situation was better balanced and industries multiplied as of the 1980s. Ricochets, from the protection of industries like Dawa, possibly helped other industries that were being set up at the time. Furthermore, it was only gradually that the Kenyan government complied with World Bank demands that it liberalise markets.[35]

As of the early 1990s, the industry got another boost from public health organisations in favour of "buying local". As of the year 2000, export promotion policies also led Kenya to increase its exports to East Africa.[36] Today 35 pharmaceuticals manufacturers are registered in Kenya, two of them producing anti-retrovirals. Thus as of the 1980s, Kenya became a regional player in the production and export of medicines.

The development of the Kenyan industry enabled the latter to play a part in that of East Africa at a time when the markets of the African community are integrating. This promising development, however, is threatened by foreign industry. Medicines from Asia are highly competitive. Indian medicines, for example, are low-priced thanks to economies of scale and lower energy costs than those in Kenya; local entrepreneurs find it hard to keep up with them. As to the Northern majors, their impact is less direct. At first sight, they seem to occupy a different segment – that of expensive branded medicines. However, confronted with Asiatic firms' generics, the firms of the North had to cut their prices and adopt strategies that enabled them to hold on to strong positions. A 2013 estimate stated that GSK, for example, according to some estimates, generated more than 40% of its overall profits in the segment of anti-infectious medicines such as Amoxil.[37] Thus Kenyan firms are facing competition from emergent countries on the one hand and from developed countries on the other; the cost factor joins the brand factor in weakening their position on the local market. Lastly, on the private market, a third of the medicines come from South Asia, and almost a third from Europe and the USA[38]; foreign competition is thus substantial. This trend is strengthened by the ways in which international aid organisations provide medicines, applying standards that local firms are unable to match. In 2014, for example, the Clinton Health Access Initiative bought rehydration solutions and zinc from local producers but declined to use other products, simply declaring that its "standards differ" from those followed by Kenyan firms.[39]

The evolution of markets and production in emergent and in developing countries both show how medicinal production is currently internationalised; productive forces are constituted almost everywhere throughout the world. This transformation is not solely the result of development policies and national measures; it is also determined by global trends in which the firms of the North played a preponderant part. As a result, this overall development is inseparable from the tension between two conceptions of the market. In one of these, the financialisation of innovation and the *princeps* brand are central; the other is centred more on generics, which account for a growing share of consumption.

Globalisation from the south

When I walked into Mr. Anand's office for the first time, I was struck by its atmosphere. First of all, the music, its volume fairly low, came from the computer's speakers: it seemed to be a piece played on the sitar, no doubt

Indian classical music. On the walls, photos of Indian monuments: the Taj Mahal and a temple I didn't recognise. On a table, a figure of the god Ganesh with his elephant's head. This décor would not be surprising in Delhi – but I was in Nairobi, in the middle of the industrial zone, in the offices of a Kenyan pharmaceutical firm. I started my interview with Mr. Anand, a man of about fifty, who told me he had been in Kenya working in pharmaceuticals since the 1980s, that he had been naturalised a Kenyan and was very happy in Nairobi. I explained my project to him, the investigation it entailed, and that I had just passed several months in India. He was amused at this and also somewhat bemused:

> *How did you manage to stay in India all that long? It's so dirty, so polluted, there's so much noise! I go back regularly with my wife, but we never stay for more than a few days, she can't stand it for longer than that.*

Four years later, I recalled this conversation when I met Mr. Anand again. He explained that his wife, who is asthmatic, could not stay in Indian cities for very long for medical reasons. He had not changed his mind about the country he was born in, but was worried about his relationship with Kenya: he felt that it was important to "do something" for this country that "had given him so much".

This sort of conversation is not unusual in pharmaceutical circles in Kenya. In the pharmaceutical sector, one meets many Kenyans of Indian origin: pharmacists, industrialists, distributors, and wholesalers. Their biographies form bridges between South Asia and East Africa; ever since the late 19th century, their frequent comings and goings have been weaving a web of transnational experience. The pharmaceutical industry produces not only molecules and medicines but also social trajectories. The import-export sector distributes both products and cultural relationships. Pharmaceutical capitalism cannot be separated from human relations without which it would not exist. Pharmaceutical markets are part and parcel of a complex of sociological, economic, political and religious relationships, and of the history that has set them up. Relationships between persons are mediated by objects. I have to take account of this historical dimension. This can lead one to examine the consequences of the transformation of global markets and modes of regulation without reducing it all to a matter of economics. This also leads one to take account not only of the role of technical objects, but also of that of colonial and postcolonial history in setting up the social relationships of "postcolonial capitalism", of which the pharmaceutical industry studied here is an example.[40]

Contacts between South Asia and East Africa date back to Antiquity when the Indian Ocean became part of the trade area linking Europe to Africa and Asia.[41] In the Middle Ages, trade intensified, gaining speed from the 16th to the 19th centuries. Gujarati merchants were regularly present on the Swahili coast.[42] In the late 19th century, the British imperial authorities started bringing in Indian labourers to build the railway from Mombasa to Kisumu on the shores of Lake Victoria at the frontier with Uganda. Of the 40,000 labourers who came from South Asia, some 10,000 remained after the completion of the railway, settling mainly in the cities. In Nairobi, Mombasa and Kisumu, they earned a living by opening small shops or selling their services as artisans. This population group increased until Kenya became independent in 1963 when the nationalist project brought with it discriminations and a growing hostility towards groups of Indian origin. Under the Kenyan constitution, Indian residents could acquire Kenyan nationality, but dual nationality was banned. Less than half the Indian population residing in Kenya acquired Kenyan nationality, and almost a 100,000 left the country, immigrating mostly to Britain. In 1962, on the eve of independence, some 177,000 Indians were living in Kenya; by 1979, they numbered only 79,000. By the end of the century, they numbered about 100,000 and were still the largest group of non-African origin in Kenya. About half of them held Kenyan nationality.[43] In 2017, Kenyans of Indian descent were recognised as the country's 44th tribe.

The history of Indian presence in Kenya during the last century is marked by colonialism which has largely shaped the relations between the Indian diaspora and the local population. Racial hierarchies, unequal economic and commercial relationships, and a tendency to oscillate between integration and rejection are some of the major consequences of the colonial episode. During the colonial period, Indian grocers (*dukkawallahs*) were in some areas the only persons to have economic relations with the local population; the latter often complained that they were being cheated.[44] Reports on cohabitation and confrontation between the Indian immigrants and the native population were more frequent than reports on relationships between the native population and British settlers. The colonial authorities attempted to control the Indians' commerce in order to collect taxes, with the argument of preventing illegal practices.[45] During the colonial period, Indians were already being categorised as a community of middlemen[46] – intermediaries between markets and between social groups defined in racial terms – and stigmatised as such: unfair advantage-seekers and exploiters in one view, dishonest and ignorant of "good commercial practices" in another. Relationships of this sort did not totally exclude forms of solidarity between Indians and Kenyans, however: in politics, for example, and in particular in the struggle for independence.[47] Nevertheless, the history of Indians in East Africa went through periods of tension – particularly after Independence – and produced racial categorisations and ethnic stereotypes linked to the economic status of the Indians.[48]

The social status of Indians in Kenya is, therefore, a noteworthy trait: Indians played an important part in Kenya's economic life. Many shops and commercial enterprises were managed by Kenyans of South Asian origin, and Indians frequently went into the liberal professions; in healthcare, they were particularly numerous. This was linked to colonial history: between 1910 and

1920, the British authorities had encouraged Asian doctors to come to East Africa, where they were usually put into subaltern positions under European practitioners. By the end of the 1920s, however, the presence of Indians in colonial services had fallen off as a result of a policy of "Africanisation". Nevertheless, a large number of Indian doctors spent their entire career in Kenya where it would seem (despite the paucity of sources documenting this) that during the 1920s, Indian doctors became an integral part of private medical practice, laying the foundations for the current situation.[49] According to Michel Adam, about a third of the doctors practicing in Kenya today are of South Asian origin.[50] The same can be said of the pharmaceutical profession, as regards both retail outlets and larger manufacturing or importing firms, a large proportion of these firms being managed by executives of South Asian origin and financed by Indo-Kenyan capital. Adam maintains that 60% of investment in industrial pharmacy is financed by capital held by the Indian diaspora.[51]

At last, the Indian population originates mainly from Gujarat, followed in order of importance by Punjab, Goa, and Bombay. What matters, in that case, is that Gujarat, famous for its diaspora in the USA, Britain, and East Africa, is currently one of the Indian states that export most formulas and active ingredients. On the western coast of India, Gujarat produces about 30% in volume of the Indian generics and about 10% in volume of the medicines exported. It is important to understand this in order to grasp India's position on the generics market, as Gujarati business is oriented particularly towards the production of finished products. This positioning and efforts in the field of regulation have made Gujarat a leader in this field in India. Gujarat has also been the fief of Narendra Modi, who became the Prime Minister of India in 2014.

The history of Indians in Kenya has clearly marked the Kenyan pharmaceutical market. The circulation of molecules, of knowledge and of people are all intimately linked. When visiting a firm in India, I met Rajani. His son, who was also there, told us that he often went to Kenya to do the firm's marketing.[52] Standing beside him, Rajani's nephew told us in turn that he had worked in Kenya for several years in one of the largest firms in the country. As a young "expat", he had liked it a lot in Kenya, but now that he had a family, he did not plan to go back to Africa. Rajani himself then emphasised on the professional links between his firm and Kenya, mentioning as an illustration that the manager – of Indian descent – of a Kenyan pharma company sat on the board of his own firm. On the Western shore of the Indian Ocean, this takes on a special meaning. In a Kenyan manufacturer's offices, finding the statue of a Hindu god or the framed photograph of an Indian guru is not unusual. Most Kenyan pharmaceutical firms – for example, Cosmos, Lab & Allied, or Universal – are based on networks of families and friends. In many cases, the firm is still headed by its founder, his son or his nephew. The major part of the management stems from the Indian diaspora. In some cases, these executives have kept their Indian nationality, and in others, they are Kenyans, born either in Kenya or in India; in some cases, they are expatriates. These circulations are not restrained to India and Kenya, as many executives of Kenyan firms have worked in other countries before coming to Kenya.

In the Kenyan pharmaceutical industry, the role of this diaspora is essential. This is partly explained by the need for investment capital in the sector; historically, in the 1970–1980 period, investment capital was more readily available in the Indian diaspora than in Kenya itself. Some commentators, however, relativise claims of this sort: in production, some firms were set up by native Kenyans, and in distribution, the presence of the Indian diaspora is less marked than in production. On the whole, however, the presence of Indians and Kenyans of Indian descent in the Kenyan pharmaceutical sector is considerable. In manufacturing, management is mainly Indian; on a different ground, in imports, at least a third of the products comes from India. In that way, Indians in the Kenyan pharmaceutical market are twice "intermediaries". As entrepreneurs, they put in relation Kenyan consumers with foreign manufacturers – when they import Indian products – but as a community, they are also held to be matchmakers. Diaspora, as a historical, social, and cultural event, therefore plays a pivotal role in the understanding of the Kenyan pharmaceutical industry. Taking it into account allows us to show that the emergence of a national pharmaceutical industry does not owe everything to economic initiatives or industrial policies. It suggests that a richer appreciation of the machinery of economic globalisation asks for a situated view upon phenomena and not only an abstract vision of markets. Above all, it enrolls pharmaceutical issues in a history of representations of otherness. It helps, therefore, to understand how the colonial history, by producing or reinforcing racial representations (Indians as intermediaries, Indians as "more or less" honest traders) has led to the elaboration of a repertoire of stereotypes. As we will see later, the market players do not hesitate to mobilise this repertoire in order to account for the illicit as a problem.

Manufacturing medicines in the global south

There are several pharmaceutical production plants in the industrial zone of Nairobi. To get there, one passes through a lively commercial neighbourhood. Men push trolleys loaded with bananas, pineapples, wooden furniture, and pallets. On the opposite side of the road, women carrying sacks of goods for sale jostle their way through the crowd of pedestrians. On the ground, shoemakers display their collections of soles stringing them up on walls. When one emerges from this bustling environment – without, however, emerging from the traffic jams – one comes on walls covered with painted advertisements for brands of milk, of paint, and of medicines. A massive plant, huge as a power station, produces Tusker beer. The road changes into a line-up of factories that produce paint, glue, and "elementary" chemicals. Hawkers approach truck drivers, workers, and cars, selling grilled maize or chocolate bars; an improvised kitchen surmounted by a protective umbrella offers *chapatis*, the Indian pancakes Kenyans are so fond of, or *ugali,* the omnipresent local wheatmeal. A cock that seems to be lost inspects some gravel. Nearby there are more factories: some of them are manufacturing plants producing "local" medicines.

The field of pharmaceuticals is developing, changing, gradually freeing itself from the richest countries' predominant influence. But what exactly does it mean to "manfacture medicines"? To what extent are the Southern firms confronted with their own challenges, changing and evolving the rules of pharmaceutical production? This has been the subject of much brisk debate on forms of innovation in the South,[53] on the specificities of the regulatory procedures applying in the manufacture of generics,[54] on the conditions under which "industrial and technological capacities" are built up,[55] on the feasibility of plans for pharmaceutical self-sufficiency in a context of increasing interdependence,[56] and on the history of pharmaceutical production in the South.[57] Too often, these discussions lead us to examine industrial pharmacy as a "local" activity with its problems linked to the spaces in which it develops. However, this tendency can be explained. One does not have to make a particularly thorough ethnographic study to realise that the environment of the Kenyan pharmaceutical industry is very different from that of industries in the North. The difference is not merely geographical; it is human, technical, financial, legislative, regulatory; and also epidemiological and meteorological. One way to avoid the neo-colonial flavour of considerations upon the localness of the developing countries' pharmaceutical industry would be to consider the multiple shifts that accompany geographic dissemination. With the shift in production, virtually everything has changed. The practice of pharmaceutical production and the production of medicine as a commodity, an object, are being transformed, as is the overall perception of the South, which is no longer seen as a periphery from which resources are extracted, but as a site of production and innovation, its initiatives carrying increasing weight on global markets.

At the same time, the entire pharmaceutical industry in both the North and the South, in the West as in the East, has characteristics that are linked to its geographical localisation. The specificity of Southern industries is doubly marked by their entry into a trans-national market ruled increasingly by practices that are supposedly "harmonious", aiming at the application of criteria that are supposedly universal – but that in fact have been "harmonised" by the firms of the countries that are wealthiest and the most technologically advanced. This domination and the forms of collaboration and competition set up with the firms of the South play a large part in fashioning the development of industries in the South. But what does it mean in the first place to manufacture medicines in the South? The Kenyan industry, as its actors introduced it to me, offers a telling example of the realities and difficulties of this activity.

For the entrepreneurs involved, the financial aspect is the most important of all, since it places a basic constraint on the development of activity and is itself constrained by the financial environment:

> *Here [in Kenya] the pharmaceutical industry involves about four to five thousand people. It is one of the main employers of university graduates. In our firm [employing some 400 people], we have about 70. Despite this we [the pharmaceutical industry] do not exist as far as the government are concerned. No aid whatever. Return on investment in this country takes time, as rates on bank loans are very stiff. So it takes at least seven to eight years for an investment to pay off in this industry. But financially nothing is done.*[58]

In this context, the government plays an important role, some of its measures plainly influencing activity by modifying the financial environment and firms' strategies of profitability. In 2013/14, value-added tax on raw materials was debated: in 2013, VAT on raw materials had been reintroduced at 16%, although it was suspended on finished products, giving rise to protests by entrepreneurs. As a result, VAT was removed again in 2014. Other disagreements between entrepreneurs and government persisted, however, as to the tax on imported technologies, and in particular as to the list of products considered to be "input material", for example.[59] Conflicts such as these illustrate the concrete dynamics of construction of financial capabilities and profitability of firms, and the part played by the State in this process.

Acquisition of equipment and human resources are two other aspects of industrial pharmacy in Kenya. Equipment is an important item in investment and is negotiated by Kenyan firms with foreign suppliers from India, China, Belgium, Germany, and Finland. Human resources also involve transfers, in this case of competencies. But it is not so much a case of recruiting researchers or doctoral students as of training personnel in issues of industrial pharmacy. In Kenya, courses in this are still in their infancy:

> *We have got some courses with UNIDO [the UN agency promoting industrial development]. Otherwise there's a training centre at Moshi in Tanzania that organises things with GIZ [the German developmental agency]. Mount Kenya University trains in industrial pharmacy and Nairobi University has a school of pharmacy, but not really industrial pharmacy. These are things that are set up bit by bit; for the time being we have above all learned from people who come in from other firms and enable us to benefit from their experience.*[60]

Other issues include the cost of registering medicines, that of procedures for marketing authorisation, the lack of protectionist measures, the productivity and profitability of production lines, and the acquisition of equipment.[61]

As with any other industrial activity, a pharmaceutical firm also has to operate from day to day, in an environment and under conditions that are highly restrained. Production capacity thus covers more than simply supplying numerous medicines and making production lines profitable. It impinges materially on the way the firm is run and on the availability and robustness of infrastructure:

> *You know, my problems are simple. For example; the plant has to be kept switched on. But here it isn't easy to see to it that there is current 24 hours out of 24. But one has to be really sure of that, otherwise it can be catastrophic. [...] We've also got big problems with theft. People who come on to the property and leave with equipment. So we have to have guards, security barriers, and so forth. My problem as an entrepreneur, in the first place, it's that.*[62]

Research and development (R&D) is the ultimate core component of a firm's technological capability. Countries of the South are often thought of as reception sites for innovations from the North rather than as sites of autonomous innovation. Yet, the sociology of science has shown that to a large extent, reformulation and reverse engineering are, in fact, forms of research and innovation and should be considered as such.[63] This is why it is important to clarify the conditions under which a firm carries out R&D and also the role assigned to this activity. In Kenya, there are R&D activities in only the largest firms, which have R&D departments employing between five and ten persons. They work mainly on formulation. This means in the first place that they are doing reverse engineering on branded medicines (rather than inventing new molecules). Laboratory teams work on gathering information, on experimenting and on practical matters. They adapt formulations to local environmental conditions (temperature, hygrometry, etc.); research departments are also involved in quality controls and in testing the stability and purity of the firm's products. Last but not least, they also do research on packaging, seeking more economical ways of preserving and transporting their products. This can involve technical difficulties:

> *You can either buy a formula, or do a search on Internet. In the latter case the formula will be incomplete, and the R&D team will have to play around with it, so that each product will be compatible with the others, to make sure that one gets a proper distribution (release). So there is a lot of hard work to be done, and it takes at least between zero and two years before one can apply for registration.*[64]

Above all, innovation is thought out in terms of adaptation to local conditions, for example, stabilisation of medicines exposed to variations in temperature:

> *Here we've got a little R&D department of about ten people. It works on formulations to make medicines appropriate for this part of the world. Often for example we have to work on formulations to make them more stable in this climate.*[65]

This interviewee stresses the fact that the aim of research carried out in his firm is not discovering but adapting – adapting products that have not been designed for Kenyan conditions. This "localisation" of innovative practice is also justified by the entrepreneurs by an epidemiological contrast between the South and the North. In the course of the same conversation, my interviewee spoke about the oncoming phase in his firm's R&D: work on the diseases of the middle classes, and in particular, diabetes. Our discussion continued, and we came to new treatments for cancer. His judgement was abrupt:

> *Cancer is a rich countries' disease. Here people are still dying very young; cancer isn't yet a big enough problem. One shouldn't forget that we are working on medicines that are essential and that our objective is quantitative: for the time being as many people as possible should get access to the main treatments.*[66]

This interview shows that Kenyan firms' research seeks above all to "adapt" products to the local environment and that this adaptation involves a confrontation between a vision of the "real" needs of the local population as they (the producers) see these needs, and their idea of needs "imported" by foreign firms and international public health organisations.[67] However this may be, it confirms a conception of research that is turned towards other aims than those of the firms that dominate international markets.

According to these factors, in Sub-Saharan African countries such as Kenya, pharmaceutical manufacturing is an activity with a pretty low return on investment rate, and it is sometimes hard for the firms to stay in the race.[68] It goes without saying that this model is not a uniform one. Some firms of emerging countries like India are today able to impose themselves on multiple markets in spite of the power of leading multinationals. Others, in Kenya, for instance, export their pharmaceuticals even before fulfilling the demand on the national market. The result of this situation is a highly heterogeneous and segmented world market, between the multinational firms in the richest countries, with their astronomical profits, and those emerging in poorer countries, without forgetting the myriad of manufacturing units of a country like India, where the most powerful companies coexist with very small units. One could imagine that such different firms could go together thanks to a clear repartition of sales territories. But there is nothing like this, for a phenomenon complexifies everything – the dynamism of pharmaceutical distribution and the multiple connections it brings between different players and the market segments they occupy.

Pharmaceutical distribution to the boiling point

It is not enough to manufacture medicines: one has to sell them. The multiple production units created around the world depend upon distribution operations to move their goods to the market. As a consequence, the internationalisation of industry goes with a crucial mechanism: the expansion of distribution and intermediation activities on markets. And if, as we have said, pharmaceutical manufacturing brings low returns on investments, this is not exactly the case for the multiple intermediation activities that sometimes generate an important added value. But in order to be profitable, these activities require particular skills from the sellers and have important consequences for the market.

In Kenya, the system of distribution seems at first sight to be a concentrated one. Set up in 2000, the Kenya Medical Supplies Authority (KEMSA), the national system of distribution for medical supplies, is the dominant operator, supplying 90% of public bodies.[69] Civil society non-profit organisations also ensure part of the distribution, in particular one faith-based NGO, MEDS (Mission for Essential Drugs and Supplies), which supplies 40% of medicines in the voluntary sector.[70] Lastly, the private market is dominated by wholesaler-importers such as Phillips, Surgipharm, Harley's, and Laborex. On closer examination, however, it turns out that this is not the whole story. In the first place, 80% of spending on pharmaceuticals takes place on the private market; this means that KEMSA covers only a small part of the overall market.[71] Furthermore, KEMSA has been running into increasingly stiff competition since 2010, when the new constitution was brought in and health services were decentralised making it possible for counties to deal with other distributors: the "push" system (KEMSA sent kits of medicines to health centres) was supplanted by a "pull" system (centres placed monthly orders according to their needs). Besides this, medicines for malaria, AIDS, and tuberculosis are to a large extent financed by international donors. These donors, when they resort to KEMSA to distribute treatments that they finance, contribute to "heterogenising" KEMSA, as they impose their own supply rules, such as prequalification. They also fragment circuits by occasionally dealing with private distributors such as Phillips, a partner in PEPFAR.[72] They sometimes even have their own chains, as in the case of the Kenya Pharma project set up by the operator Chemonics, through which USAID distributed ARV and other medicines between 2009 and 2015.

Lastly, whereas about ten major operators dominate the private sector, the number of small distributors is much higher; in 2010, the total number of wholesalers was 212.[73] Additional operators hold import permits issued through PPB – in the course of the interviews, operators put the number at about a hundred, and occasional importers, wholesalers, and retail pharmacists do not hold import permits and still take part in the market's activity. An association of importers/distributors claimed in an interview to have 250 members.[74] To this should be added a large number of retail pharmacies: the

Kenya Pharmaceutical association groups some 3000 registered pharmacies, but estimates that the number in activity is probably twice that.[75] To import, one needs an import licence, but no distinction is made between wholesalers, importers, and distributors; the three operations can be carried out by the same player. On the whole, the Kenyan distribution network is then a fragmented one, with numerous intermediaries. This leads to a double competition: that between firms wishing to export to Kenya and that between importers for firms' custom. Actually, the Indian firms I have met work with both large distributors and smaller retailers in Kenya who engage in the import business with or without licences.

This fragmented situation and the resultant multiplicity of distribution networks produces effects that vary from one market segment to another, but it tends to make local industry more fragile. Above all, it gives distributors an advantage over local manufacturers. Several observers of the market have pointed out that the reactivity of importers to variations in demand on a changing market such as that in Kenya weakens local manufacturers, who cannot adapt as easily as importers can.

According to one analyst:

> *Distributors prevail over manufacturers, everywhere. Distributors are tigers. They set the prices, foresee market trends and then control the market [...] They are the ones who can make life very difficult for you.*[76]

Significantly, prosperous importers in the sector work in buildings that are brand new, spacious, employing large teams. It would seem that in Kenya, distribution is a field that is highly profitable and is recording constant growth.

The Indian situation somehow mirrors that of Kenya, showing the additional clout of distributors. India has made its mark on international markets thanks to its competence in the production of generics. Over the past 20 years, it has become a major operator. The volume of its exports has recorded growth of about 20% a year for the past decade. Today India is the tenth-biggest exporter in the world, exporting 20% of the overall volume of generics to the world market.[77] Its trade in pharmaceuticals is largely directed towards highly industrialised countries: 38% to the USA and 12% to the EU.[78] Few Indian firms, however, are capable of exporting to the wealthiest countries; some 40% export to other countries of the South or to "semi-regulated" markets.[79] Trade with African countries is growing. In 2015, about 20% of Indian pharmaceutical exports went to Africa,[80] the majority going to South Africa, Nigeria, and Kenya.

Solidarity with patients in other parts of the South, and Africa in particular, has led to India's being dubbed "the pharmacy of the developing world". But this apparently humanitarian attitude has been questioned and should be interpreted, rather, in its economic context: that of a national industry expanding on international markets.[81] Effects of India's "strategic decoupling" to protect its developing industry have been particularly positive, though mainly because India already had a large domestic market.[82] At present, the re-coupling of Indian industry to the global economy that began in 1991, and saturation of the domestic market, have been forcing Indian firms to broaden their outreach.[83] The first indication of this trend is the rise in Indian firms' marketing expenditure as of the late 1990s; the second indication is the multiplication of exports, in particular to semi-regulated markets. As a result, despite investments and the occasional transfers of know-how between India and Africa, Indian firms tend to see intercontinental relations less as partnerships in development than as markets to be won. In an interview with a firm in Gujarat, a manufacturer explained this to us:

> *Why take that path [of collaboration and technology transfer]? It's far simpler as it is! We don't have to make big investments; over there the currency is very unstable; for us it's far more practical to sell directly.*

Some Indian producers even sell nothing whatever in India and have directed all their activity abroad, in particular to emerging and developing countries, following growth strategies adapted to the saturation of the Indian market.[84] This does not really change their posture: what is at stake is, first and foremost, the growth of their activity, irrespective of consequences on production in the countries that import their wares.

In this framework, two central traits of the organisation of the circulation of Indian pharmaceuticals in Kenya bring out the sheer diversity of the paths to Kenya followed by Indian medicines, and at the same time, the strategic role of intermediaries. The first of these traits is Indian manufacturers' need to find importers, distributors, and advertisers to provide them with access to private markets and to be able to respond to calls for tenders put out by procurement agencies and by donor organisations. On the Kenyan private market, this means that different distribution models coexist. Usually, it is Kenyan importers who come to India to find contacts and set up partnerships, but it can also happen that Indian manufacturers approach importers to offer their products in Kenya. Partnerships can take various forms: the prevailing one, in Kenya and for Indian exporters, is the authorised agent in charge of sales on the local market. In this model, a firm contracts with an importer/distributor, who becomes their sole authorised distributor on the Kenyan market; the resultant relationship is intended to last over a medium to long term, often for several years. Gujarati firms exporting to Kenya, however, sometimes use several distributors, according to the latter's local linkages, to their own growth phase, and to their strategy:

> *We have two importers to Kenya. There is Mr Ashok [my interviewee hands me a business card], and the firm M, that imports and handles the marketing. We take over registration, pay the administrative fees, and M looks after the logistics of the actual transport.*[85]

The former of the two importers mentioned in the interview belongs to a firm of Kenyan producers; when we point this out, our interviewee replies evasively: "*Yes, apparently he finds it simpler to import finished products as in any case he has to import everything to Kenya as a manufacturer*". It sometimes also happens – though this seems to be relatively rare – that an Indian manufacturer responds directly to a Kenyan call for tenders without going through a distributor. Several patterns of importation and distribution co-exist, and operators who are not necessarily the same as those involved in importing undertake the distribution of medicines in Kenya.

The second trait underscoring the Indian industry's need to expand – and the importance that this lends to intermediaries – is the subcontracting by Indian firms, which is noteworthy. This corresponds to the internationalisation and development of both major firms and a host of Small and Medium Entreprises (SMEs). Medicines can be manufactured by some firms on behalf of others, who are licensed to distribute and to market them. Arrangements of this sort were extensively developed with multinationals from the North who wanted to cut their production costs; at the same time, it enabled Indian firms to reach their desired levels of production. This is, the case of the arrangement between Dr. Reddy and GSK for products sold in several African countries, in the Middle East, the Asia-Pacific region, and in Latin America. Similar agreements link AstraZeneca and Torrent, Pfizer and Aurobindo, Pfizer and Biocon, Boehringer Ingelheim and Cipla.[86] Usually, this is the case with all forms of production outsourcing – a practice that has become central today in organising production on an international scale. Loan-licensing and third-party manufacturing are widespread in India; they consist of marketing under a brand-name medicine produced by a third firm. The difference between loan-licensing and third-party manufacturing is that in the case of loan-licensing the licence-holder does not possess the means of production but usually provides the raw materials; he is responsible for the quality and the supervision of operations; on the other hand, in third-party manufacturing, it is simply the customer who places an order who also markets the product.

This atomisation of production operations, and the emergence of markets in developing countries, promote the emergence of a market for intermediaries who sell and distribute medicines that they have not produced. Here, the situation in India differs from that in Kenya. In India, distribution is determined by an essential fact: the industry faces a growing need to find outlets if it is to keep the production plant running at profitable levels. As in Kenya, however, this strengthens the position of intermediaries. Firms often have recourse to the latter to open up new markets for them, signing contracts to enable them to keep their investments (in capital and labour) profitable; this, in turn, involves recourse to yet other intermediaries: other producers who externalise some of their operations or marketing firms that do not possess productive apparatus. This situation shows the increasing importance taken on by intermediate business in trans-national pharmaceutical markets.

These markets have multiplied, as have relations of interdependence, and geographical zones have proliferated. The markets in question have also become more complex, both juridically/legally and technically, as production and distribution have been "crossed" and mingled. Intermediate business now makes an essential contribution to the value added by sales of generic medicines. To illustrate this importance on the Indian market, wholesalers' and retailers' margins on branded generics are currently very large, in some cases reaching between 201–1016% when compared with 25–30% on branded *princeps*. The latter remains more expensive than the branded generics, but weak price control in India leads intermediaries to take margins that are far larger for branded generics than for *princeps*. In the case of the latter, the value added is captured mainly by the brand.[87] In Kenya, this can be observed both in the number of products registered and in the structuring of prices. In 2009, 12,008 medicines were registered,[88] and the 2007 registers showed 187 anti-malarial medicines produced by 113 manufacturers in 20 different countries.[89] Moreover, Kenya was one of the countries in which distribution and retail margins were highest, representing 70% of the final price, due mainly to costs linked to transport and distribution.[90]

This overview of distribution operations brings a remark that can sum up most issues met on the contemporary market: in the globalised pharmaceutical markets, the most important thing is access to distribution channels in order to move medicines to the market. This chapter has shown that the pharmaceutical industry went global during the last decades with the multiplication of manufacturing units around the world. We also noticed that such an activity, although indispensable, is often very far from the imagination of a highly sophisticated innovation industry bringing billions of dollars and is close to industrial production. As a result, pharmaceutical globalisation manifests itself in the coexistence of heterogeneous market segments, between multinational firms from the richest countries, the powerful and international industry of countries like India, and that of countries like Kenya, whose reach remains national or regional. The market is, therefore, plural: there are different pharmaceutical markets, where different players operate, following distinct rules. But distribution brings another note. Through the multiplication of distribution networks, their internationalisation and their interconnection, production activities happen to be competing de facto. This is particularly true for the poorer markets, in which the local/national industry is competing with European, American, and Indian firms, and sometimes with other regional firms. As a consequence, the contemporary market – or rather markets – are interconnected, and a harsh competition opposes players supposed to operate in different fields and territories. In that context, the most important for firms is not to manufacture medicines – an increasingly common activity – but to access distribution channels to move their goods to the market. The question, then, is why this competition for distribution channels leads to the exacerbation of the illicit medicines problem?

Notes

1 Bhattacharya, N. (2016). Between the bazaar and the bench: Making of the drugs trade in colonial India, ca. 1900–1930. *Bulletin of the History of Medicine*, 90/1, pp. 61–91.
2 *Chemist and Druggist*, 34, 1889, 239, cited in Nandini Bhattacharya, *Op. Cit.*
3 Gambardella, A. (1995). *Science and innovation, the US pharmaceutical industry during the 1980s*. Cambridge: Cambridge University Press.
4 Rajan, K. S. (2012). Pharmaceutical crises and questions of value: Terrains and logics of global therapeutic politics. *The South Atlantic Quarterly*, 111/2, Spring 2012, pp. 321–346.
5 Pignarre, P. (2003). *Le grand secret de l'industrie pharmaceutique*. Paris: La Découverte; Rajan, K. S. (2012). Pharmaceutical crises and questions of value: Terrains and logics of global therapeutic politics. *The South Atlantic Quarterly*, 111/2, Spring 2012, pp. 321–346.
6 Naci, H., Carter, A. W., & Mossialos, E. (2015). Why the drug development pipeline is not delivering better medicines. *BMJ*, h5542, ISSN 1756–1833.
7 Berndt, E. R., Nass, D., Kleinrock, M., & Aitken, M. (2015). Decline in economic returns from new drugs raises questions about sustaining innovations. *Health Affairs*, February, 34/2, pp. 245–252.
8 Austin, M. (2012). *Licensing, selling and finance in the pharmaceutical and healthcare industries. The commercialization of intellectual property*. Farnham: Gower.
9 Joseph, R. K. (2011). *The R&D scenario in Indian pharmaceutical industry*. RIS-DP 176, December.
10 Dhar, B., & Rao, C. N. (2002). *Transfer of technology for successful integration into the global economy. A case study of the pharmaceutical industry in India*. United Nations, UNCTAD/ITE/IPC/MISC. 22.
11 Badiger, A., Kadekodi, G. K., & Nayanatara, S. N. (2006). *Economic reforms and drug policy: A micro level analysis*, New Delhi: IIPA, CMDR, and UNDP.
12 Joseph, R. K. (2011). *The R&D scenario in Indian pharmaceutical industry*. RIS-DP 176, December.
13 Datar, A. L. (1972). *India's economic relations with the USSR and Eastern Europe 1953 to 1969*. Cambridge: Cambridge University Press. pp. 70–71.
14 Joseph, R. K. (2011) *The R&D Scenario in Indian Pharmaceutical Industry*, RIS-DP 176, December.
15 Guennif, S., & Ramani, S. V. (2010). *Catching up in pharmaceuticals: A comparative study of India and Brazil*, UNU-MERIT Working Papers, no. 019, UNU-MERIT, Maastricht.
16 Sampat, B. N. (2012). The accumulation of capabilities in Indian pharmaceuticals and software: The roles that patents did (and did not) play. In H. Odagiri, A. Goto, A. Sunami, & R. R. Nelson (Eds.), *Intellectual property rights, development, and catch-up*. Oxford University Press.
17 Chaudhuri, S. (2005). *The WTO and India's pharmaceuticals industry: Patent protection, TRIPS, and developing countries*. New Delhi: Oxford University Press; Abrol, D. *et al.* (2011). Globalization of the Indian pharmaceutical industry: Implications for innovation. *International Journal of Institutions and Economies*, 327, 3/2, July, pp. 327–365.
18 Joseph, R. K. (2011) *The R&D Scenario in Indian Pharmaceutical Industry*, RIS-DP 176, December.

19 Sagonowsky, E. (2017). The top 15 generic drugmakers by 2016 revenue. *FiercePharma Manufacturing*, 16 May.
20 Horner, R., & Murphy, J. T. (2017). South–North and South–South production networks: diverging socio-spatial practices of Indian pharmaceutical firms. *Global Networks*, March, Preprint.
21 Ecks, S. (2008). Global pharmaceutical markets and corporate citizenship: The case of Novartis' anti-cancer drug Glivec. *BioSocieties*, 3/2, pp. 165–181.
22 Cited in M. Berger *et al.* (2010). *Strengthening pharmaceutical innovation in Africa.* Council on Health Research for Development (COHRED), New Partnership for Africa's Development (NEPAD), p. 33.
23 www.tradingeconomics.com/sub-saharan-africa/health-expenditure-per-capita-us-dollar-wb-data.html.
24 Kaplan, W., & Laing, R. (2005). Local production of pharmaceuticals: industrial policy and access to medicines – An overview of key concepts, issues and opportunities for future research. *Health, Nutrition and Population (HNP), discussion paper*. Washington, DC: World Bank.
25 M. Mackintosh, G. Banda, P. Tibandebage, & W. Wamae (Eds.) (2015). *Making medicines in Africa: The political economy of industrializing for local health.* London: Palgrave Macmillan.
26 Greene, J. (2011). Making medicines essential. *BioSocieties*, 6, pp. 10–33; Nitsan, C. (2012). *The World Health Organization between North and South.* Ithaca: Cornell University Press.
27 Peterson, K. (2014). *Speculative markets: Drug circuits and derivative life in Nigeria.* Durham: Duke University Press.
28 Berger, M., *et al.* (2009). Strengthening pharmaceutical innovation in Africa. *Council on Health Research for Development (COHRED), New Partnership for Africa's Development (NEPAD).*
29 M. Mackintosh, G. Banda, P. Tibandebage, & W. Wamae (Eds.) (2015). *Making medicines in Africa: The political economy of industrializing for local health.* London: Palgrave Macmillan. pp. 8–9.
30 Interview of the chairman of a pharmaceutical firm, Nairobi, 20 February 2014.
31 Chorev, N. (2020). *Give and take. Developmental foreign aid and the pharmaceutical industry in East Africa.* Princeton: Princeton University Press.
32 As of 1981, the Kenyan government published an initial list of essential medicines.
33 Buy drugs from local firms. *The Standard*, 19 September 1981.
34 Drug firms fight against stiff foreign competition. *The Nation Weekend Magazine*, 16 May 1982.
35 Swamy, G. (1994). Kenya structural adjustment in the 1980s. *Policy Research Working Paper, 1238, World Bank.*
36 Simonetti, R., Clark, N., & Wamae, W. Pharmaceuticals in Kenya: The evolution of technological capabilities. In M. Mackintosh, G. Banda, P. Tibandebage, & W. Wamae (Eds.) (2015). *Making medicines in Africa: The political economy of industrializing for local health.* London: Palgrave Macmillan.
37 Frost & Sullivan. *Innovative brands remain robust within Kenya's private pharmaceutical market.* 2 October 2013. Retrieved from www.frost.com/prod/servlet/press-release.pag?docid=285641444.
38 Kariuki, J., Njeru, M. K., Wamae, W., & Mackintosh, M. (2015). *Improving the supply chains for the health sector: What role for locally manufactured and imported*

medicines and medical supplies in Kenya. Nairobi: African Centre for Technology Studies.

39 Interview of the global malaria manager, Clinton Health Access Initiative, Nairobi, 21 February 2014.

40 I. K. Mitra, R. Samaddar, & S. Sen (Eds.) (2017). *Accumulation in post-colonial capitalism*. Singapore: Springer.

41 Beaujard, P. (2017). Echanges dans l'océan Indien; l'Afrique de l'est du 8e au 15e siècle. In Catherine Coquery-Vidrovitch (Dir.), *L'Afrique des routes. Histoire de la circulation des hommes, des richesses et des idées à travers le continent africain*. Paris: Musée du Quai Branly, Actes Sud. pp. 110–121.

42 Markovits, C. (2004). *The global world of Indian merchants, 1750–1947. Traders of Sind from Bukhara to Panama*. Cambridge: Cambridge University Press.

43 Nowik, L. (2010). Les Indiens d'Afrique de l'est: Combien sont-ils? In M. Adam (Ed.) *L'Afrique Indienne. Les minorités d'origine Indo-Pakistanaise en Afrique orientale*. Paris: Karthala. pp. 109–190.

44 Aiyar, S. (2015). *Indians in Kenya. The politics of diaspora*. Cambridge: Harvard University Press, pp. 71–76.

45 Oonk, G. (2007). 'We Lost our Gift of Expression'. Loss of the Mother Tongue among South Asians in East Africa, 1880–2000. In G. Oonk (Ed.), *Global Indian diasporas. Exploring trajectories of migration and theory*. Amsterdam: Amsterdam University Press. pp. 67–88.

46 Oonk, G. (2006). South Asians in East Africa (1880–1920) with a particular focus on Zanzibar. Towards a historical explanation of economic success of a middlemen minority. *Journal of African and Asian Studies*, (5) 1, pp. 57–89.

47 Aiyar, S. (2015). *Indians in Kenya. The politics of diaspora*. Cambridge: Harvard University Press.

48 Fouéré, M.-A. (2010). Les Indiens sont des exploiteurs et les Africain des paresseux! Production des catégories raciales et enjeux socioéconomiques en Tanzanie. In M. Adam (Ed.), *L'Afrique Indienne. Les minorités d'origine Indo-Pakistanaise en Afrique orientale*. Paris: Karthala. pp. 371–408.

49 Greenwood, A., Topiwala, H. (2015). *Indian doctors in Kenya, 1895–1940: The forgotten history*. London: Palgrave Macmillan.

50 Adam, M. (2010). Des Indiens des comptoirs aux Indo-Africains. pp. 15–78 In M. Adam (Ed.), *L'Afrique Indienne. Les minorités d'origine Indo-Pakistanaise en Afrique orientale*. Paris: Karthala, p. 52.

51 Ibid.

52 Interviews of the General Manager and the Marketing Manager of a pharmaceutical firm, Ahmedabad, Gujarat, 21 November 2015.

53 Cassier, M., & Correa, M. (2009). Éloge de la copie: Le reverse engineering des antirétroviraux contre le VIH/sida dans les laboratoires pharmaceutiques brésiliens. *Sciences sociales et santé*, 27/3, pp. 77–103; Abrol, D., *et al.* (2011). Globalization of the Indian pharmaceutical industry: Implications for innovation. *International Journal of Institutions and Economies*, 327, 3/2, July, pp. 327–365.

54 Ray, A. S., & Bhaduri, S. (2003). The political economy of drug quality: changing perceptions and implications for Indian pharmaceutical industry. *Economic and Political Weekly*, pp. 2303–2309; Iyer P. K. (2008). Regulatory issues in the Indian pharmaceutical industry. In P. Banerjee (Ed.) *India, Science and Technology 2008*, NISTADS, CSIR; Jeffery, R., & Santhosh, M. R. (2009). Architecture of drug

regulation in India: What are the barriers to regulatory reform? *Journal of Health Studies*, vol. 2, pp. 13–32.

55 M. Mackintosh, G. Banda, P. Tibandebage, W. Wamae (eds) (2015) *Making Medicines in Africa: The Political Economy of Industrializing for Local Health*, London: Palgrave Macmillan.

56 Joseph, R. K. (2016). *Pharmaceutical industry and public policy in post-reform India*. London: Routledge.

57 Greene, J. (2014). *Generic. The unbranding of modern medicine*. John Hopkins University Press; Greene, J. (2016). Pharmaceutical geographies: Mapping the boundaries of the therapeutic revolution. In J. A. Greene, F. Condrau, & E. S. Watkins (Eds.), *Therapeutic revolutions: Pharmaceuticals and social change in the twentieth century*. Chicago: University of Chicago Press.

58 Interview of the CEO of a pharmaceutical firm in Nairobi, 21 February 2014.

59 Wamae, W. (2014). Value-added tax in the pharmaceutical industry: What does it really mean for Kenya's industralisation? *Working Paper, ACTS*, September.

60 Interview of the manager of a pharmaceutical firm, Nairobi, 14 February 2014.

61 Coulibaly, A. (2010). L'industrie pharmaceutique et la production pharmaceutique en Afrique de l'Ouest: Potentiels contraintes et perspectives d'évolution. *Passerelles*, 11, 2, pp. 11–13.

62 Interview of the manager of a pharmaceutical firm, Nairobi, 14 February 2014.

63 Cassier, M., Correa, M. (2009). Éloge de la copie: Le reverse engineering des antirétroviraux contre le VIH/sida dans les laboratoires pharmaceutiques brésiliens. *Sciences Sociales et Sante*, 27/3, pp. 77–103.

64 Interview of the manager of a pharmaceutical firm, Nairobi, 14 February 2014.

65 Interview of the manager of a pharmaceutical firm, Nairobi, 21 February 2014.

66 Interview of the manager of a pharmaceutical firm, Nairobi, 14 February 2014.

67 I emphasise the fact that there are merely manufacturers' epidemiological projections; Julie Livingston has shown elsewhere how important cancer actually is in African countries. Livingston, J. (2012). *Improvising medicine: An African oncology ward in an emerging cancer epidemic*. Durham: Duke University Press.

68 Chaudhuri, S., & West, A. (2015). Can local producers compete with low-cost imports? A simulation study of pharmaceutical industry in low-income Africa. *Innovation and Development*, 5/1, pp. 23–38.

69 Kariuki, J., Njeru, M. K., Wamae, W., & Mackintosh, M. (2015). *Local supply chains for medicines and medical supplies in Kenya: Understanding the challenges*. Nairobi: African Centre for Technology Studies.

70 Ministry of Medical Services and Ministry of Public Health and Sanitation. (2010). *Sessional Paper on National Pharmaceutical Policy*, June.

71 Syam, N. (2014). Regional pooled procurement of medicines in the East African community. *Research paper 53*. Genève: South Centre.

72 PEPFAR: Presidential Emergency Plan for Aids Relief. US aid plan set up in 2003, during the presidency of George W. Bush.

73 Ministry of Medical Services and Ministry of Public Health and Sanitation. (2010). *Sessional Paper on National Pharmaceutical Policy*. June.

74 Interview of the chairman of the Kenya Pharmaceutical Distributors Association, Nairobi, 14 May 2012.

75 Interview of the chairman of the Kenya Pharmaceutical Distributors Association, Nairobi, 14 May 2012.

76 Interview of an expert in pharmaceutical industrial policies and a UNIDO consultant, 29 January 2016.
77 Bose, A. S. (2017). Why pharmaceutical exports from India to Europe grew during economic crisis? *Management and Labour Studies*; Indian Brand Equity Foundation. (2017). *Pharmaceuticals Sectorial Report*, April. Retrieved from www.ibef.org/industry/pharmaceutical-india.aspx.
78 Bose, A. S., *Ibid.*
79 Mazumdar, M. (2012). *Performance of pharmaceutical companies in India: A critical analysis of industrial structure, firm specific resources, and emerging strategies.* New York: Springer.
80 Calculation based on Pharmexcil data. Retrieved from www.pharmexcil.com/trade-statistics.
81 Kottakkunnummal, M. (2016). Seeing like an Indian generic pharmaceutical company. Generics as humanitarian goods in Africa. *Economic and Political Weekly*, 9 April, 51/15, pp. 56–63.
82 Horner, R. (2014). Strategic decoupling, recoupling and global production networks: India's pharmaceutical industry. *Journal of Economic Geography*, 14(6), pp. 1117–1140; Abbott, F. (2017). Indian policies to promote local production of pharmaceutical products and protect public health. WHO Report.
83 Mazumdar, M. (2012). *Performance of pharmaceutical companies in India: A critical analysis of industrial structure, firm specific resources, and emerging strategies.* New York: Springer.
84 This point is also made by Chaudhuri, S. (2015). Can foreign firms promote local production of pharmaceuticals in Africa? In M. Mackintosh, G. Banda, P. Tibandebage, & W. Wamae (Eds.) (2015). *Making medicines in Africa: The political economy of industrializing for local health.* London: Palgrave Macmillan.
85 Interview of the manager of a pharmaceuticals production firm at Baroda (Gujarat), 23 November 2015.
86 Joseph, R. K. (2011). The R&D scenario in Indian pharmaceutical industry, RIS-DP 176, December, pp. 15–16.
87 Singal, G. L., Nanda, A., & Kotwani, A. (2011). A comparative evaluation of price and quality of some branded versus branded–generic medicines of the same manufacturer in India. *Indian Journal of Pharmacology*, 43/2, pp. 131–136; Kotwani, A. (2013). Tracking medicine prices in the supply chain. Who benefits from the free market in India? *Economic and Political Weekly*, 28 December, pp. 104–112.
88 Ministry of Medical Services and Ministry of Public Health and Sanitation. (2010). *Sessional Paper on National Pharmaceutical Policy*, June.
89 Ministry of Health, PPB and the Division of Malaria Control (DoMC). (2007). *Antimalarial medicines in Kenya: Availability, quality and registration status*, cited in UNIDO (2012) *Kenya Pharmaceutical Sector Development Strategy*, p. 1.
90 IMS Health. (2014). *Understanding the pharmaceutical value chain*. p. 21.

3 Selling at all costs

The battle for distribution channels

In June 2009, a shipment containing 30 tons of medicines (two containers) was inspected by the Kenyan authorities at the Kilindini port in Mombasa. This shipment was destined to the national agency managing pharmaceutical supplies after a tender which was won in the former year by the Kenyan pharmaceutical firm Dawa Limited. The inspection, as realised by the pharmaceutical inspectors, revealed several irregularities.[1] First, the import permit for the shipment was expired and changes had been brought *a posteriori,* which amounted to falsification. Even more serious, the declared importer was Dawa and the exporter was Shanghai Schangen Trading Corporation (declared origin Shanghai in China), but the packaging, bearing the Dawa brand, indicated that the medicines had been manufactured in Kenya. Above all, the manufacturer was not the exporter but another Chinese firm – Yansu Zwe Kantai Pharmaceutical Company Limited – which was not registered in Kenya. The authorities declared that this was counterfeiting case since the origin of the medicine had been deliberately hidden and the medicine presented in a deceiving manner as fabricated by Dawa, which was not the case. But the counterfeiting act denounced in this situation was not random counterfeiting: Dawa had just counterfeited its own products! It claimed to have manufactured products that it actually imported.

This curious "self-counterfeiting" case highlights the kind of problems that emerge from the market structure described in the former chapter. In the global South, the globalisation of industrial pharmaceutical manufacturing has gone with a renewed competition to access distribution channels. The violence of this competition and the ease of access to medicines (and not to the circuits that allow to sell them) confronts market players to arbitrages. For a manufacturing firm like Dawa, it can be more profitable to import medicines than to produce them. This episode shows how important the distribution channels are for pharma entrepreneurs. The problem of illicit medicines results from the conflicts and irregularities that are inextricably linked to this situation. Illicit medicines are only one symptom of the competition for distribution, a competition in which everyone tries to capture the profits that are

DOI: 10.4324/9781003194767-5

formed in the distribution process. The illegal strategy mobilised by Dawa here is only the underside of a legal strategy that consists in influencing legislation in order to define according to one's own interests the medicines that should be authorised to circulate and those that should not be. As a consequence, the illicit is not only related to criminality or State failure: it is a direct manifestation of the kind of competition which is happening in internationalised, but highly heterogeneous markets.

It would, however, be difficult to make such an assertion without trying to know how competition for distribution channels leads to a surge in the illicit. In order to explain the passage from one to the other, it is necessary to show how the market players manage to domesticate it, to impose themselves in it. How are they proceeding?

Good practices and regulatory weapons

In the course of recent decades, regulations framing pharmaceutical productive activity have multiplied, at the instigation of both national governments and international institutions such as the WHO, the ICH (International Conference on Harmonisation), and the PIC/S (Pharmaceutical Inspection Co-operation Scheme). Regulation of Good Manufacturing Practices (GMPs), however, is by no means new. In the USA, the Biologics Control Act was passed in 1902, after some 20 years of lobbying and a case in which 12 infants died as a result of contamination.[2] The Food and Drug Administration (FDA) set the first standards of GMP early in the 1940s, following cases of cross-contamination,[3] and the WHO, in 1967, following the 20th World Assembly on Health, issued the first regulation of international ambit.[4] The purpose of GMPs was to normalise the production of effective, trustworthy medicines. These guidelines were to be both marks of trust and barriers guarding the entrance to the market.[5] In the 1970s, the guidelines were applied by firms in the USA producing *princeps* medicines in order to increase the cost of the generics that were competing with their products.[6] Since then, the most powerful firms have kept on pushing for more stringent GMPs, a strategy that helped in eliminating challengers lawfully. These regulations have weighed on the regulatory capacities of governments in the South, as we shall presently see.

In Kenya, the regulatory work developed in the course of the decade 1980 to 1990, starting with the registration of medicines in the territory. In 1981, rules governing registration were established after several controversies on the circulation in Kenya of medicines that were banned or were strictly regulated in other countries.[7] At the time, firms whose costs were rising had already protested against this increase.[8] In 1992, a national laboratory for quality control was set up to test pharmaceutical substances.[9] In 1994, the Kenya National Drug Policy made respect of GMPs[10] a condition for registration of firms. Registration procedure became stricter for local manufacturers and importers – at least in theory; it is hard to find out what actual effect these measures had. Product specifications had to be submitted on registration and inspection could follow; but until recently, local firms have not in fact been made subject to production standards. "*before that, issue of the licence was based on a 'come and check' procedure, and manufacturers devised arrangements with the PPB*".[11] In 2008, the government established a new National Pharmaceutical Policy. In 2012, the Kenya Pharmaceutical Sector Development Strategy was set up, one of its central components being a roadmap obliging local firms to respect the GMP.[12] In 2012, certain local firms obtained PIC/S accreditation and one of them obtained a WHO pre-qualification certifying that it respected the good practices of fabrication established by the organisation.

> *It was really to deal with quality and the problem of different standards. One had to be sure that only one standard was explicitly intended. If we [Kenyan industry] could ensure that an international standard was being applied, then there was no problem. It would give equal opportunities to companies in developing the sector. There are no local standards. We have to fight against this perception of standards as being local.*[13]

The government's current strategy consists in boosting the image of the Kenyan industry by "delocalising" its image through enforcement of international standards such as the WHO GMP. Some stakeholders feel that today respecting these standards is essential if local firms are to survive international competition, as these standards now have to be applied by central procurement agencies. As Cosmos, the leading Kenyan firm producing antiretrovirals did not have pre-qualification, the proportion of its sales to the government went into a constant decline from 30% announced in 2003 to 20% in 2005; this trend persisted throughout the decade ending in 2010. The same pattern prevailed in anti-malarials based on artemisinine; in 2011, the number of local firms producing Artemisinin-based combination therapy (ACTs) dropped from ten to zero following a move to the AMFm co-payment mechanism (Affordable Medicines Facility malaria) that involved dealing with prequalified suppliers.[14] Furthermore, GMP put additional pressure, in terms of profitability and productivity, on Kenyan firms facing competitors selling prequalified products at low prices. In this context, the preferential 15% that NGOs could add to their prices, if their medicines were manufactured locally plays only a marginal role. A particularly striking example is that of Universal, a company that succeeded in obtaining WHO pre-qualification for its line of ARV. In an interview with the general manager, he shared his mixed feelings:

> *In one way, it's a very good thing that we got WHO pre-qualification. It forced us to become much more professional, to raise our standards of quality and tighten up our procedures. But to this day we have sold no ARV. [...] Competition from India is harsh, and international donors prefer low prices that prevent us from selling.*[15]

Local industries' dependence on imports makes their prices less competitive, confining them to piecemeal sales to public health institutions in the case of medicines such as ARV.[16] Examples such as these bring out the difficulties Kenyan firms come up against once they adapt to harmonisation of standards of production.

In India, the main regulatory authority controlling the quality of medicines on the market is the *Central Drugs Standards Control Organization* (CDSCO) and the regulation GMPs for the Indian market is defined through Schedule M[17], the first version of which was published in 1988. In 2001, the Ministry of Health and Family Welfare issued a revised version, closer to WHO recommendations; it was applied progressively from 2002 to 2005. Since 2005, it has been applicable to sales in India. As of 2005, India has been subject to the intellectual property rules contained in the agreement on TRIPS. Small and medium enterprises protested against this particular modification of the rules; subsequently, numerous manufacturing units were obliged to close down.[18] Schedule M diverges from the WHO GMPs on several points – in particular, that of water treatment and the role of quality controls – though some stakeholders feel that it is no less demanding.[19] The main remaining problem is that of lining up the practice of SMEs with the recommendations of Schedule M as a drug inspector in Gujarat explained:

> *The big problem is that of sick units. [...] A large number of firms have got growth problems, to enlarge their market, because of competition from firms in other states in India. Following standards is not always easy, and one also has to do good work in marketing, otherwise medicines don't sell. The market here is full of small manufacturers and it is still expensive to export, so sometimes the manufacturers put themselves in unstable positions ... normally they have to respect Schedule M. But in those cases, it's a bit difficult.*[20]

The observance and application of GMPs throughout the country take place within the fluctuating relationship between enterprises and the government. This fluctuation is partly materialised by the drug inspectors' work as actors in the state's intervention. The latter regulates first and foremost entrance to the market, keeping certain firms out and letting others in, according to the state of negotiations, as the above interview shows. Good practices become a mode of regulation that can have drastic effects, such as closing down firms while being based on a relatively slack system of constraints, its application depending both on controls and their interpretation by the government authorities. From this point of view, the harmonisation of GMPs does not only play a role in the standardisation of quality, it is also a tool against competitors. But the regulation of practice is not the only domain that is strategically investigated by pharmaceutical firms.

Intellectual property, keep out

In Kenya, intellectual property, though not totally absent from producers' concerns, was by no means massively present at the time when my investigation was underway. At the time, the World Bank deemed Kenya one of the "least developed countries"; a status that changed in 2015. Meanwhile, as one of the "least developed countries", it was entitled to make unrestricted use of TRIPS flexibilities in matters of copyright. This was asserted locally by the Industrial Property Act passed in 2001, which gave priority to "access" rather than intellectual property – a result of lobbying, during the debates entailed by the bill, by a coalition in favour of the broadest possible access to essential medicines. One concrete result of this was the licence granted voluntarily by GlaxoSmithKline and Boehringer Ingelheim to the local firm Cosmos Limited after the latter applied to the Kenyan government for a compulsory license to manufacture the lamivudine, zidovudine, and nevirapine molecules, and then to the Universal Corporation to produce ARV combining the zidovudine and lamivudine molecules.[21] The CEO of Cosmos Limited linked explicitly the granting of the patent to the post-2001 period – that followed the case brought by Big Pharma against South Africa and subsequently dropped, and the Doha Declaration – to a context favourable to developing countries in matters of intellectual property.

> *It was the time of the Doha Round. At first I wanted a compulsory license, but nothing came of it. But afterwards there were the events in South Africa, and there was the Industrial Property Act, and eventually it was GSK who issued a voluntary licence.*[22]

This is why it is important to take into account the "international climate", which contributes to making certain operations – for example, transfers of know-how, licensing agreements – either possible or impossible. However, in this situation, the Kenyan manufacturers were not given free rein. From 2006 to 2008, Cosmos was also involved in a battle with Pfizer, who accused the firm of intellectual property infringement for producing azithromycin, an antibiotic that belonged to the WHO essential medicines list.[23] Cosmos' lawyers resorted to the argument of TRIPS flexibilities, but it was dismissed by the Court. For the argument to be valid, Cosmos should have applied officially for a compulsory license delivered by the government, which had not been the case. In 2008, soon after the patent expired, the Kenyan firm was declared guilty of intellectual property infringement and the goods manufactured during the patent validity had to be destroyed. The irony of the situation was that Pfizer had mobilised for the case the patent held with the African Regional Intellectual Property Organisation (ARIPO). However, at the time of the lawsuit, the organisation had not asked Pfizer to renew their fees – Pfizer had sued a Kenyan firm for a patent upon which it had not paid its fees![24]

In India, the copyright issue played a central part in debates on pharmaceuticals, though more pronouncedly than in Kenya. Since its entry into the WTO took effect in 2005, India has been obliged to respect the agreement on TRIPS. A considerable amount of literature has been devoted to the consequences of the agreement on the Indian pharmaceutical industry, which until then had enjoyed substantial latitude in manufacturing medicines.[25] Most commentators highlight the increasing pressure that is being brought to bear on the Indian government by industry and by certain governments – in particular that of the USA – to apply a conception of intellectual property that suits the interests of firms of the North. An example: India has for some 15 years been on the Special 301 "priority watch list" of the US Trade Representative that indicates the countries where respect of copyright is not adequately enforced.[26] Contentious points are in particular section 3(d) of the Indian patent law, which enables the licensing authority to reject applications when it feels that they do not embody enough real innovation and also provides for recourse to compulsory licensing – used on only one occasion – a right guaranteed to governments by TRIPS. In recent years, conflicts have revealed the pressures brought to bear by firms and foreign governments on the Indian authorities. When the Indian government invoked Section 3(d) in 2006, Novartis took it to court; the case lasted for seven years.[27] The compulsory license granted to the firm Natco for its Nexavar anti-cancer drug was also used to underscore the rights of governments as regards this practice.[28]

When Narendra Modi was elected in 2014, the Indian government adopted a more conciliatory attitude towards the USA in copyright matters, though preserving Indian leadership in generics policy. In January 2015, an application for copyright by the firm Gilead for the sofosbuvir molecule (used to treat hepatitis C) was rejected; it was eventually granted in May 2016. Unofficial communiqués spread the news that the Indian government had renounced further recourse to compulsory licenses. The new IP law was initially decried as giving in to the demands of multinational majors.[29] At the same time, section 3(d) was retained. In this context, manufacturers mobilised resources with a view to marketing medicines in accordance with their desiderata. For example, the fact of being near Bangladesh, classified as one of the "least developed countries", but where the pharmaceutical industry is well established, enables manufacturers to set up very favourable licencing agreements.

> *For us, copyrights are something we have to consider, but that is not necessarily going to prevent us from putting products on the market. For example, until then to send to Kenya was not very complicated because Kenya was classified as one of the LDCs. And for many manufacturers there is always as solution – Bangladesh. As it is an LDC, you can manufacture there whatever you want to! For example they've got sitagliptine – an anti diabetic drug that's a real blockbuster that we Indians can't make. But all you have to do is to make an arrangement with firms there and you can market after that.*[30]

Here too, the manufacturing activity is conditioned by international standards and debates, and by governments' determination or lack of determination to counter them, even though stakeholders in emergent countries like India have ways of getting round constraints that are imposed on them.

Pirates and scammers

The tensions surrounding GMPs and intellectual property principles often go along with derogatory qualifications of Southern firms: insufficiently skilled, insufficiently abiding to the rules, these firms would not be up to the task. This discourse, broadcasted by the media, market players and observers, characterises industrial pharmacy in the South first and foremost by its lacks. This is not a recent thing: "*Pharmaceutical industry shows healthy signs*", the *Kenya Times* reported on 25 February 1991, following up its headline with a subtitle: "*but still lacks technological capacity*". This discourse contributes to the depreciation of the firms in emerging and developing countries. Furthermore, it is also often employed to qualify the States that host these industries, as well as their regulatory authorities, as shown here by a member of the Kenyan pharmaceutical society: "*From a legal point of view, we've got fantastic laws; the challenge is to apply them. There is a huge gap, a big lack of capacity of PPB to apply regulations*".[31]

Lack of capacity of the firms, of the State: critiques and accusations against companies and authorities are numerous. They indicate another space in which the international competition between firms – and the devaluation of Southern firms – is at play: the field of communication strategies.

The "anti-piracy" discourse promoted in the 1980s and 1990s by the US pharmaceutical industry, shows how important this field is. The 1980s have been pivotal years for the GATT's negotiations; they corresponded to a very aggressive promotion of the strategic interests of Northern firms, especially in the case of the pharmaceutical industry.[32] During this period of time, the industrial firms in the richest countries tried to impose a way of understanding that would fit their interest. They elaborated a metaphoric language and a world view that systematically denigrated their challengers. For some observers, at that time "The dominant and most aggressive metaphor of the debate was piracy".[33] Promoted by the US government and industry, this metaphor directly aimed at the foreign generic industry, which was being accused of copying medicines that were patented in other countries. Such a metaphor allowed to close any debate upon intellectual property, accusing wrongdoers of being criminals and marking any discussion upon alternatives to patentability with the seal of immorality. This bashing enterprise largely influenced the debates upon generic medicines in the Southern countries, as illustrated by this question raised in 1991 in the *Kenya Times* (the article mentioned above):

> *The question of generics versus brand names is a touchy one. Experts argue that brand names have the attributes of authenticity precision efficacy and corroborativeness which means that any complaints about a particular drug*

> *can always be directed to the manufacturer who shoulders full responsibility for his product. On the other hand, generics are anonymous and could open the gate wide for all manner of unscrupulousness.*[34]

The industry leaders' attacks on generic production resulted in a permanent suspicion regarding the legality and quality of medicines produced in the South. The Pretoria lawsuit initiated at the pharmaceutical industry against the South African government at the turn of the 21st century, the huge failure it became for the industry made it more difficult to resort as bluntly to the "piracy" argument.[35] However, the world view that took shape through this discourse in the 1980s and 1990s did not vanish. In Kenya, we can hear it resonating with old stereotypes, formed or reinforced during the colonial period. Market players – manufacturers, distributors, as well as consumers – mobilise this repertoire of stereotypes to maintain derogatory views upon some generic actors, and this affects, in particular, the Indian industry. This discourse is mostly relying upon identification processes that frequently associate pharmacy to "indianity" in Kenya.[36] It manifests itself in multiple configurations, through which terms such as "medicine", "Indian", "national" are moving and renegotiated by the social actors.

In retail pharmacy, it is generally felt that in Kenya, selling medicines – or rather owning a pharmacy – is an Indian profession. This stereotype is widespread, as a large number of retail pharmacies have Indian names and are owned by Indian families. Gidraph G. Wairire has identified pharmacies as the sixth most important type of enterprise owned by Kenyan Indians, after the hardware business, general dealerships, retail clothing, car spares dealerships, and the retail trade in books and stationery.[37] Some 25% of dispensing chemists in Kenya are of Indian origin – a figure that suggests a substantial presence of the Indian minority group not only in pharmaceuticals but also in the liberal professions, for example, medical doctors and lawyers.[38]

Big Pharma has exploited this ethnicisation. I interviewed the security manager of a European pharmaceuticals firm on the subject of falsified and counterfeited medicines. He explained that in Kenya, the problem was important, as the market there was "semi-regulated".

> *"Above all", he said, "there is a problem, as a lot of people are involved in illegal business, and because the market has been 'cornered' by a few lobbies of businessmen of South Asian origin".*

This remark "superimposes" images: that of the production layer on that of distribution, linking problems of quality and legality to the geographical determination of a market. The resultant discourse should be understood in its relation to stereotypes of Asian industry put into circulation over the past two decades by the pharmaceutical majors of the North. It was important for these majors to be able to argue that quality was guaranteed by Northern branding, and to be able to associate illegality and poor quality with production in the South. My interviewee simply superimposed on one another these representations of quality, of persons, and of roles played on the Kenyan market.

This superimposition of issues of quality, perceptions of persons, and cultural attributes also affect the public in general and consumers in particular. It reveals a racialisation of medicines. A Kenyan of about 20, discussing my research, criticised "Indian medicines" not only as dubious in quality but also on the grounds that they were those most currently used in cities like Nairobi.

> *They give us the worst. Most Kenyan medicines are bad, but there are also the Indian medicines, that are copies. People, the government don't want to spend for us, so we sell only copies of medicines made by Indians who are just trying to rip us off.*[39]

Once again, the judgement is severe and at the same time puzzling. It should be interpreted as an expression of a multiple nexus: the perceived socio-economic position of the Indian diaspora in Kenya; discourse on India as the main exporter of medicines to Kenya; and India as a manufacturer of generics with the same ingredients as branded medicines. In some ways, this interpretation opposes the idea that India would be "the pharmacy of the Third World" as Indian firms, like those owned by Indians in Kenya, merely seem to have humanitarian aims. An important aspect of my respondent's remark was also indicated by the confusion it maintained between things, people, and cultures. He was criticising medicines that "came" from India, but I do not think he knew that Kenyan manufacturers could be Indians or of Indian origin. On the other hand, he was criticising medicines imported from India on the basis of an idea of the role played by Indians in Kenya in the course of colonial and post-colonial history. This confusion reveals a link, a muddled crisscrossing of different levels and activities: Indians as manufacturers working in Kenya, Indians as importers of medicines, and Indians in India manufacturing medicines and exporting them to Kenya. On a day to day basis, the public attaches little importance to whether or not the medicines have been manufactured in India or in Kenya by Kenyans or by Indians and sold by Kenyans or by Indians. What matters here is the more general association between medicine and Indians and the suspicion as to the quality of medicines that this link justifies. This process is "fed" by a continual circulation of signs between things, countries, and persons.

These multiple discourses regarding "Indian medicines" attest to the importance and the complexity of the qualification of the industry in the Global South. The strategies put in place by the most powerful industrial actors go along with entangled representations built in a longer term of colonial and post-colonial relations. The discourse produced in this association of industrial strategies and popular stereotypes contributes to depreciate the industry in the South. However, whereas Northern firms try to eliminate their opponents with regulatory and intellectual property lobbying as well as communication strategies, the market players belonging to poorer countries are not left without any means. Their profit strategies, in this context, can bring them on the edge of legality.

Making profit, capturing regulation

Parallel import consists in importing from a third country a product whose price is lower than that in the country to which it is being imported. This enables countries in which prices of medicines are very high to strengthen competition by putting downward pressure on them. When in Kenya, the law on intellectual property was rewritten after Kenya joined the WTO in 2001, it integrated recourse to parallel imports into the Industrial Property Act (IP Act), section 58(2); though formerly forbidden under intellectual property legislation dating from 1989,[40] this flexibility was allowed by the TRIPS at the time of the Doha Declaration in 2001[41]; thus in Kenya, parallel imports of pharmaceutical products are now allowed. From a strictly legal point of view, however, the status of parallel imports is nonetheless vulnerable, as only the IP Act allows it; neither the Pharmacy and Poisons Act nor the Trademarks Act so much as mentions it.[42] As a form of flexibility, parallel import can be used in cases involving patent rights and brand rights. As a result, recourse to parallel import can give rise to legal conflict; a number of operators have tried to amend the flexibility, basing their arguments on the Trademarks Act.

A noteworthy case opposed Lords Healthcare to Salama Pharmaceuticals, illustrating the problems raised by parallel importing. Lords was an agent for the Indian firm Cipla, distributing its Budecort-200 branded inhaler (registered in Kenya by Lords Healthcare), used in asthma treatment. In 2006, while Lords were the sole distributors in Kenya by virtue of its agreement with Cipla, the distributors lost a tender for 2400 units of this product called for by Kenyatta Hospital. It subsequently appeared that another firm, Salama Pharmaceuticals had won the tender for the same product under the same brand name. The complaint was lodged on the basis of the trademark Act, arguing that Lords Healthcare was the manufacturer and holder of exclusive rights to the brand, and that the similarity between the two products involved could deceive customers and harm them. The defence responded that the complainant was not the manufacturer of the product; that furthermore, the brand had been registered only with PPB, and that this did not confer any particular right on the plaintiff, as the defendant, acting as parallel importer, had also registered the product with the same agency; and lastly, that the products were not similar, but identical, which fact could not harm consumers. The court eventually dismissed the complaint.[43]

As to the promoters of parallel imports, a group of distributors, the Kenya Pharmaceutical Distributors' Association, has often taken a stand, claiming recourse to this right. The chairman of the association justifies this, referring to the exorbitant prices of medicines in Kenya. He adds that the problem also involves Indian generics, as these too are following a brand logic and pricing strategies. He stresses that there is no link between parallel import and quality issues, as parallel imports are subject to the same controls as other medicines carried out by the regulatory authorities.[44] On the other hand, operators from multinational Western firms represented by the Kenya Association of Pharmaceutical Industry, and Kenyan distributors working directly with them, have criticised parallel imports. In their view, the latter is problematic as they prevent complete identification of the product, as it is not imported by the official agent of the brand. Furthermore, these imports penalise the local agent handling the product, who has carried the cost of registration and marketing. The local agent suffers as a result of unfair competition from operators who do not incur the same expenses.[45] Other observers feel that parallel imports are simply "illegal" as they fail to respect intellectual property:

> *In fact for me I call it "illegal importations", what they call parallel importations. There's a definition of parallel importations and we have actually over the years as KAPI discussed with the government, the regulator, to ask "what do you mean by parallel importation?" There's a law (the IPAct), which defines what parallel importation is, and we did develop guidelines and said, "fine, if you want to call it Parallel importation, this is what it is" and in any case the owner of the brand should be notified. Because what we do, we register the drug, we pay high fees (1000 dollars, and also 300 dollars every year to keep the product registered), and then somebody else walks to the regulator and gets an authority to get them from another source and put them on the market. So it kills… First of all we have reps in the field and the doctors are prescribing the medicines. But the product is not coming from our warehouse, it's coming from somebody else's warehouse. Despite the fact that we have agreed on that process, the regulator has continued to flout his own law, to give these illegal importers legitimacy. Through this process that is how the counterfeit end up here. Because these people they would go to India, maybe to a wholesaler and buy the drugs and bring them here and many of them fly, they go to Dubai, they bring consignments, they squeeze… sometimes they bribe the custom people …*[46]

Another argument against parallel imports underscores that the use made of them is linked less to concern for public health than to a mere market strategy:

> *It started off as, quote-unquote, "parallel importation". There are some people who said, especially since 2002, that medicines in this country are very expensive, that Big Pharma are overpricing medicines, and some of them went to India and said that "drugs are costing this amount". But you know in India the government is subsidizing medicines. So through that, and through cartels linked to political people and regulators, they developed a case for "parallel importation" in which case they would be authorized to import our medicines. They are not the registration owners and they*

> *would then import, from India or China or wherever, in the name of parallel import, they would then put the products on the market. Sometimes at 90% of the price whereas in fact, if they followed the dogma of the price they bought from India or Pakistan, they would have to put it at 50 or 60% [of the price]. So in fact it's a profiteering game. Without any marketing expense or anything.*[47]

Above all, several operators in multinational firms stress the overall link between parallel imports and the circuits of illicit medicines. Nevertheless, as another Sanofi executive in Kenya explained to us several years after this interview, even though his firm was highly critical of parallel imports, it had not made this question a top priority.[48]

These debates were graphically illustrated in 2002 and 2006 when amendments to the IP Act were mooted to remodel the law on parallel import by requiring the agreement of the rights holder.[49] Initially, the amendment was passed in June, late at night, when many MPs were absent,[50] and it was part of a bundle of amendments.[51] In August, it was rejected by President Daniel Arap Moi. The second time, the proposal was submitted as part of another parcel of amendments and was rejected by the Assembly.[52] In an attempt to limit criticism of the parallel import system at the same time as promoting it as a form of flexibility, the government set up a number of working groups. In one of these, formed in September 2006, a number of members opposed or promoted parallel imports.[53] The workgroup issued practical guidelines in 2008.[54] In the prevailing context, however, these guidelines were never applied: the anti-counterfeit law was being mooted and protests had broken out against it. The conflict went on. In 2014, after a new campaign by groups opposing parallel imports, the dispute resumed afresh and a new working group was set up. In September 2015, the PPB issued a new document listing the contentious points contained in the 2008 document and proposing a new regulatory framework for parallel imports.[55] In July 2016, the intention was to put these new guidelines into application in the course of the coming months.[56] To knowledge, in 2020, this had not yet been done.

So far, the conflict upon parallel imports looks like a "traditional" trade dispute. But in order to understand more fully the animosity of participants in the debates, it is necessary to put them back in the context of Kenyan pharmaceutical regulation and to introduce a new character: Julius.

Julius is a specialist in pharmaceutical regulation, a high ranked officer in the National Quality Control Laboratory (NQCL). Formerly, he had worked at PPB from 2000 to 2010. In 2005, PPB needed to improve its expertise in legal and pharmaceutical matters. At the time, it was usually the police who dealt with violations of pharmaceutical regulations, but the police often lost their cases because officers were not sufficiently competent in the field. Julius and a colleague were sent to England to take master's degrees. The training took place in both England and Kenya between 2006 and 2010. Julius continued after that at the Kenya School of Law, becoming a barrister in

2015. Meanwhile, in 2007, when he came back from England, he was posted to NQCL before returning to PPB, where he was put in charge of imports.

On taking up this new position, he told me in an interview, he soon noticed that the department had issued import permits for medicines that were not registered or that had failed to pass GMP inspections, and also that medicines had been registered after having been assessed negatively by the NQCL because they had not come up to its standards. His superior, however, insisted that permits be awarded. Reacting to this, Julius set up a system that made it possible to trace the origins of permits. At the time, from 2008 to 2010, the Permanent Secretary of the Ministry was James Ole Kiyiapi, who was in the future to run as a candidate for the presidency of Kenya. Julius contacted him and explained the system of illegal import permits that had been set up at PPB. Kiyiapi mandated the Efficiency Monitoring Unit (EMU), a body in charge of evaluating public institutions, to investigate. Julius was identified as the whistle-blower, a privileged EMU informer. However, according to him, somebody, probably from PPB, contacted EMU before his visit. "*So when the group came, they came to see me and told me, with knowing nods, 'Oh, so you're the one, OK, OK ...'*"[57] During this period, Julius claims, he was threatened both verbally and physically by colleagues at PPB. His situation became more serious still in June: soon after his visit to EMU, Kiyiapi, who was involved in a conflict with the minister of medical services, was transferred to the ministry of education. Julius thus lost an important supporter and was transferred to the management of a hospital in 2010, accused of having insulted the Chairman of the Kenya Pharmaceutical Distributors Association (KPDA), of having demanded bribes in exchange for import permits, of having threatened the Registrar of PPB in a circular, and of having issued import permits for medicines that had expired; according to him, it was his superior who had authorised these permits:

> *One day he came into my office and asked me to grant an import permit to a NGO he was acquainted with, but three things were missing to complete the application. So I refused, but when he insisted I finally let it be signed – the document had not been approved by the person in charge of imports (i.e. me), but was signed directly by my superior.*[58]

The EMU report was published in March 2011 and changed the situation. It was highly critical of PPB and of the registrar, who was accused of having registered under his responsibility medicines that had failed the NQCL quality tests, and in particular KamoxClav, a combination of amoxicillin and clavulanic acid produced by the Indian firm Flamingo. Aglowmed, another Indian firm, had continued distributing medicines in Kenya without respecting the GMP, according to a PPB inspection report. Financial transactions were also noted, tending to strengthen the hypothesis of a system of corruption. Soon after these revelations, Julius was restored to his former post,[59] and the parliamentary sub-committee on health called on the PPB management to clarify the situation. Two stormy sessions took place in August 2011; at one of them, a PPB agent was expelled after being aggressive to MPs; then, the session was simply adjourned because the PPB representatives had not been properly prepared.[60] A case brought against the PPB Registrar in September 2011 ended in 2014 with a dismissal, the court considering that it was not competent to judge accusations brought by the EMU report.[61]

Julius sometimes sees himself as the most competent authority on regulation in Kenya. He has a poor opinion of the Kenyan pharmaceutical market, which in his view is "*basically unregulated*". He willingly repeats that the industry is not really satisfied with him. He is particularly critical of what he terms "*unregistered parallel imports*" that are, according to him, not registered as such and come into the category of illegal importations. It should be pointed out that his action against PPB was taken in the context of rivalry between PPB and NQCL that we will deal with in Chapter 4. Furthermore, Julius's rhetoric often comes close to that used by KAPI, referring, for example, to parallel imports as "*so-called parallel imports*" and "*what I call counterfeit medicines*".[62] This being said, his discourse is centred on the presence of unregistered medicines in Kenya and on the active part played by certain PPB officials in accepting compensation for granting import permits. The EMU report and other interviews of former PPB officials lend substance to this hypothesis.

Stories like Julius' show that the capture of value linked to the development of distribution networks is by no means confined to manufacturers or to importer-distributors. Value-capture involves official bodies and builds up substantial connections or bridges between distribution networks and heterogeneous forms of regulation, between "*briefcase import*" and regulatory bodies, for example. Economic capture can be pursued through "legal" means such as regulatory influence, intellectual property and communication, as seen earlier; it also takes place either in the process of exacting registration, import and control fees, or in the process of corruption.[63] The leading players in the industry perfectly know how to influence regulations and they invest huge amounts of money in communication strategies. However, less powerful firms are not left without any means. Some market players even resort to illicit practice in order to overcome national regulatory hurdles. In any case, the main goal is to "capture" regulation in order to access distribution channels and, *in fine*, maximise profits.[64] As a result, multiple illicit cases are determined by different causes: regulation and good practices, intellectual property, corruption, and so forth. Under that light, the anti-counterfeiting policies that got reinforced during the last 20 years could be only one new episode of the pharmaceutical profit saga. They illustrate the conflicts for accessing distribution channels and the strategic operations of regulatory capture. But the imposition of these policies does not stem only from industrial and trade strategies. In order to understand them, we then need to take into account deeper changes that affect international public health policies.

Notes

1 Kareithi, A., & Mwai, E. (2009). Dawa Ltd yet again in drug scam. *The Standard*, 24 June; Kenya National Assembly Official Record, 25 June 2009.
2 Immel, B. K. (2001). A Brief History of the GMPs for Pharmaceuticals. *Pharmaceutical Technology*, July, pp. 44–52.
3 Swann, J. (1999). The 1941 Sulfathiazole Disaster and the Birth of Good Manufacturing Practices. *Pharmacy in History*, 41/1, pp. 16–25.
4 Lantenois, C., & Coriat, B. (2014). La "préqualification" OMS: Origines, déploiements et impacts sur la disponibilité des antirétroviraux dans les pays du Sud. *Sciences Sociales et Santé*, 32, 1, March.
5 Brhlikova, P., Harper, I., & Pollock, A. (2007). Good manufacturing practices in the pharmaceutical industry, Working paper 3. *Workshop "Tracing Pharmaceuticals in South Asia"*. University of Edinburgh, 2–3 July.
6 Carpenter, D. (2010). *Reputation and power, organizational image and pharmaceutical regulation at the FDA*. Princeton: Princeton University Press. p. 715.
7 Pharmacy and Poisons Act (Cap. 244), The Pharmacy and Poisons (registration of drugs) rules, 1981. The Kenya Gazette Supplement No. 55, Legal Notice 147, 25 September 1981.
8 Drug laws put plants at risk. *Daily Nation*, 2 April 1982.
9 The Pharmacy and Poisons Board (Amendment) Act, 1992, No. 12 of 1992, 28 October.
10 Ministry of Health. *Kenya National Drug Policy*, 15 July 1994. Retrieved from http://apps.who.int/medicinedocs/documents/s16443e/s16443e.pdf.
11 Interview of an expert in pharmaceutical industrial policies and a UNIDO consultant, 29 January 2016.
12 UNIDO, Republic of Kenya. (2014). *Kenya GMP roadmap. A stepwise approach for the pharmaceutical industry to attain WHO GMP standards.*
13 Interview of an expert in pharmaceutical industrial policies and a UNIDO consultant, 29 January 2016.
14 The report that mentions this, points out with marked technocratic coldness: "While this may be perceived as a possible success of AMFm in terms of reducing the amount of non-quality assured ACTs in the market, it has a clearly negative impact on the local pharmaceutical industry". BroadReach. (2011). Market analysis of public and private sector capacities to expand access to subsidized acts in Kenya, *Project Report*, December.
15 Interview of the general manager of Universal Corporation, Nairobi, 21 February 2014.
16 Osewe, P., *et al.* Improving access to HIV/AIDS medicines in Africa. World Bank, 2008, Chapter 3.
17 The first version of Schedule M was published in 1988. In 2001, a revised version closer to WHO recommendations was published by the health department of the Ministry of Health and Family Welfare, and applied progressively between 2002 and 2005.
18 Joseph, R. K. (2016). *Pharmaceutical industry and public policy in post-reform India*. London: Routledge.
19 Vasireddy, U. (2015). Comparison of guidelines of Indian GMP with WHO GMP. *4th International Summit on GMP, GCP & Quality Control*, October 26–28, Hyderabad,

India. Retrieved from http://gmp-gcp-quality-control.pharmaceuticalconferences.com/abstract/2015/comparison-of-guidelines-of-indian-gmp-with-who-gmp.

20 Interview of a drug inspector, 23 November 2015.

21 Osewe, P. L., Nkrumah, Y. K., & Sackey, E. K. (2008). Improving access to HIV/AIDS medicines in Africa. Trade-related aspects of intellectual property rights flexibilities. *World Bank*, pp. 32–35.

22 Interview of the General Manager of Cosmos Ltd., Nairobi, 20 February 2014.

23 Pfizer Inc. v. Cosmos Limited. (2008, April 25), Case 49, 2006, decision of the Kenyan Industrial Property Tribunal at Nairobi.

24 Njuguna. (2008). Kenya: Tribunal finds Pfizer's azithromycin dihydrate patent infringed. Afro-IP, 2 July. Retrieved from http://afro-ip.blogspot.in/2008/07/kenya-tribunal-finds-pfizers.html.

25 See in particular: Chaudhuri, S. (2005). *The WTO and India's pharmaceuticals industry: Patent protection, TRIPS, and developing countries*. New Delhi: Oxford University Press; Abrol, D., *et al.* (2011). Globalization of the Indian pharmaceutical industry: Implications for innovation. *International Journal of Institutions and Economies*, 327, 3/2, July, pp. 327–365; Joseph, R. K. (2016). *Pharmaceutical industry and public policy in post-reform India*. London: Routledge.

26 Gopakumar, K. M. (2016). Nothing special (301) to report. *The Hindu Business Line*, 15 April; Joseph, R. K. (2016). *Pharmaceutical industry and public policy in post-reform India*. London: Routledge.

27 Ecks, S. (2008). Global pharmaceutical markets and corporate citizenship: The case of Novartis' anti-cancer drug Glivec. *BioSocieties*, 3/2, pp. 165–181; Rajan, K. S. (2017). *Pharmocracy. Value, politics, and knowledge in global biomedicine*. Durham, NC: Duke University Press.

28 Joseph, R. K. (2016). *Pharmaceutical industry and public policy in post-reform India*. London: Routledge.

29 Abrol, D. (2016). Who Gains from the Modi Government's Intellectual Property Rights Policy? *The Wire*, 22 mai. Retrieved from http://thewire.in/2016/05/22/who-gains-from-the-modi-governments-intellectual-property-rights-policy-37795/.

30 Interview of a manager of a pharmaceutical firm, Gujarat, 23 November 2015.

31 Interview of the Chairman, Nairobi Branch, Kenya Pharmaceutical Association, Nairobi, 24 February 2014.

32 Weissman, R. (1996). A long, strange TRIPS: The pharmaceutical industry drive to harmonize global intellectual property rules, and the remaining WTO legal alternatives available to third world countries. *University of Pennsylvania Journal of International Law*, 17/4, pp. 1069–1125; Drahos, P., Braithwaite, J. (2002). *Information feudalism. Who owns the knowledge economy?* London: Earthscan.

33 Weissman, R., *Ibid*, p. 1088.

34 Should we or should we not use generics? *Kenya Times*, 25 February 1991.

35 Owen, T. (2013). From "Pirates" to "Heroes": News, discourse change, and the contested legitimacy of generic HIV/AIDS medicines. *The International Journal of Press/Politics*, 18/3, pp. 259–280.

36 I use the notion of "Indianity" in reference to that of "Italianity" proposed by Roland Barthes when analysing a system of signs referring to a "cultural knowledge" and associating an idea or a product to a geographical source. Barthes, R. (1964). La rhétorique de l'image, *Communications*, 4, pp. 40–51.

37 Wairire, G. G. (2010). Commerçants et industriels d'origine Indo-Pakistanaise au Kenya. Regards sociologiques. In M. Adam (Ed.) *L'Afrique Indienne. Les minorités d'origine Indo-Pakistanaise en Afrique orientale*. Paris: Karthala. pp. 277–302.
38 Adam, M. (2010). Des Indiens des comptoirs aux Indo-Africains. In M. Adam (Ed.), *L'Afrique Indienne. Les minorités d'origine Indo-Pakistanaise en Afrique orientale*. Paris: Karthala. pp. 15–78.
39 Informal conversation with F., Summer 2013, Nairobi.
40 Intellectual Property Act. (1989). Cap. 509 (Kenya).
41 Industrial Property Act, Act No. 3 of 2001 (Kenya).
42 The Trademarks Act, Cap. 506 (Kenya).
43 Republic of Kenya in the High Court of Kenya at Nairobi (Milimani Commercial Courts), Civil Suit 334 of 2007, Lords Healthcare Limited, plaintinff, versus Salama Pharmaceuticals Limited, Defendant, Ruling, 22 September 2008.
44 Interview of the chairman, Kenya Pharmaceutical Distributors Association, Nairobi, 14 May 2012.
45 Interview of the Regulatory Affairs & Imports Manager of one Import and Distribution firm, 21 February 2014.
46 Interview of the Regional Director of a large European pharmaceutical company, Nairobi, 8 May 2012.
47 Interview of the Regional Director of a large European pharmaceutical company, Nairobi, 8 May 2012.
48 Interview of the Head of Security of a large European pharmaceutical company, 1 February 2016.
49 Gerhardsen, T. I. S. (2006). Kenya fights to retain IP flexibilities for medicines imports. *IP Watch*, 9 August. Retrieved from www.ip-watch.org/2006/08/09/kenya-fights-to-retain-ip-flexibilities-for-medicines-imports/; voir aussi: Ministry of Health Task Force. (2006). *The proposed amendments to Kenya's industrial property act 2001: Impact on access to medicines.*
50 Lewis-Lettington, R., & Munyi, P. (2004). Willingness and ability to use TRIPs flexibilities. Kenya case study. *DFID Health Systems Resource Centre*, September.
51 The Statute Law (Miscellaneous Amendments). Act (No. 2 of 2002).
52 The Statute Law (Miscellaneous Amendments). Bill 2006.
53 Pharmacy and Poisons Board. (2006). *Task-force report on parallel importation, counterfeits and illegal trade in pharmaceuticals.*
54 Pharmacy and Poisons Board. (2008). *Guidelines for parallel importation of medicines in Kenya.*
55 Pharmacy and Poisons Board. (2015). *Proposed framework for regulation of parallel importation of medicinal substances in Kenya*. Version 1, September.
56 Jamah, A. (2016). Kenya to allow imports of cheap drugs. *The Standard*, 5 July.
57 Interview of Julius, Nairobi, 14 September 2016.
58 Interview of Julius, Nairobi, 14 September 2016.
59 Republic of Kenya in the High Court of Kenya at Nairobi, Judicial Review Division, Miscellaneous Civil Cause No. 131 of 2011.
60 Ndonga, W. (2011). MPs, pharmacy board meeting poisoned by tempers. *Capital News*, 16 August. Retrieved from www.capitalfm.co.ke/news/2011/08/mps-pharmacy-board-meeting-poisoned-by-tempers/; Wambui, N. (2011). Venomous encounter for poisons board with MPs. *Capital News*, 30 August. Retrieved from www.capitalfm.co.ke/news/2011/08/venomous-encounter-for-poisons-board-with-mps/.

61 Republic of Kenya in the High Court of Kenya at Nairobi, Judicial Review Division, Miscellaneous Civil Cause No. 214 of 2011.

62 Interview of Julius, Nairobi, 14 September 2016.

63 This point is developed in the case of the South-East Asian market in: Quet, M., *et al.* Regulation multiple. Pharmaceutical trajectories and modes of control in the ASEAN. *Science, Technology and Society*, 32/3, 2018.

64 The issue of regulatory capture has been widely discussed. See Abraham, J. (2008). Sociology of pharmaceuticals development and regulation: A realist empirical research programme. *Sociology of Health & Illness*, 30/6, pp. 869–885.

Part 2

Pharmaceutical security

Between public health and the market

The conflicts over anti-counterfeiting policies have shown that there is no consensus on illicit medicines as a public problem. We have already discussed in the previous section one alternative understanding to the usual dominant discourse on counterfeiting. Transformations in distribution bring in new problems, in quality, registration, transport, and in the sales strategies adopted by firms. This market context gives a new importance to illicit medicines. To this first type of alternative explanation, centred on pharmaceutical markets and trade strategies, I will now add a second. The public problem of illicit medicines has over the past two decades been framed by a concern for "security", the aim of which is to ensure that certain operators control markets. This redefines the business of quality control. To develop this counter-narrative, I will now analyse the dynamics of security, paying attention simultaneously to discursive mechanisms and practices that produce particular configurations of power.

In his course on *Security, Territory, Population*, Michel Foucault pointed out a shift in power towards procedures intended to securitise population groups.[1] Together with several other authors, he opened up a research field that has been broadening ever since: the analysis of security dynamics.[2] Since then more and more work has been done on security policy and practice, in fields as diverse as urban policy,[3] international relations,[4] migrations,[5] digital archiving,[6] food,[7] and epidemic.[8] Issues proper to security processes in fields as diverse as these do not necessarily correspond; they are often produced by dynamics specific to the activities concerned. Yet, seen in Foucault's perspective, they do share one characteristic: they are not so much the result of overdetermined global strategies as of local articulations, conflicts, contradictions and overlapping discourse, the logics of which – always only partial and contingent – we have to reconstruct if we are to understand them.[9] Subsequent work has detailed Foucault's conception of power, using various theoretical and conceptual approaches, such as the theory of discursive performativity,[10] and theories of modes of government[11] and of bio-politics[12] directly inspired by Foucault. This work underscores the diversity of causes – both objective and socially induced – of insecurity in the globalised world: industrial and environmental catastrophes,[13] new infectious diseases and pandemic risks,

DOI: 10.4324/9781003194767-6

terrorism and bio-terrorism,[14] and economic gambles. These studies show how the social construction of insecurity is linked to the durable importance of elements that structure the social world: the State,[15] infrastructures,[16] and vital systems.[17] They describe security as the fruit of administrative and political practices such as preparedness and crisis management.[18] These policies take shape in complex articulations of technology, ideology, and economics such as the "war–development–security" nexus,[19] or that of "security–disease–commerce".[20] More generally, these studies help to show that security policies tend to produce precisely the effects that they are supposed to prevent: preparedness builds up unpreparedness,[21] bio-politics leads to a sense of vulnerability and infelicity,[22] and security professionals produce a sense of insecurity[23]; all of this brings about a transformation in depth of democratic regimes, de-democratising them and making exceptionalism part of normal government.[24]

An essential contribution of all this work on practices of securitisation has been the analysis of power. Attention is being paid to ample movements that are making security a commonplace in public policy, without overlooking local issues and practice in which "security" and its orientations are imposed, negotiated, and redefined. In this part of the book, I will adopt this approach, considering power as a pervasive force that configures regulatory texts; fashions public and media discourse; formulates scientific knowledge, political strategy, and practical routines; and configures technological tools. All of this constitutes the process of securitisation that characterises the current dynamics of pharmaceutical markets in relation to the broader field of international public health.

A noteworthy characteristic of this particular configuration of power is the importance taken on by words such as "fake", "counterfeit", and "generic", and their definitions, and also the mechanisms relaying discourse on illicit medicines, in industry, publicity, and law. To assess this importance, one has to take into account the fact that the terms used to qualify cases of "fake medicine" stem from particular assessments that presuppose different tools of regulation. *Substandard*, for example, designates medicine that does not meet the norms it is supposed to respect. This can be intentional, a deliberate refusal to respect manufacturing or distribution standards, but it can also be unintended, a defect due to damage suffered during transport or conservation. An *adulterated* medicine is one the composition of which has been altered, either at the time of production (by under-dosing, or contamination by extraneous matter) or during its distribution (expiry, or deterioration due to exposure to inappropriate temperatures). An *unregistered* medicine is one that has been put into circulation without having been recorded by the regulatory authorities, either because of diversion of the product, of non-respect of customs procedures, or of the relevant firms not having deemed it profitable to register the medicine for a given territory, or because the medicine has been imported by individual patients more or less informally, without having been authorised to be marketed. A *falsely labelled* medicine is one that carries erroneous information as to its nature or properties; this can be due to an imitation of the labelling of a branded medicine, or to divulgation of erroneous information as to its composition. The notion of *spurious* medicine is employed mainly in India, where the Section 17-B of the Drugs and Cosmetics Act, 1940, as amended in 1982, defines several typical cases: medicines manufactured under a name belonging to another medicine; medicine imitating another medicine; medicine the packaging of which does not indicate its composition correctly, or attributes it to another manufacturer. Finally, the more general notions of *falsified* or *fake* medicine, designating objects sold as medicines but which are not medicines, or are not what they are presumed to be.

In actual practice these terms are often intermingled, creating highly problematic confusion and bias. Dealing with illicit medicines entails normative activity: laws, standards, and directives have to be produced by governmental authorities and communicated to firms – an activity that is itself determined by designations and interpretation of the problem. The mainspring of this configuration of authority lies in the circulation of terms and formulae in imposing a specific language and in applying an interpretation by means of coercion and punishment.[25] All of this is done under the influence of a double association: that – explicit – of "brand" with "quality" and that – implicit – of "generic" with "dubious quality". This change enshrines a reassertion of brand as a sign of distinction and implicitly puts blame on suppliers of "poor" or "bad" medicines – sometimes even going so far as to associate them with "pharmaceutical terrorism". At the same time, it establishes intellectual property (IP) as the main means of improving the quality of medicines. Understanding this phenomenon can be facilitated by using the notions of "frame" and "framing", defined as impositions of interpretative schemata on social reality.[26] The exercise of power is based on the transformation of discourse used to describe reality.[27] In reformulating the problem of illicit medicines, we can thus observe the ways in which power can be exercised by acting on language.

The imposition of a "security" framework on the problem of illicit medicines, however, is not solely a matter of discourse and its transformations. It also depends on a significant set of other phenomena, for example, police seizures, the application of new inspection practices, redistribution of responsibilities among various government agencies, and the creation of organisational partnerships. The re-framing studied here is thus not merely discourse and representation. Discourse and non-discourse crisscross, and technical arrangements combine with operators' strategies. The strength of the power complex lies in the chains of reformulations that transform the problem of fake medicines into one of counterfeiting, which is subsequently framed by a law prescribing specific forms of intervention. All of this is linked, in particular, to the pivotal function of legal activity in access to medicines.[28] Juridical activity connects discourse to concrete action; this in turn makes the reformulation and circulation effectuated by discourse a crucial matter. This characterises a power formation that has an unusual mechanism: involving political economy and the geopolitical power relationships we have described, it also involves institutional strategies and personal practices, and last but not least epistemic and communicational effects due to the circulation of discourse in public space. I suggest to qualify the power of this formation as a *discursive and practical hegemony*, with hegemony understood as a form of constraint imposing dominant norms without recourse to physical force. I will simplify this analysis, limiting it to some of its strategic sites, that is, regulation/law, the media, science, and practical operations.

"Pharmaceutical security" as a discursive and practical hegemonic formation concerns the movement of medicines. It is revealed in knowledge (e.g., studies of illicit and substandard medicines), in media discourse (e.g., news items on arrests of traffickers), in regulation (e.g., the Kenyan law on counterfeit), in training courses (offered e.g. by the research institute combating counterfeit medicines), in technological tools (used e.g., to analyse the chemical composition of medicines), and in operations of supervision (e.g., inspection of medicines on the market and in retail pharmacies). It is through these dynamics of pharmaceutical security that procedures of regulation, control, and analysis ensure discrimination between "good" and "bad" medicines. Securitisation thus apparently results from, on the one hand, an increasing convergence and integration of healthcare, technological, and commercial interests in the current concern for public health, and on the other hand an identification of this concern with the economic interests of the dominant operators on the market, that is, the pharmaceutical enterprises of the North.

My demonstration in this part of the book will borrow from the sociology of public problems, communication sciences and media studies, and the socio-anthropology of science. I will proceed in two stages. Firstly, I will analyse the form that the problem of "fake medicines" has taken on (Chapter 4[29]), paying particular attention to activity concerning regulations, the media, and science. I will show how the framing in terms of IP and counterfeiting imposed itself before being denounced by activists on access to treatment. Next, I will characterise the extent to which this framing actually organises practices, taking as an example a study of the regulatory work dealing with the circulation of medicines between India and Kenya (Chapter 5). Framing affects operators well beyond the reach of legislative and institutional innovation: domination of the approach in terms of anti-counterfeiting, for example, leads to a redefinition of the shares of expertise attributed respectively to customs and to pharmaceutical authorities. The interest of this approach lies in its showing exactly how security is constructed: not only by a "top-down" or "bottom-up" process, but in the "constant interplay of top and bottom".[30] This interplay is shown up by simultaneously analysing on the one hand the global problem of management by intermediary agents, with their ways of responding to policies, and on the other hand overall frames such as that of counterfeiting. If, as Ken Booth maintains, security is what one does with it,[31] then it is advisable to gain a better grasp *both* of the ways in which the meaning of threats is produced *and* the meaning of the solutions adopted to deal with the problem is proposed.

Notes

1 Foucault, M. (2004). *Sécurité, territoire, population. Cours au Collège de France, 1977–1978*, Paris: Seuil/Gallimard.
2 Ewald, F. (1986) *L'État Providence*, Paris, Grasset; Dourlens, C., et al. (1991). *Conquête de la sécurité, gestion des risques*, Paris: L'Harmattan.
3 Bonelli, L. (2008). *La France a peur. Une histoire sociale de l'insécurité*, Paris, La Découverte; Laurent Mucchielli (dir.) (2008) *La frénésie sécuritaire. Retour à l'ordre et nouveau contrôle social*, Paris: La Découverte.
4 Lipschutz, R. D. (ed.) (1995). *On security*, New York: Columbia University Press; Krause, K. (1998) Critical theory and security studies: The research programme of 'critical security studies, *cooperation and conflict*, September, 33, 298–333; Ceyhan, A. (1998). Analyser la sécurité: Dillon, Waever, Williams et les autres, *Cultures & Conflits*, pp. 31–32, printemps-été.
5 Bigo, D. (1998) Sécurité et immigration: vers une gouvernementalité par l'inquiétude?, *Culture et conflits*, pp. 31–32, printemps-été.
6 Boullier et alii, D. (2004) L'institution de la sécurité ou comment s'en désintéresser, *Les Cahiers du numérique*, 4, pp. 219–238.
7 Keck, F. (2008). Risques alimentaires et catastrophes sanitaires. L'Agence française de sécurité sanitaire des aliments, de la vache folle à la grippe aviaire, *Esprit*, 3–4, pp. 36–50.
8 Torny, D. (2012). De la gestion des risques à la production de la sécurité. L'exemple de la préparation de la pandémie grippale, *Réseaux*, 1, p. 171.
9 Foucault, M. (2004) *Sécurité, territoire, population. Cours au Collège de France, 1977–1978*, Paris: Seuil/Gallimard.
10 Waever, O. (1997). *Concepts of Security*, Copenhagen: Institute of Political Sciences, University of Copenhagen.
11 Bigo, D. (1998). Sécurité et immigration: vers une gouvernementalité par l'inquiétude?, *Culture et conflits*, pp. 31–32, printemps-été.
12 Dillon, M., & Lobo-Guerrero, L. (2008). Biopolitics of security in the 21st century: An introduction, *Review of International Studies*, 34(2), 265–292.
13 Aradau, C., & Munster, R. v. (2011). *Politics of catastrophe, Genealogies of the unknown*, London: Routledge.
14 Collier, S. J., Lakoff, A., & Rabinow, P. (2004). Biosecurity: Towards an anthropology of the contemporary, *Anthropology Today* 20, 5, pp. 3–7; Masco, J. (2014). *The theater of operations. National security affect from the cold war to the war on terror*, Durham: Duke University Press.
15 Schendel, W. v. & Abraham, I. (Eds.) (2005) *Illicit flows and criminal things. States, borders and the other side of globalization*, Bloomington: Indiana University Press.
16 Aradau, C. (2010) Security that matters: critical infrastructure and objects of protection, *Security Dialogue*, 41(5), pp. 491–514.
17 Collier, S. J., & Lakoff, A. (2008). The vulnerability of vital systems, how "critical infrastructure became a security problem p.17639 in M. D. Cavelty, K. S. Kristensen (Eds.) *Securing the homeland. Critical infrastructure, risk and (in) security*, London: Routledge.

18 Collier, S. J., & Lakoff, A. (2008). Distributed preparedness: The spatial logic of domestic security in the United States, *Society and Space*, 26/1, pp. 7–28.
19 Duffield, M. (2001) *Global governance and the new wars. The merging of development and security*, London: Zed Books.
20 King, N. B. (2002). Security, disease, commerce: ideologies of postcolonial global health, *Social Studies of Science*, 32, pp. 763–789.
21 Collier, S. J., & Lakoff, A. (2008). Distributed preparedness: The spatial logic of domestic security in the United States, *Society and Space*, 26/1, pp. 7–28.
22 Caduff, C. (2014). On the verge of death: Visions of biological vulnerability, *Annual Review of Anthropology*, 43, pp. 105–121.
23 Bigo, D. (1998). Sécurité et immigration: vers une gouvernementalité par l'inquiétude?, *Culture et conflits*, pp. 31–32, printemps-été.
24 Aradau, C., & Blanke, T. (2010). Governing circulation: A critique of the biopolitics of security, In M. de Larrinaga, M. Doucet (Eds.) *Security and global governmentality: Globalization, governance and the state*, London: Routledge.
25 Krieg-Planque, A. (2009). *La notion de « formule » en analyse du discours. Cadre théorique et méthodologique*, Besançon: Presses Universitaires de France-Comté.
26 Literature on the forms of framing is abundant. See, for an overall idea: Goffman, E. (1974). *Les cadres de l'expérience*, Paris: Minuit; Gamson, W. A., & Modigliani, A. (1989). Media discourse and public opinion on nuclear power: A constructionist approach, *American Journal of Sociology*, 95/1, pp. 1–37; Entman, R. (1993). Framing: Toward clarification of a fractured paradigm, *Journal of Communication*, 43(4), pp. 51–58.
27 Klemperer, V. (1996). *LTI, la langue du Troisième Reich. Carnets d'un philologue*, Paris: Albin Michel [1947]; Faye, J.-P. (1973). *La critique du langage et son économie*, Paris: Galilée.
28 Biehl, J. (2013). The judicialization of biopolitics: Claiming the right to pharmaceuticals in Brazilian courts, *American Ethnologist*, 40/3, pp. 419–436.
29 Gusfield, J. (2009). *La culture des problèmes publics. L'alcool au volant: la production d'un ordre symbolique*, Paris: Économica [1981]; Céfaï, D. (1996). La construction des problèmes publics. Définition de situations dans des arènes publiques, *Réseaux*, 14, pp. 43–66; Neveu, E. (1999) L'approche constructiviste des « problèmes publics. Un aperçu des travaux anglo-saxons, *Etudes de communication*, 22, pp. 41–58; Neveu, E. (2015) *Sociologie politique des problèmes publics*, Paris: Armand Colin.
30 Mazzella, S. (2005). Vie et mort du droit d'asile territorial, *Sociétés contemporaines*, 2005/1, 57, pp. 105–120.
31 Booth, K. (1997). Security and self: Reflections of a fallen realist, pp. 83–119 In K. Krause, M. C. Williams (Eds.), *Critical security studies: Concepts and cases*, Minneapolis: University of Minnesota Press.

4 The regulatory turn to security

Safety versus security

In the early 1980s the Kenyan pharmaceutical business was running into turbulence. On 7 July 1980, *The Standard*, a daily newspaper, headlined: "Crisis Hits Pharmacies", and announced that "*A major crisis is looming within the Government pharmaceutical services which could lead to a paralysis in several hospitals*".[1] The alert was triggered by the resignation of several hospital pharmacists at the Kenyatta Hospital and several other establishments to protest against a lack of clarity as to their functions, the weaknesses of training in the pharmaceutical professions, the excessive number of medicines in circulation and their dubious quality, a result of the lack of proper supervision. The pharmacists were also protesting against the fact that they were not involved in calls for tenders, and that this led to debatable selections, to oversupplies as well as to supply shortfalls. The background was one of criticism of the government's practice in matters of regulation. A tender had been won by a local firm, Anpi Ltd., whose offer was less competitive than others (its prices were higher and its previous orders had not been fully honoured)[2]; the use of the Depo Provera contraceptive was criticised, as in many countries it was banned[3]; the government had attacked foreign firms that were using Kenya as a "dumping ground" for surplus medicines, medicines that had expired or were banned in other countries.[4] Over this period of change in government, the attitude of the new Health Minister, Arthur Magugu, was strong-willed[5]; as criticism built up, he multiplied surprise visits to healthcare centres and announced a policy that broke away from that of his predecessor. At his instigation a crucial change to pharmaceutical regulation came into force on 1 April 1982. Medicines on sale in Kenya would now have to be checked and registered. This decision was supposed to mark the "*the end of the road for the drug dealers who have been earning millions of shillings through the importation, manufacture and selling of sub-standard drugs in Kenya*".[6]

Some 30 years later, on 2 December 2009, the Kenyan government inaugurated an Anti-Counterfeit Agency (ACA) to keep track of "*the circulation of dangerous goods, a large number of which bear health and environmental risks*".[7] Counterfeit medicines were one of these "dangerous products",

DOI: 10.4324/9781003194767-7

a central argument used to justify the creation of the ACA. The problem the agency was intended to deal with, however, was very different from that which the health authorities had been facing 30 years previously. The current battle was against the proliferation of products violating copyright, which were considered dangerous for health and the environment. The main arguments used by the new agency identified counterfeiting with a criminal activity, accusing it of weakening the Kenyan economy, of threatening safety and security, and of bringing about a loss in jobs.[8] Pharmacy was thus no longer considered to constitute a separate domain from that of the economy; it was now linked to concerns that had previously been seen as extraneous. Furthermore, the method suggested for solving the problem was also very different from that previously applied; the focus was no longer on respecting registration of goods based on quality checking, but on respecting patents, copyrights, and their holders, and enforcing regulations through a police-like force.

Comparing the two events shows how the treatment of issues of quality and legality has evolved over the past 30 years.

The anthropologist Julia Homberger sees in this a passage from pharmaceutical *safety* to pharmaceutical *security*[9] – the latter corresponding to the criminalisation of regulatory infringement, the emphasis upon economic stakes and IP, and the increasing mobilisation of public–private partnerships and police forces. Such a shift, from safety to security, not only affects pharmaceutical policies in developing countries but also concerns public-health practices as a whole. How was it enacted? A fast-forward explanation would no doubt point to the lobbying role of pharmaceutical firms which are dominating the market – we saw how easily they were campaigning and using communication tools. However, as seducing as such explanation may seem, it would leave aside a number of crucial mechanisms. The following chapter tries to account for the security shift in a nuanced way, in order to show the multiple processes that have led to a security framework of the public problem of illicit medicines.

A multi-faceted problem

Before going further, a short historical contextualisation may be needed. Historians studying pharmaceuticals have shown that the issue of legitimacy is an integral part of the history of medicines, producing frontiers between the legal and the illegal, the toxic and the anodyne, and the standard and non-standard.[10] The line separating licit from illicit, for example, has been constantly transformed, as Maurice Cassier has shown in the conflicts between the patents system and registration of medicines in the Codex in the early 19th century,[11] or as others have pointed in the case of debates regarding the quality and legality of quinine in British India.[12] At the time concern for public health was already closely linked to a particular notion of the order of society and to the central importance of the state, as the "medicinal police" shows – a practice dating from the mid-18th century, in the case of France.[13] Already operators with different – but convergent – objectives were involved: industrialists, pharmacists, public authorities, etc.[14] Because of this, we have to situate in a timeline examples of discourse qualifying illicit practices. During the 1930s in France, for example, the industrialisation of pharmacy and the mass commercialisation of products that could create new risks broadened the whole problem of health safety, and after World War II this caused a considerable stir. The history of public-health crises reveals that the potential dangers and legitimacy of medicines do not spare the branded industry, and are not confined to the generic industry that was to boom later.[15] With the creation in 1948 of the World Health Organization (WHO), these preoccupations moved into a transnational discussion, giving rise to differing appreciations and proposals such as pharmacovigilance and drug utilisation studies.[16]

Apart from this, the issue of illegitimacy enters into configurations that vary with geographical location, covering different sets of problems. I refer here to the work of Jeremy Greene on the emergence of the generics market in the USA, an emergence I suggest to compare with that of the generics market in Kenya sometime later. According to Greene, in the USA the emergence took place during the 1960s and 1970s, and concern over the anonymity that was threatening medicines gave rise to the publication of a host of articles on illicit medicines.[17] He describes one of these articles, published in the newspaper *Parade*; it documented the role of the mafia in a "zombie" market for medicines suspected of being based on chalk or flour. Greene reminds his readers that while fears linked to illicit medicines go back a long way, for a relatively long time major manufacturers have also been suspected. He cites Lucille Wendt, a member of the Kefauver committee, famous for its criticism of Big Pharma in 1961, and who denounced "*'Counterfeiting!'[…] a euphemistic term for getting government agencies to police the trademarks of the major drug manufacturers*". The same criticism has been made of recent anti-counterfeit laws. The history of generics in the USA shows that already by the early 1960s anti-counterfeit policies were being hotly debated.

In most African countries, construction of the problem of fake medicines has also been going on for some time. It has been gathering impetus, and was reformulated at the turn of the millennium.[18] In the case of Kenya, a survey of the corpus of the daily press between 1979 and 1990 shows that between 1980 and 1990 attention was focused mainly on the quality of pharmaceuticals and, in particular, on the distribution of expired medicines. Accused of being responsible for this were donor organisations that sent those medicines to African countries, which wealthy countries no longer wanted, their healthcare authorities intending on clearing their shelves of products earmarked for destruction. Nitsan Chorev has found that the problem of medicines unauthorised in certain countries and nonetheless sold in developing countries served as a WHO argument in favour of developing local production in the mid-1970s.[19] During this period, medicines denounced as "fake" were rarely copies of existing medicines. Between the late 1990s and the early 2000s, however, the problem was increasingly formulated in terms of counterfeiting, and the role of foreign producers – particularly Chinese and Indian – was increasingly denounced. There has thus been a shift in framing in countries like Kenya between 1980 and today. Let us see now how it happened.

Anti-counterfeiting goes to the WHO

To give an initial idea of the security framing that was progressively imposed as of the 1990s, let us take the evolution of the treatment of the issue by the WHO, which is a model organisation in the fields of public health and pharmacy. The international community has been looking increasingly closely at the problem of "fake" medicines, and this interest became "autonomous" as of the later 1980s. At the same time, it has been reformulated in terms that had until then been used only rarely in the field of public health, or at least by the WHO. The notion of "counterfeit" is a case in point. Occasionally used in the post-war period to describe illicit medicines, it had remained marginal.[20] In 1985, however, it was officially introduced to the WHO at its Nairobi conference.[21] During this conference it was used without being defined, but it was considered a crime to counterfeit medicine and the WHO authorities were advised to collect data and inform governments of the nature and extent of the problem. On 13 May 1988, a resolution was taken concerning the rational use of drugs (WHA41.16). One of its paragraphs requested the general management to initiate programmes for prevention and detection of activities linked to circulation of "*falsely labelled, spurious, counterfeited or substandard pharmaceutical preparations*".[22] In the first documents to come out, the problem of counterfeiting was subordinated to a different issue: the rationalisation of pharmaceutical policy. The Nairobi conference passed a resolution, WHA41.16, 1988, emphasising the importance of the role of governments in formulating and applying national pharmaceutical policy.[23] At the time the WHO formalised and was promoting the notion of "essential medicines"[24]; this involved the need to regulate prices of medicines, modes of prescription, and administration; among these concerns, counterfeiting was still only a minor theme.

The theme broadened, however, early in the 1990s at the first WHO meetings on counterfeit medicines; within the organisation, it was the industry that took the initiative on this question.[25] In April 1992 WHO and IFPMA (International Federation of Pharmaceutical Manufacturers) together organised a workshop to deal exclusively with this issue. The workshop came up with a new definition of counterfeit pharmaceuticals (see Table 4.1 for a definition by WHO-IFPMA). The notion of counterfeit and the presuppositions with which it is fraught began to be accepted more frequently in the organisation in its discussion of the problem of illicit medicines. The report indicated that the "anti-counterfeit" provisions in the draft of the Agreement on Trade-Related Aspects of Intellectual Property Rights (TRIPS) of the General

Table 4.1 Main definitions of counterfeit, WHO and IMPACT

WHO-IFPMA 1992	*IMPACT 2007 (Lisbon, Portugal, 2^e^ general meeting of IMPACT)*	*IMPACT 2008 (Hammamet, Tunisia, 3^e^ General Meeting of IMPACT)*
A counterfeit medicine is one which is deliberately and fraudulently mislabelled with respect to identity and/or source. Counterfeiting can apply to both branded and generic products and counterfeit products may include products with the correct ingredients or with the wrong ingredients, without active ingredients, with insufficient quantity of active ingredients or with fake packaging.	A medical product is counterfeit when there is a false representation in relation to its identity (1), history or source (2). This applies to the product, its container or other packaging or labelling information. Counterfeiting can apply to both branded and generic products. Counterfeits may include products with correct ingredients/components (3), with wrong ingredients/ components, without active ingredients, with incorrect amounts of active ingredients, or with fake packaging. Quality defects or non-compliance with Good Manufacturing Practices/ Good Distribution Practices (GMP/GDP) in legitimate, authorised medical products should not be confused with counterfeiting. For example: (1) any misleading statement with respect to name, composition, strength, or other elements; (2) any misleading statement with respect to manufacturer, country of manufacturing, country of origin, marketing authorisation holder; (3) this refers to ingredients or any other component of a medical product.	A medical product is counterfeit when there is a false representation in relation to its identity (1), or source (2). This applies to the product, its container or other packaging or labelling information. Counterfeiting can apply to both branded and generic products. Counterfeits may include products with correct ingredients/components (3), with wrong ingredients/ components, without active ingredients, with incorrect amounts of active ingredients, or with fake packaging. Quality defects or non-compliance with Good Manufacturing Practices/ Good Distribution Practices (GMP/GDP) in legitimate, authorised medical products should not be confused with counterfeiting. For example: (1) any misleading statement with respect to name, composition, strength, or other elements; (2) any misleading statement with respect to manufacturer, country of manufacturing, country of origin, marketing authorisation holder, including use of falsified documentation in the manufacture or trade of the product; (3) this refers to ingredients or any other component of a medical product.

Agreement on Tariffs and Trade (GATT) agreement that was then being worked out provided a "sound legal framework" based on an effective international protection of brands together with penalties and sanctions, including imprisonment. Representatives of GATT took part in the meeting between WHO and IFPMA, signalling by their presence that the theme of IP had now intruded into the concerns that the WHO was dealing with.

The WHO reports on the counterfeiting issue in pharmaceuticals during the 1990s revealed in the first place the institution of the problem of illicit medicines as an autonomous matter. The problem was no longer treated merely as an aspect of a country's pharmaceutical policy. It was also during this period that a penal, policing approach to the question of "false medicines" made its appearance. The "Counterfeit Drugs" report in 1992 – signed by Dr R. Arnold, representing the IFPMA – recommended taking steps for the "detection, prosecution, judgement, punishment" of offenders. The terms "detection, prosecution, judgement, punishment", though not synonymous, do overlap to some extent, their partial redundancy underscoring the criminal dimension of the struggle against illicit medicines, making the latter a matter for police surveillance.

As of the year 2000, the Organisation's "security-conscious" approach was confirmed. A work group was set up within the WHO, with the collaboration of IFPMA, the International Pharmaceutical Generic Alliance, the World Self-Medication Industry, and Pharmacists without Borders.[26] This led to the submission of a technical document to the World Health Assembly in 2001. A major development took place in February 2006 in Rome during the International Conference on Combating Counterfeit Medicine, with the support of the WHO, AIFA (the Italian Medicines Agency) and IFPMA. During the conference, in the "Rome Declaration", it was announced that a taskforce was to be launched in September[27]: IMPACT (International Medical Products Anti-Counterfeiting Taskforce). It is however important to note that the IMPACT taskforce was never ratified by the members' assembly – which has resulted in several critiques. In November 2006 this new entity proposed a definition of counterfeit products in *Principles and elements for national legislation against counterfeit medical products* (see Table 4.1, definition by IMPACT 2007). This new definition lists multiple forms of defects and infringements and widens that given in 1992 in order to include any product whose presentation is erroneous. It is therefore contradictory: on one hand, the notion of "deliberate" infraction is suppressed, which tends to include any infringement, and on the other hand, the quality defects of "authorised and legitimate" products are distinguished from counterfeiting. In December 2008 in Tunisia, this definition was modified and complemented to meet objections to the first definition formulated at the World Health Assembly in May 2008 (see Table 4.1, definition by IMPACT 2008). The new definition attempted, in particular, to distinguish patenting issues from those of counterfeiting. Contradictions persisted, however, as the notion of counterfeiting was still being applied to issues of extensive adulteration in which the actual intention of the producer was difficult to discern.

Criticism incurred by the WHO treatment of the issue of illicit medicines and, in particular, by the existence of the IMPACT group led the WHO to adjust its position between 2008 and 2010. A report was issued in 2008 with the aim of "*sorting out the concepts of counterfeit, generic, and substandard medicines, and assessing the extent to which current definitions confuse or do not confuse the issues involved*".[28] In 2009 and 2010, a work group was set up to reassess the WHO positions on the issue of counterfeit medicines. At the 63rd World Assembly, in May 2010, the notion of "counterfeit" was replaced by that of "Substandard/Spurious/Falsely-labelled/Falsified/Counterfeit" (SSFFC), an acronym confirmed until further notice by a resolution passed in 2012 (WHA65.19). The acronym in question exemplifies the terminological difficulties WHO was facing in its oscillation between an overall and a detailed approach, the overall approach associating, for example, quality issues with those of branding, and the detailed approach focusing on types of issues that were disconnected from one another conceptually. Eventually in 2017, the "delicious acronym" (in the words of Marie-Paule Kieny, Assistant DG, Health Systems and Innovation) was dropped in favour of "substandard" and "falsified". This episode closed a controversy that had lasted since 2006, but which in fact had started up well before that, in developments dating back to the 1980s.

The evolution of the WHO exemplifies the hesitation and ongoing modification of the WHO's stance on the counterfeit medicines issue. To start with, the organisational principles involved were contested by several member-countries, which accused the WHO directorate of not having involved members sufficiently, and of having assigned too important a role to private operators in various initiatives it had taken on the question. Secondly, during the period some matters of pharmaceutical quality had been criminalised. In the 1992 report, the accent had been placed on the criminal aspect:

> *The counterfeiting of any product is a crime. Counterfeiting of pharmaceuticals is a particularly serious criminal offence and handling such counterfeits is an unethical practice because it endangers human health.*

Thirdly, the security approach to "fake medicines" was marked by the resounding success of the notion of counterfeiting, its definition and application to the field of public health – which was also in part a regression as of the 2010 period.

The contested success of the notion in the WHO (which was subsequently to drop it) had several consequences that we will now have to disentangle. The first of these consequences was conceptual, influencing the way people think about "fake medicines". Definitions of "counterfeit" vary, but those given in the TRIPS agreement and by the European Union (EU) concern trademarks. Because of this, when the WHO deals with "fake medicines", it imports a notion linked to IP and, in particular, to copyright law. The notion of counterfeit was already blurred in the 1992 definition, which concerned not only medicines counterfeiting brand names but also poor-quality products and packaging that featured misleading information. At the IFPMA-WHO symposium in 1992 counterfeit medicine was defined as a product that had intentionally been falsely labelled as to its identity and source. Identity was not defined precisely. Gopakumar and Shashikant note that the definition can apply to both the international common denomination and the brand name, mixing up issues of IP and those of quality.[29] The IMPACT definitions attempted to deal with this terminological problem, distinguishing unintended quality defects that should not be considered acts of counterfeiting (counterfeit in this respect should be distinguished from substandard), and also kept this issue clear of patenting issues (definition IMPACT 2008). In the WHO, the terms used and their definitions are important. They provide a basis for practice, particularly when the latter impinges on the field of law. The definition of counterfeit should be seen as performative, and as circulating. For example, it is well known that the WHO-IFPMA definition, though not ratified by the World Health Assembly, was used as a guide in various WHO documents and, in particular, in the *Guidelines on import procedures for pharmaceutical products* (1996),[30] the *Guidelines for inspection of drug distribution channels* (1999),[31] and the *WHO good distribution practices for pharmaceutical products* (2006),[32] and also in technical reports validated by the executive committee. As to the definition formulated by IMPACT in 2008, it was taken up by the pharmaceutical industry despite the fact that the WHO had not validated it and that it embodied a contradictory vision of the problem: IFPMA defends the IMPACT definition dating from 2008.[33] Above all, however, the initial closeness of the notions of counterfeit and IP promotes uses that despite being inappropriate lend added weight to a reading of the problem in terms of counterfeiting. For example, the European Community customs report on seizures of counterfeit pharmaceuticals in 2007 reports a 34.6% increase in counterfeit products produced in India, and a 39.21% increase in counterfeit products produced in Switzerland.[34] This estimate is linked to an inclusion of products seized because of patent disputes; without this detail, Switzerland could have joined India and China on the list of "pirate" countries!

The WHO case is particularly revealing: there was shifting in the matter of illicit medicine. At the same time, similar shifting took place in many other international organisations.[35] Several of these set up working groups on counterfeiting, following the World Customs Organisation (WCO) approval in June 2006 of the launch of the SECURE standards project aimed at strengthening IP rights. Between 2005 and 2009, successive G8 summits also emphasised the importance of combating counterfeiting.[36] The Council of Europe worked on counterfeit policy between 2008 and 2010, leading to the Medicrime convention.[37] Between 2006 and 2012, negotiations between various governments on Anti-Counterfeiting Trade Agreement (ACTA) were also symptomatic of the change. Decisions were made in the context of increasing pressure from firms to combat counterfeiting, including pharmaceutical counterfeiting. The Global Conference on Counterfeiting and Piracy, for example, has been in existence since 2004, an initiative of the International Chamber of Commerce, in partnership with organisations such as Interpol and the WCO. The WHO case is nonetheless the most striking example, as it is supposed to concern itself solely with public health, but has shown during this period just how difficult it can be to carry out this mission without being exposed to pressure from private firms and corporate interests that are seeking to impose IP as a privileged normative principle.

Confusing "counterfeit" with "generic"

Illicit medicine as a public issue, the ways in which it becomes known and is managed – all of this depends to a large extent on the terms used to describe the problem and the definitions assigned to these terms: in other words, on practices of formulation.[38] The particular connection between, on the one hand, legal issues of IP and, on the other hand, that of representation and supervision of the problem of fake medicines boils down to a problem of language. This aspect should be taken seriously in any discourse on "fake medicines" and analysed in detail, together with its multiple implications. I have examined the ways in which the media dealt with the problem in different countries in order to understand the construction of the issue on an international scale. Using a method tried and tested in communication and media studies, and discourse analysis, I have assembled a corpus of English-language press articles published in India and Kenya by looking up key terms. These articles are admittedly biased, as the English-language press does not deal with exactly the same subject matter; local languages have had to be omitted, as the various bodies of text have to be comparable. My main interest in analysing the transnational press was to grasp hegemonic trends in discourse on the public issue of illicit medicines, while paying attention to local variations.

At the WHO, the main problem is the intrusion of IP issues into the question of pharmaceutical quality, using as a gateway the notion of counterfeiting and its definitions. In the media, a comparable intrusion takes place; though somewhat different, it is complementary. Same traits are common to both organisational and communicational (media) spaces: the problem seen as criminal and increasing recourse to the notion of counterfeit. Before the year 2000, there is little mention in the Indian press of IP rights. The main themes here are access to medicines, price control, generics, and government regulation of the prices and sale of medicines. The terms "counterfeit" and "counterfeiting" are completely absent. In only two articles of the corpus is the notion of IP central; it is mentioned in only 3% of them. Before the year 2000 there is no relevant article in the digitised Kenyan corpus; comparison with India is thus impossible. Interviews with activists in Kenya and India, however, tend to confirm the intuition that the problem of illicit medicines is not dealt with as *counterfeiting* in either of these countries.

After 2001, this all changes. Framing of the issue in terms of counterfeiting begins. In the Kenyan corpus, after 2005 counterfeiting is the principal subject of almost 20% of the articles. The term "counterfeit" ranks fourth in frequency in this corpus, coming after "State" and "Public health".[39] The notion of IP occurs less frequently, being the main topic of 3% of the articles. The framing of the problem of illicit medicines in terms of counterfeiting is markedly hegemonic in the Kenyan press, which however does not go into detail in matters of copyright, a more technical subject. In the Indian press, the notion of counterfeit is completely absent until 2001, when it appears as the main subject of 4% of the articles collected. The notion of IP, on the other hand, is present in 34% of the articles, and is the main topic in 20% of them, 11 times more frequently than before 2001. Despite the fact that Indian journalists refuse to apply the notion of counterfeiting – to avoid any confusion between the latter and generics, a matter of national importance – IP rights apparently became an unavoidable issue after 2001 in both India and Kenya.

It is thus over the past decade that a framing of the problem of fake medicines in terms of IP and counterfeiting has been massively imposed. This imposition can be found in both collections, showing no doubt that it is a worldwide trend, though it admittedly varies from place to place. The Kenyan press, for example, applies the notion of counterfeit massively. The Indian press, on the other hand, avoids it, preferring to treat the subject as a matter of IP.

In criminalising the issue, for example, the terms used to describe it are particularly striking: it is a "scourge", a "pharmaceutical crime", and even "pharmaceutical terrorism". Danger of death is frequently mentioned, linked to a variety of incidents. The victims of the "scourge" are the patients, consumers, and users of the medicines. Economic issues, however, are nonetheless also evoked: the problem hampers the development of countries and violates the rights of legitimate producers. Numerous operators committed to this stance stress the presumptive places of origin of fake medicines (mainly South and East Asia, and the Middle East), stigmatising as "pirates" the producers and distributors concerned. As to corrective measures recommended, much of the discourse stresses the need to organise international collaboration and to apply laws more strictly. IP is presented as the most effective weapon in the combat against the proliferation of illicit medicines, and stricter regulation as an urgent need. Anti-counterfeit discourse denounces a problem that it considers to be of major importance; the solutions proposed consist in strengthening the law by technological means. More generally, as Homberger and Cossa note, anti-counterfeit discourse shifts its focus from safety to security, promising first and foremost to securitise consumer goods.[40]

Like the WHO, the press offers a framing of the problem in terms of counterfeiting, reformulating the issue of illicit medicines by inscribing it in the semantic field of crime and economic interest. A further issue, also underscored by many healthcare activists, is that counterfeit medicines can be confused with generics, and as a result of this confusion jeopardise access to affordable treatment. I have studied this particular problem using the Prospero software. It enabled me to follow the evolution of the notion of counterfeit medicines over the course of time, according to the writers (mainly journalists) who use it, and to associations between this notion and others, such as "generic". In my collections of press articles, associations between

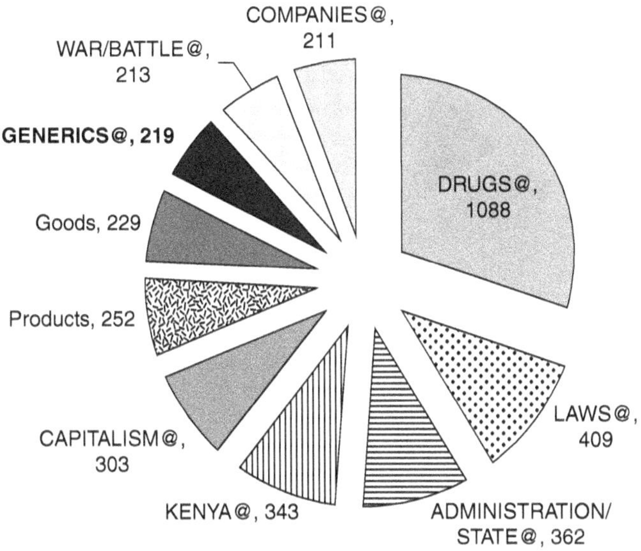

Figure 4.1 Entities most often linked to "counterfeits" in the corpus of the Kenyan press.

the two notions are very common. There are discrepancies, however, between press treatment in Kenya and in India. The association between generics and counterfeits is reciprocal in the Kenyan press, whereas in India this is not the case. In the Kenyan press, when counterfeiting is mentioned, generics are also referred to, and massively so (see Figure 4.1). When generics are mentioned, counterfeiting is one of the topics most often broached (Figure 4.2). In the Indian press, on the other hand, when the subject of generics is brought up in the debate on counterfeiting (Figure 4.3) – usually to denounce confusion between the two – counterfeiting is not associated with issues concerning generics (Figure 4.4). Besides this, the Indian press adopts a rigorously legal and technical approach, using terms such as "patent" and acronyms such as "IP" (intellectual property) that figure in legal debates (Figures 4.3 and 4.4) that are completely absent from the Kenyan corpus (Figures 4.1 and 4.2). In addition, the Indian corpus shows an extensive association between technology (Figure 4.3) and counterfeiting: technology is usually presented as the solution to the problem of counterfeiting. This is not the case in the Kenyan corpus (Figure 4.1).

Although the recurrent association of two terms in the media can contribute to blurring their differences, it does not necessarily give rise to confusion, as the terms can be explicitly opposed to one another in statements such as "*Generics are not counterfeits*". The joint presence, when examined more closely, can nonetheless cause blurring, as the following examples show:

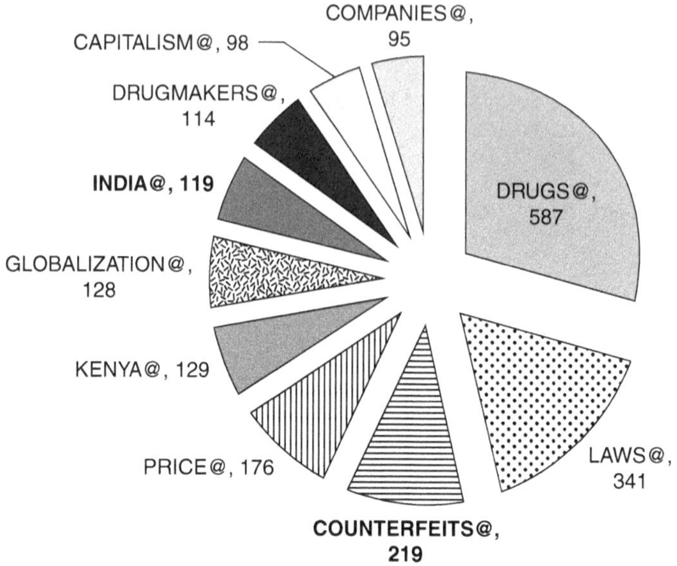

Figure 4.2 Entities most often linked to "generics" in the corpus of the Kenyan press.

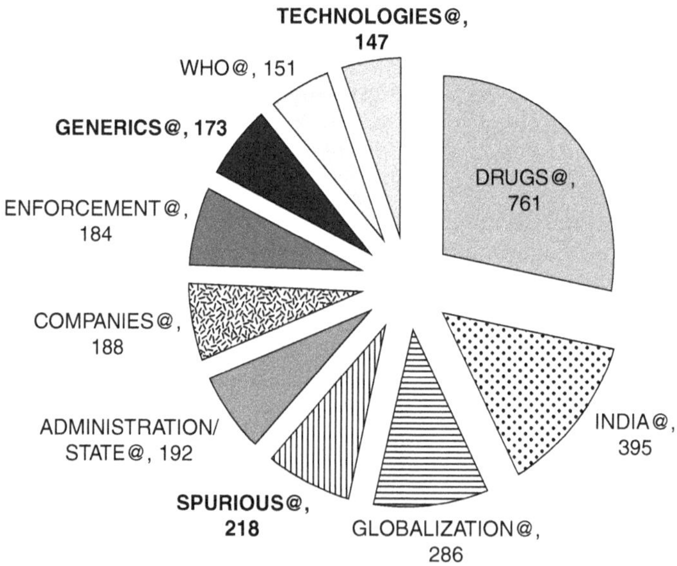

Figure 4.3 Entities most often linked to "counterfeits" in the corpus of the Indian press since 2008.

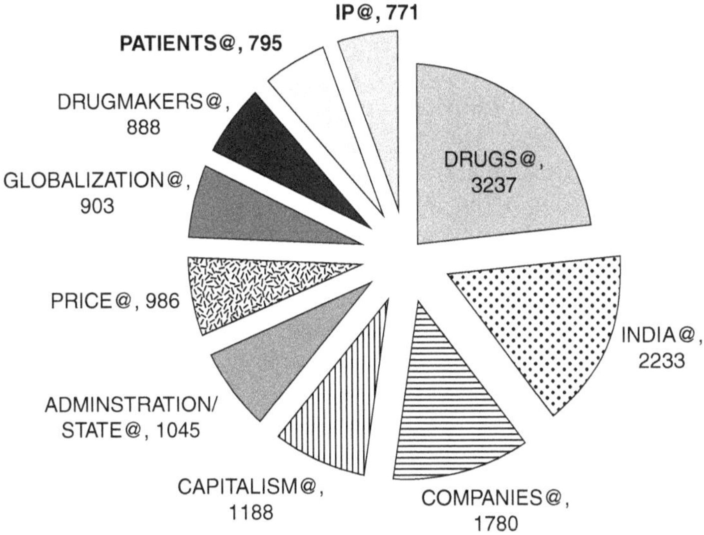

Figure 4.4 Entities most often linked to "generics" in the corpus of the Indian press since 2008.

> *Medical care the world over is prohibitively expensive and many people are increasingly turning to* ***generic drugs*** *and herbal medicine. As a result, unscrupulous traders have cashed in on this desperation to circumvent the system and sell* ***counterfeits*** *repackaged as genuine medicine.*
>
> *(Kenyan press)*

> *Complexity of counterfeit supply chain has intensified especially with the emergence of Internet-based sales channels and the transnational payment gateways to procure* ***generics*** *and APIs from patent-insecure nations to convert them into* ***counterfeits****.*
>
> *(Indian press)*

These two examples show that an association between "generics" and "counterfeit" is not based uniquely on a joint presence of the two terms, but also on the production of a blurring effect that can give rise to confusion. In the first passage, as in the second, though generic medicines are not presented as counterfeits, the two notions are nonetheless closely linked. In one case, generics and counterfeits are seen as symptoms of the same effect (turning consumers away from branded medicines, the "originals"). In the other case, generics can be converted into counterfeit medicines in a way that is not explicitly stated. Thus, although an anti-counterfeit framing tends to be imposed in the press, a certain non-distinctness is maintained between generic and counterfeit medicines.

As far as public knowledge is concerned, treatment in the press has further consequences. A substantial proportion of articles – in order to give a clearer idea of exactly what is at stake – offers quantitative assessments of the extent of the problem of illicit medicines. As data tend to be meagre, the statistics cited and published in different press organs are often identical. Among the most frequent assessments are the following: (1) counterfeit medicines are said to constitute a global market of 75 billion dollars up by 90% on the figures for 2005, according to the WHO; (2) according to the same source, 30% of medicines in Kenya are counterfeit, and in India 35%; (3) according to the EU, 75% of counterfeit medicines would come from India.

Closer examination of these figures shows up inconsistencies in these proportions, however. To take some examples from the Kenyan press corpus:

> *the latest WHO report says about **30 per cent** of all medicines in the market are counterfeits.*
>
> *(The Standard, 25 April 2011)*

> *The Pharmacy and Poison board has found that about **10 per cent** of the drugs in the market were counterfeited.*
>
> *(Daily Nation, 03 November 2011)*

> *The Pharmaceutical Society of Kenya contends that **half of all anti-malarial** drugs in Kenya are counterfeit.*
>
> *(Business Daily, 26 October 2011)*

> *Incidents of counterfeit malaria and tuberculosis medicines given free of charge in government hospitals have gone **down to zero**, said the Pharmacy and Poisons Board.*
>
> *(Business Daily, 26 October 2012)*

And in the Indian press corpus:

> *The World Health Organisation (WHO) had recently put the spurious pharma business at Rs 4,000 crore, or **35 per cent** of the domestic industry size. However, WHO admitted in a letter to the government that this figure was based on a news report two years ago, and not based on any research.*
>
> *(The Financial Express, 13 August 2003)*

> *According to WHO estimates, counterfeits in India have been estimated at **20–25%** of the market volume, which translates to a very large volume owing to the large size of the Indian pharmaceuticals market. Based on these estimates, the counterfeit drugs market in India is worth Rs 6,500 crore annually.*
>
> *(The Financial Express, 14 September 2009)*

> *According to Government estimates **0.46 per cent** of all medicines sold to customers are spurious. But an earlier survey of 10,000 samples, funded by the World Health Organisation and undertaken by the International Pharmaceutical Federation, had concluded that **3.1 per cent** of drugs in India were counterfeit.*
>
> *(Business Line, 27 January 2010)*

These figures are patently inconsistent, varying by as much as 300% in the case of the Indian market. There are contradictions between different sources and between different estimates coming from the same source. The WHO estimates, for example, vary in the space of a few years, from the idea that the market for fake medicines accounts for 35% of the total – to that of 20–25%.

Besides the statistics produced, sundry "incidents" are another way in which the press represents the problem of illicit medicines. Customs seizures and police raids offer other approaches to the problem. Statistics on isolated cases of this sort are unrelated to one another, and give different pictures of the situation, complementing the overall statistical one. The following are a few examples.

> ***Kenya**: The Pharmacy and Poisons Board has impounded counterfeit drugs (4000 tablets of Cialis) worth Sh1.5 million at the Eldoret International Airport.*
>
> *(The Standard, 21 November 2010)*

> *A record pile of counterfeit drugs were burnt last night as the Government upped its war against illegal medicine. The **40 tonnes** of drugs whose value is estimated at **Sh17 million** were destroyed under the close watch of Inspector Dennis Otieno of the Pharmacy and Poisons Board.*
>
> *(The Standard, 11 August 2009)*

> ***India**: In one of the searches, about **2,700 bottles** of a spurious cough syrup were seized in Cuddalore and **228 bottles** in Coimbatore on Saturday.*
>
> *(The Hindu, 22 March 2010)*

> *The Delhi Police have arrested three persons for allegedly being involved in selling spurious medicines and **seized drugs worth Rs 40 lakh** from them.*
>
> *(Hindustan Times, 14 June 2011)*

The media treatment is the same as for illicit drugs, but in this case – that of fake medicines – the quantities are not decisive, as undifferentiated treatment tends to even out the actual extent of the problem, flattening it. Seizures of 200 bottles of cough mixture and of 40 tons of medicines are treated in much the same way. The main result is that echoes in the media are amplified, the slightest intervention of the authorities creating an event and maintaining a permanent level of alert and a constantly flashing alarm.

Treatment of the issue in English-language press in Kenya and India thus also reveals a second determinant in framing: association and confusion. Recurrent association of the issue of IP, and confusion between heterogeneous categories of illicit medicines – substandard, counterfeit, generic – are also part of the framing operation. The press tends to promote a certain way of looking at the problem by imposing on it a determinate semantic field, despite variations from one country and situation to another.

Detecting, measuring, qualifying the illicit

The third important dimension of the construction of the problem of "fake" medicines in public space is the identification and description of the problem. It is on the putative authority of their sources that statistics and estimates are announced and put into circulation, as we have already seen.[41] The field of science, seen as a privileged space in the production of knowledge, is an essential link in the construction of illicit pharmaceuticals as a problem. As we shall shortly see, actual knowledge of the problem of illicit medicines brings with it uncertainty in many forms; often it is produced by means of methods that are in no way unassailable. By its very nature, it is difficult to get to know an illicit practice such as the distribution of doubtful medicines. There are admittedly many scientific surveys and estimates, but the data they come up with is often hard to understand. We will thus have to examine in greater detail the ways in which these data are actually produced.

In the scientific field, the problem of illicit medicines is seen from a dual point of view, both societal and pharmaco-epidemiological. The main fields and disciplines concerned are international public health, tropical medicine, pharmacology, epidemiology, and analytical chemistry. Relevant articles deal with many themes, ranging from general considerations on the policy of pharmaceutical regulation to biochemistry; the corpus is a heterogeneous collection of articles on medicines that are unregistered or have expired, on issues of information centred on medicines, on the stability of products, on the impacts of time and temperature on their alteration and expiry, on unregistered medicines used by medical personnel in Northern countries with supervisory protocols, on forms of contamination of medicines known as traditional, and on the black market for steroids in sports circles. The methods used to answer all these questions are also very varied: interviews and questionnaires, chemical analyses of substances using various sampling methods, socio-political analysis of information systems, comparative (or non-comparative) testing of identification techniques, listing of medicines stocked in households, and so forth. Despite this extreme diversity, most scientific publications dealing with illicit medicines fall into one of the three following categories: (1) opinion pieces; (2) tests of technologies used for detection, for evaluation of quality, and for identification or authentification of medicines; and (3) surveys aiming at measuring the prevalence of illicit medicines in particular geographical zones.

Opinion pieces are not scientific articles, even when they are published in specialised journals; compared to the general press, they are only a little more specialised. Reading them nonetheless helps us grasp the ways in which the issue of illicit medicines makes its way into the field of science. The corpus contains one article dating back to 1952, but until the 1990s occurrences are rare (there are only 36 articles dated between 1952 and 1990).[42] On perusing the corpus it emerges that the problem of fake medicines and, in particular, its formulation in terms of pharmaceutical counterfeiting, though not entirely absent between the 1950s and the 1980s,[43] becomes a regular feature in the specialised press only as of the early 1990s. An article published by Martijn ten Ham, head of the Drug Safety Unit of the Drug Management and Policies Division of the WHO, kingpin of the entry of our thematic into this organisation, marks the beginning of the growth of the importance of the theme.[44] In the course of the 1990s publications dealing with the theme of illicit medicines become more numerous: most of them are centred on developing countries. By the end of the century articles and debates multiply in the specialised press. Most of them deal with incidents and results of surveys, arguing in favour of stricter regulation. They rarely use with any precision notions such as "substandard", "false", and "counterfeit"; these terms are usually used as complements or even as equivalents. Seen from this angle, the field of science reawakens public discourse to the issue of illicit medicines as of the 1990s, contributing to a discourse that has hitherto been vague, and focusing attention mainly on the "fake" and "counterfeit" medicines circulating in the countries of the South.

The second category of articles deals with the detection of illicit medicines, and the ways of distinguishing the authentic from the false. This category is relatively absent from the corpus until the turn of the century. It gains importance as of 2005/2006, with a growing number of articles in publications on pharmaceutical analysis, biochemistry, and analytical chemistry. These articles are part of a current of research that offers technical solutions to problems of identification and authenticity.

The main techniques used are liquid chromatography and mass spectrometry that involve destructive sampling. Some articles, however, propose non-invasive techniques such as Raman spectrometry (which consists in playing a ray of light on an object and analysing the frequency that has been modified by the chemical composition of the object). The aim of this current in research is to provide effective, economical ways of checking medicines, and of making this testing as mobile as possible. It indicates a renewal of interest in the struggle against counterfeiting, its tools, and methods of detection. It also brings to the fore the importance accorded to proprietary technologies, such as the "minilab" (that makes it possible to do initial testing on the site under investigation), and the "truscan" (a portable Raman spectrometry apparatus). I will return to these devices later; for the time being we can note that the scientific field is increasingly being marked by the definition of the public issue of illicit medicines.

The third category of articles – surveys of prevalence – appears in the late 1990s; during this decade available data often concern the estimates or evaluations that follow seizure operations. The surveys consist in evaluating quantities of fake, substandard, and counterfeit medicines circulating on such and such a market. In some cases, the survey takes the form of interviews, dealing with estimates and representations of the problem; in other cases, samples are taken and chemical analysis performed on them. The main methodological problem faced concerns the sampling techniques (how are the medicines collected?) and analysis (what criteria and techniques of analysis have the researchers used in evaluating the samples?), linked to the definition of the objects analysed. In some cases, purposive sampling based on suspicion leads authors to refuse to provide statistics, and to disconnect their work from assessments of prevalence.[45] This is by no means always the case, however. One survey concludes, for example, that 38% of alternative medicines are adulterated by the presence of corticosteroids; but the samples have in most cases been submitted by patients and doctors who suspected that corticosteroids were present.[46] Another article, based on a selection of 70 samples of anti-tuberculosis drugs from 6 different countries, reports that 10% of the samples analysed were substandard.[47] This, however, was a result obtained by combining an initial analysis carried out by the Centre for Disease Control (CDC) that isolated 22 samples (33%) that the Centre considered substandard, with a subsequent analysis of 40 samples by the Food and Drug Administration (FDA), 19 of these in the substandard group. The figure of 10% given in the article thus indicates that 4 of the 40 medicines tested by the FDA turned out to be substandard, whereas about half of the samples had already been tested as substandard by the CDC. This indicates not so much that 10% of anti-tuberculosis drugs were substandard, as that the CDC and the FDA (which classifies as substandard a lot fewer drugs) do not use the same methods of evaluating!

Research circles are aware of these limitations, and attempts at systematic study are usually accompanied by a critique of the data, their paucity, and the lack of rigour in the field.[48] An article reviewing various studies identifies by means of restrictive criteria some 50 surveys based on sampling; it underscores in most cases a weakness in methodology and confusion between substandard and counterfeit medicines.[49] Another review, carried out on 28 surveys of quality of anti-malarial drugs between 1999 and 2011, finds that 22 of the 28 studies are based on convenience sampling, that is, without previous random screening; this means that they favourised selection by suspicion.[50] Taken together, however, these studies help to build a statistical idea of the quantity of illicit medicines in circulation in such and such a country or region of the world.

After the WHO and the general press, scientific publications provide a view of a third dimension of the framing process applied to illicit medicines. Firstly, the scientific press confirms the dating (the early 1990s) of the renewal of interest taken in scientific circles in the issue of false medicines.

This renewal comes together with inaccurate qualification, and often in terms of counterfeiting. It corresponds first and foremost to two types of technical articles: articles on methods of detection, and those on the prevalence of illicit medicines. Increased interest in detection methods indicates that issues of technical instrumentation have gained importance – and these issues themselves are linked to the sales concerns of the suppliers of technical equipment. At last, the multiplication of surveys of prevalence, despite the methodological difficulties involved and the limited scope of the results obtained, leads to a production of statistics that are subsequently taken up in other fields. Indeed, as we will see in the following section, the autonomy of the academic field being limited on such issues, there is a certain degree of porosity between the surveys of scientific articles on the one hand and surveys published by international organisations, foundations, and government agencies on the other. This favours the homogeneisation of hegemonic discourse.

The security framework

The analysis of definition issues at the WHO, treatment of the problem in the general press, and questions raised by detection and measurement in the academic field reveal noteworthy evolutions in the treatment of the problem of illicit medicines since the 1990s. However, the rationale of international organisations, the media and the academic field are not homogeneous. Each field follows its own rules and goals and provides "framing elements" to the issue, rather than imposing a complete frame. To understand the emergence of a security framework, one has therefore to take into account the multiple meeting points between discourse – meeting points which are defined by the circulation of words, definitions, and statistics throughout the social world. Figures produced in the scientific arena respond to those given by regulatory authorities, foundations, and agencies – governmental and non-governmental – also engaged in the production of knowledge regarding the circulation of illicit medicines.

These discursive circulations are not free of contradictions. If, for example, we look at the sources of the three figures on "counterfeits" most often published in the Kenyan press, we find that certain operators have manipulated the data. This is obvious in, for example, the 2012 report by Management Sciences for Health (MSH), the USAID technical operator in Kenya (a report financed by USAID and the FDA). These statistics are taken up, with the sources indicated, in a report that I was handed in Nairobi in April 2012[51]:

> *Counterfeit medicine is a growing threat across the world, accounting for up to USD 75 billion in sales in 2010*. WHO estimates that more than 30 percent of the medicines for sale in some areas in Africa can be counterfeit**. In Kenya alone, about USD 65 to 130 millions worth of counterfeit medicines are being sold each year***.*[52]

The sources advanced – WHO and US Pharmacopeia – are standard references in matters of health and medicine, giving the figures cited legitimacy and authority. In reality, the following is what one finds in the source documents:

> *Worldwide sales of counterfeit medicines could top US$ 75 billion this year, a 90% rise in five years, according to an estimate published by the Center for Medicine in the Public Interest in the United States of America (USA)*.*

The "$75 billion" do not come from a WHO estimate, but from an American group financed by the pharmaceutical industry and simply *cited* in a WHO report. The figure also crops up in the Indian press, where it is also attributed to the WHO. In the rest of the paragraph concerned, the MSH report attributes to WHO an estimate according to which more than 30% of medicines sold in certain parts of Africa are counterfeit. In reality, these estimates come from a report that WHO supported but that was published by the IMPACT group: "*Many countries in Africa and parts of Asia and Latin America have areas where more than 30% of the medicines on sale can be counterfeit*"**. As we have already seen, the IMPACT group is an initiative in which many operators in industry and international organisations have been involved, WHO being a partner that had distanced itself towards the end of January 2012. The group was never officially attached to the WHO, though it always used the WHO logo on its publications. Last but not least, the third part of the paragraph attributes to US Pharmacopeia (the institution that sets pharmaceutical standards in the USA) an estimate of the number of counterfeit medicines sold in Kenya every year. The US Pharamacopeia publication is actually a press review that reproduces an article on the Kenyan market published in the Nigerian newspaper *Business Day*:

> *Approximately 30% of the drug market is counterfeit, according to the Kenyan Association of Pharmaceutical Industry, who says that USD $130 million worth of counterfeit pharmaceuticals is being sold each year***.*

The Kenyan Association of Pharmaceutical Industry (KAPI) is the organisation that promotes foreign pharmaceutical laboratories' interests in Kenya; it was at the time headed by a Sanofi representative. There is – to say the least – a discrepancy between figures given by KAPI and those of US Pharmacopeia.

We note in the same paragraph of this MSH report, in condensed form, a sample of the practice of erroneously attributing sources with a view to justifying industrial groups' estimates by passing them off as studies made by creditable institutions such as WHO and US Pharmacopeia. Distortions of this sort are recurrent in the Kenyan and Indian press: figures produced by the industry are attributed to reputable public-health institutions; this is part of the framing of the debate on illicit medicines. It is linked to the "need" for statistics to lend apparent substance to discourse on the importance of the problem. An operator in the sector stresses this:

> *We use a lot of figures too, I assure you that some of them are … um …, but we use them anyway. Because behind it, when you are doing information, going to see authorities or whatever, well, they want figures. If you don't tell them "one medicine out of two on Internet is counterfeit", or "ten percent of world trade", or "5 to 7%" … you see what I mean? But that's how it is […] people need figures or danger. That gets a reaction in the media, a reaction from politicians.*[53]

On another level, it is also noticeable that some operators seize on available definitions as a strategy, together with their implications, in order to strengthen ideas that favour stringent IP rights. They play at superposing normative positions that are contradictory, mixing health concerns with those of commerce and of the law that at the same time set up competition between different value systems. This superposition can be seen, for example, in the report on the "Opinion formers' conference on counterfeit medicines" (co-organised in London on 26 October 2009 by the Wellcome Trust and the American Pharmaceutical Group).[54] This report mixes together several positions. To start with, it reproduces the definition of counterfeit given by WHO/IFPMA in 1992.[55] It goes on to distinguish between generic, counterfeit, and substandard. It recognises that the proportion of counterfeits is lower than that of substandard medicines, but nonetheless stresses that the risks linked to counterfeit medicines are considerably greater, and thus have a "higher overall impact". This appears to give higher priority to health issues. Next, the report proposes to separate health issues from those of copyright:

> *Intellectual property can be divorced entirely from discussion of counterfeit drugs. Although trade and intellectual property rights are important factors affecting access to pharmaceutical products, they can be considered separately from the criminal production and distribution of counterfeit medicine.*

This seems to strengthen the thinking in terms of health. Immediately after this, however, the report emphasises the role that IP can play in the battle against pharmaceutical piracy; this re-directs the debate towards commercial considerations:

> *As counterfeiters are passing off their products as someone else's, they are typically infringing trademark; counterfeit medicines are one strand of a wider "pirating" industry. In practice, trademark infringement can be used to counter trade in counterfeit medicines.*[56]

The overall result is to superpose health, commercial and legal issues, producing yet another framing effect.

A third framing effect is obtained by formulating the problem of quality by viewing it through the lens of authenticity and ownership. This can be seen in the report entitled "Keeping it real". Its authors identify, among the main causes of counterfeiting, the difficulty of pointing out quality to consumers. They explain that:

> *In principle, manufacturers that are able to provide assurances regarding the quality of their goods should have a competitive advantage. (…) That is one of the main functions of a brand. But to signal quality effectively, manufacturers need to be able to ensure that their brands are not being counterfeited. The main mechanism for so doing is registration and enforcement of trademarks.*[57]

Further on, the authors stress the role played by technologies that preserve identity, reasserting that "*the most fundamental cause of the spread of fake drugs in less developed countries has been the inability of manufacturers to protect the identity of their products*".[58] By doing this they reframe quality and health issues as issues of identification that could be dealt with by means of authentification technologies. This association between quality, identity, and branding also occurs frequently in our corpus; it is one of the main characteristics of anti-counterfeit discourse.

The circulation in society of figures and of definitions on one hand, and the practice of reformulating issues on the other, play an essential part in framing. As it does not remain enclosed within a clearly delimited space, it fashions the overall context in which regulation is carried out. This framing work can be seen at work in a series of legal texts: laws (the Kenyan anti-counterfeit act, and analogous measures in Uganda and the East African Community), conventions (Medicrime in the EU), and multilateral agreements (ACTA). These measures pursue a large range of objectives, targeting different geographical, economic, and social milieus; all apply some degree of constraint. They share the objective of regulating markets and countering the proliferation of counterfeit products, including medicines. Affinity between, on the one hand, the terms employed, the definitions adopted, the figures produced, and on the other hand, the regulations put in place to deal with them indicates a situation that is performative. Reformulation of the problem of illicit medicines is followed by transcription into coercive laws, regulations, agreements, and trade pacts.

Furthermore, some operators play a particular role in this framing process. This can be seen on an individual level. Michèle Forzley, an expert in health and law, heads a consulting firm that has a large private clientèle and promotes stringent IP rights. She wrote the report on which the work of the WHO task force is based.[59] The lobbyist Roger Bate, an economist, a member of the American Enterprise Institute, a neoconservative think tank, has also devoted numerous publications to counterfeit medicines, and is widely cited.[60] At last, institutions and government agencies have been targeted by strategies that influence the framing process. One criticism of the Kenyan law points out the pressure brought to bear on the government and parliament by industrial groups (and, in particular, the Kenya Association of Manufacturers). Such lobbying strategies have enabled anti-counterfeit discourse to be imposed within institutions.[61]

These discursive circulations have allowed for the problem of illicit medicines to be reformulated trough a "security" lens – and we see that trade strategies have been only one among many elements of this reformulation process. Discourse at the WHO, media interest in illicit medicines, and attempts in the academic field to describe and measure the problem, all show that change has taken place in the discursive space within which the illicit medicines issue is managed. More than that, a "security" framework has appeared. This approach consists first in the overestimation of pharmaceutical regulatory infringement, through an extensive redefinition of these practices and through the production of *questionable* data. It also implies the criminalisation of non-standard practices and the proposal to associate police forces more fully to regulation enforcement. At last, the security turns facilitate the confusion of trade and health issues. Such a confusion benefits to some actors who, pretending to protect public health, manage to impose a conception of pharmaceutical regulation which favours their own interests.

But the security turn as it is presented here is mostly a discursive turn. This discursive dimension accounts only for one part of the transformations that have happened. The discursive flow irrigates the field of social practices – but the latter are by no way the direct expression of the former. In order to understand the consequences of the security shift, we therefore have now to turn towards its material dimension: we will show how it affects the monitoring and control activity of pharmaceutical flows.

Notes

1 Njururi, B. (1980). Crisis hits pharmacies, *The Standard*, 7 July.
2 Magugu Blacklists Anpi Pharma Ltd., *The Weekly Review*, 11 April 1980.
3 Ban this Drug, Ministry urged, *Daily Nation*, 26 June 1980.
4 Kenya is not a dumping ground!, *The Standard*, 1 February 1980.
5 Jomo Kenyatta, President of Kenya, died in August 1978. Daniel Arap Moi acted as president during the transition, and became president in November 1979. The cabinet was appointed ensuring a degree of continuity, but there were some changes, such as the entry of Arthur Magugu, who, however, was not to remain Minister of Health for very long; he became Minister of Finance in 1982.
6 Tougher rules for drug dealers, *Daily Nation*, 1 April 1982.
7 War on fake goods stepped up as new board takes office, *Business Daily*, 3 December 2009.
8 Promotion leaflet for the Anti-Counterfeit Agency, When you Buy Counterveit Goods …, 2013.
9 Hornberger, J., & Cossa, E. (2012). *From drug safety to drug security. The policing of counterfeit medications*, Johannesburg, African Centre for Migration and

Society; Hornberger, J. (2018). From drug safety to drug security: A contemporary shift in the policing of health, *Medical Antropology Quarterly*, 32/3, pp. 365–383.

10 Chauveau, S. (2006). Contrefaçons et fraudes sur les medicaments (19e–20e siècles), 711–728 *in* Gérard Béaur, Hubert Bonin, Claire Lemercier, *Fraude, Contrefaçon et contrebande de l'antiquité à nos jours*, Genève: Droz.

11 Cassier, M. (2004). Brevets pharmaceutiques et santé publique en France: opposition et dispositifs spécifiques d'appropriation des médicaments entre 1791 et 2004, *Entreprises et histoire*, 2, 36, pp. 29–47.

12 Barton, P. (2007). "The Great Quinine Fraud": Legality Issues in the "Non-Narcotic" Drug Trade in British India, *Social History of Alcohol and Drugs*, 22/1, pp. 6–25; Roy R. D. (2017) *Malarial Subjects. Empire, medicine and nonhuans in British India*, pp. 1820–1909, Cambridge: Cambridge University Press.

13 Chauveau, S. (2004). Genèse de la « sécurité sanitaire »: les produits pharmaceutiques en France aux XIXe et XXe siècles, *Revue d'histoire moderne et contemporaine*, 51/2, pp. 88–117.

14 Chauveau, S. (2004) *Ibid.*

15 Bonah, C., & Gaudillière, J.-P. (2007). Faute, accident ou risque iatrogène? La régulation des événements indésirables du médicament à l'aune des affaires Stalinon et Distilbène, *Revue Française des Affaires Sociales*, 3, pp. 123–151; on thalidomide, Carpenter, D. (2010). *Reputation and Power, Organizational Image and Pharmaceutical Regulation at the FDA*, Princeton: Princeton University Press.

16 Demortain, D. (2015). Les heurts de la transnationalisation, pp. 109–122 In S. Boudia, E. Henry (dir.) *La mondialisation des risques*, Rennes: Presses Universitaires de Rennes; Kessel, N. (2015). Les risques médicamenteux entre effets secondaires et consommation pharmaceutique, pp. 123–136 In S. Boudia, E. Henry (dir.) *La mondialisation des risques*, Rennes: Presses Universitaires de Rennes.

17 Greene, J. (2014). *Generic. The unbranding of modern medicine*, Baltimore: Johns Hopkins University Press.

18 Baxerres, C. (2015). Contrefaçon pharmaceutique: la construction sociale d'un problème de santé publique In A. Desclaux, M. Egrot (dir.) *Anthropologie du médicament au Sud. La pharmaceuticalisation à ses marges*, Paris: L'Harmattan, pp. 129–146.

19 Baxerres, C. (2015). Contrefaçon pharmaceutique: la construction sociale d'un problème de santé publique In A. Desclaux, M. Egrot (dir.) *Anthropologie du médicament au Sud. La pharmaceuticalisation à ses marges*, Paris: L'Harmattan, pp. 129–146.

20 Eisenberg, W. V., & Tillson, A. H. (1966). Identification of counterfeit drugs, particularly barbiturates and amphetamines by microscopic, chemical, and instrumental techniques, *Journal of Forensic Sciences*, 11/4(October), pp. 529–551.

21 WHO (1987). *The rational use of drugs. Report of the Conference of Experts, Nairobi, 25- 29 November 1985*, WHO, Geneva; Siva N. (2010). Tackling the booming trade in counterfeit drugs, *Lancet*, 376, pp. 1725–1726 cité par Carine B. (2015). Contrefaçon pharmaceutique, la construction sociale d'un problème public, pp/ 129–147 In Alice Desclaux, & Marc Egrot (dir.) *Anthropologie du médicament au Sud, la pharmaceuticalisation à ses marges*, Paris: L'Harmattan.

22 World Health Organisation (1992). *Counterfeit drugs report of a joint WHO/IFPMA workshop*, Geneva: WHO, Annexe 1.

23 Sauwakon R., Stephen B. S., & Krisantha W. (2001). Do national medicinal drug policies and essential drug programs improve drug use? a review of experiences in developing countries, *Social Science and Medicine* 53, pp. 831–844.
24 Velasquez, G. (1991). Origine et évolution du concept du médicament essentiel promu par l'OMS, *Tiers-Monde*, 32, 127, pp. 673–680.
25 World Health Organisation (1987). *The rational use of drugs – report of the conference of experts, Nairobi 25–29 November 1985*; World Health Organisation (1992). *Counterfeit drugs report of a joint WHO/IFPMA workshop*, Geneva: WHO; World Health Organisation (1999). *Counterfeit drugs. Guidelines for the development of measures to combat counterfeit drugs*, Geneva.
26 Bale, H. (2001). *Consumption and trade in off-patented medicines*, Working Paper 65, mai, ICRIER, www.icrier.org/pdf/bale65.PDF.
27 The participants of the WHO International Conference 'Combating Counterfeit Drugs: Building Effective International Collaboration' (2006). *Declaration of Rome. Conclusions and recommendations of the WHO International conference on combating counterfeit medicines*, 18 February, Retrieved from www.who.int/medicines/services/counterfeit/RomeDeclaration.pdf?ua=1.
28 World Health Organisation (South East Asia Regional Office) (2008). *Defining "counterfeit medicines" from the perspective of public health*, SEA-TRH-007.
29 Gopakumar, K. M., & Sangeeta S. (2010). *Unpacking the issue of counterfeit medicines*, Penang: TWN p. 43.
30 WHO Expert Committee on Specifications for Pharmaceutical Preparations – WHO Technical Report Series, No. 863 – Thirty-fourth Report, Annex 12, 1996.
31 WHO Expert Committee on Specifications for Pharmaceutical Preparations – WHO Technical Report Series, No. 885 – Thirty-fifth Report, Annex 6, 1999.
32 WHO Expert Committee on Specifications for Pharmaceutical Preparations – WHO Technical Report Series, No. 937 – Fortieth Report, Annex 5, edition 2006.
33 www.ifpma.org/global-health/counterfeits/definition.html.
34 European Commission, Taxation and Customs Union (2007). *Report on Community Customs Activities on Counterfeit and Piracy. Results at the European Border – 2007*.
35 Sell, S. K. (2008) *The global IP upward ratchet, anti-counterfeiting and enforcement efforts: The state of play*, 9 June, Retrieved from www.twnside.org.sg/title2/intellectual_property/development.research/SusanSellfinalversion.pdf.
36 G8 Gleneagles (2005). *Reducing IPR Piracy and counterfeiting through more effective enforcement*; G8 Heiligendamm (2007). *Growth and responsibility in the world economy*; G8 Hokkaido (2008). *Report of Discussions. G8 Intellectual Property Experts' Group Meeting*; G8 La Maddalena to L'Aquila (2009). *Report of Discussions. G8 Intellectual Property Experts Group Meeting*.
37 Convention du Conseil de l'Europe sur la contrefaçon des produits médicaux et les infractions similaires menaçant la santé publique, STCE n°211, 28 October 2011.
38 This section is based on an analysis of a quantitative-qualitative corpus carried out by means of the Prospero computer programme. Chateauraynaud, F. (2003). *Prospéro. Une technologie littéraire pour les sciences humaines*, Paris, Ed. du CNRS.
39 In the Prospero software, used here to analyse the corpus, an "entity" is a group of terms referring to the same signifier. The entity "counterfeit" (and words of the same family) covers, for example, "imitation", "contraband medicine", "illegally copied", "lookalike", "misbranded", "pass-off (medicine/product)", "pirated", "counterfeit/spurious" "counterfeit/substandard".

40 Hornberger, J., & Cossa, E. (2012). *From drug safety to drug security. The policing of counterfeit medications*, Johannesburg: African Centre for Migration and Society.

41 In this section, I am using a monitoring of scientific articles and the construction of a corpus of articles from the scientific press taken from the WOS and PubMed databases. The corpus has subsequently been complemented manually in the course of my reading. It consists in 1188 articles dating from the period between 1952 and May 2014.

42 This number is low; this is partly due to the fact that the corpus is founded on databases that feature relatively few articles published before the 1980–1990 decade.

43 See, for example, Eisenberg, T. (1966). Identification of counterfeit drugs, particularly barbiturates and amphetamines by microscopic, chemical, and instrumental techniques, *Journal of Forensic Sciences*, 11/4, pp. 529–551.

44 Ham, M. t. (1992). Counterfeit drugs, implications for health, *Adverse Drug Reactions and Toxicological Reviews*, 11/1, pp. 59–65.

45 Newton, P. N. *et al.* (2011). Poor quality vital anti-malarials in Africa – An urgent neglected public health priority, *Malaria Journal*, 10, p. 352.

46 Gupta, S. K. , Kaleekal, T., & Joshi, S. (2000). Misuse of corticosteroids in some of the drugs dispensed as preparations from alternative systems of medicine in India, *Pharmacoepidemiology and Drug Safety*, 9/7, pp. 599–602.

47 Laserson, K. F., Kenyon, A. S., Kenyon, T. A., Layloff, T., & Binkin, N. J. (2001). Substandard tuberculosis drugs on the global market and their simple detection, *International Journal of Tuberculosis and Lung Diseases*, 5/5, pp. 448–454.

48 Shakoor, 0., Taylor, R. B., & Behrens, R. H. (1997). Assessment of the incidence of substandard drugs in developing countries, *Tropical Medicine and International Health*, 2/9, pp. 839–845.

49 Almuzaini, T., Choonara, I., & Sammons, H. (2013). Substandard and counterfeit medicines: A systematic review of the literature, *BMJ Open*, 3, e002923.

50 Nayyar, G. M. L., Breman, J. G., Newton, P. N., & Herrington, J. (2012). Poor-quality antimalarial drugs in southeast Asia and sub-Saharan Africa, *Lancet Infectious Diseases*, 12, pp. 488–496.

51 SPS (Strengthening Pharmaceutical Systems) Program (2012). *Safety of medicines in sub-Saharan Africa: Assessment of pharmacovigilance systems and their performance,* submitted to the US Agency for International Development by the Strengthening Pharmaceutical Systems (SPS) Program, Arlington, VA: Management Sciences for Health, p.22.

52 * WHO (2010). *Bulletin of the World Health Organization: Growing threat from counterfeit*, Medicines, 88, pp. 247–248. Retrieved from www.who.int/bulletin/volumes/88/4/10-020410/en/index.html.

** WHO, *Counterfeit Drugs Kill.* May 2008. www.who.int/impact/FinalBrochureWHA2008a.pdf.

***US Pharmacopeia (USP), *Media Reports on Medicine Quality*, 2011, Retrieved from www.usp.org/sites/default/files/usp_pdf/EN/PQM/pqm-media-report.pdf.

53 Interview with a member of IRACM, Paris, 26 June 2014.

54 www.wellcome.ac.uk/stellent/groups/corporatesite/@policy_communications/documents/web_document/WTX057518.pdf.

55 A counterfeit medicine is one which is deliberately and fraudulently mislabelled with respect to identity and/or source. Counterfeiting can apply to both branded and generic products and counterfeit products may include products with the correct ingredients or with the wrong ingredients, without active ingredients, with insufficient active ingredients or with fake packaging.

56 Wellcome trust, (2009). American pharmaceutical group, *opinion formers' conference on counterfeit medicines: Perspectives and action*, London: Wellcome trust, pp. 4–5.

57 Harris, J. *et al.* (2009). *Keeping it real. Combating the spread of fake drugs in poor countries*, London: International Policy Network, pp. 4–5.

58 *Ibid*, p. 22.

59 Forzley, M. (2005). *Combating counterfeit drugs: a concept paper for effective international collaboration*, World Health Organization, Health Technology and Pharmaceuticals, September. According to Sangeeta Shashikant of Third World Network, this article is itself based on a study published in 2003 with the support of the US Patent and Trademark Office, and sponsored by the International Intellectual Property Institute, a *think tank* that defends the interests of American industrial majors. See Shashikant, S. (2009) Counterfeit taskforce may block legitimate access to generics, *SUNS*, 6623, 22 January.

60 Bate, R. (2008). *Making a killing. The deadly implications of the counterfeit drug trade*, AEI Press; Bate, R. (2012). *Phake: The deadly world of falsified and substandard medicines*, Washington: AEI Press.

61 These strategies feature in the multiple communication campaigns run by pharmaceutical enterprises. One of the most spectacular, broadcast in 2009 by Pfizer (makers of the famous drug Viagra) shows a man who, having taken medicine he had received by post, spits out a rat.

5 The exercise of pharmaceutical control

Performing security

Between October and December 2008, four consignments of Indian generic medicines were seized by Netherlands customs. One of these, bound for Brazil, was of losartan potassium produced by Dr Reddy's Laboratories. Losartan is patented neither in India nor in Brazil.[1] The consignment was seized at the request of an anonymous company on suspicion of copyright violation. According to the denunciation, there was a possibility that it was bound not for Brazil, but for the European market. The original medicine, Cozaar, was patented in the Netherlands by DuPont. When it was established that it was only in transit, it was released. In May 2009 another consignment from India, bound for Vanuatu, was seized in transit at Frankfurt in Germany.[2] It was of amoxicillin, and was suspected of counterfeiting a brand. When GlaxoSmithKline (GSK), owners of the original patent for Amoxil, the brand name, admitted that there had not been a violation, the consignment was released. These cases show that even when the laws in the country of production and the country of destination permit a medicinal product to be bought and sold, transit via Europe can affect its status, legitimacy, and value. This shows how important the actual performance of checking can be, bringing an object into contact with a regulatory framework, an interpretation procedure, and an individual or collective intervention. The seizures were based on suspected violation of a patent (losartan potassium) and a copyrighted brand name (amoxicillin/Amoxil). In one case the customs officials were tipped off by an anonymous report, and in the other acted on suspicion formulated at the time of checking.

This series of incidents introduces an aspect of securitisation applied to pharmaceutical markets that complement the acts qualifying, quantifying, and regulating the issue that have been introduced in Chapter 3 of this book. As the examples show, regulations are relayed by their application, and between the rule and its application there is some play. To understand this relaying and this play, one has to take into account the actual situations in which the practices of checking are embedded. In the present case, the checking is a result of a regulatory framework, of the presence of medicines in a European

DOI: 10.4324/9781003194767-8

transit area because of the low cost of transport in the European transportation system, of the authority granted to customs officials to act on suspect goods, of the training these officials have received, and of the intervention of an anonymous party concerned by intellectual property rights. These incidents are all localised and occur in ways that sometimes have not been foreseen by the regulators. This is why we have to look at actual practices if we are to assess correctly the issues involved in security-based framing and their impact on the circulation of pharmaceuticals. With this in mind, in this chapter, I will follow the monitoring and checking activity carried out on pharmaceuticals by regulatory operators in India and in Kenya.

Monitoring and checking – inspection activity – involves a vast ensemble of knowledge, methods, and organisational forms. This chapter will introduce the reader to the categories of operation to which is subject the circulation of pharmaceuticals between two countries. It will start with the trajectories monitored in the case of medicines circulating between India and Kenya. My approach will pursue those adopted for customs inspection[3] and for expertise on pharmaceutical regulation.[4] Three arguments will be outlined. Firstly, that monitoring and sampling operations seek to ensure the movement of pharmaceuticals. Police seizures and sampling carried out in the course of quality control operations, though different in nature, both form part of a range of subtraction practices that paradoxically aim at ensuring that the overall circulation of pharmaceuticals remains intact. Secondly, that the field of control and practices of subtraction is currently displaying three trends: towards privatisation (an effect of the public-private partnerships); towards policing (as a result of police intervention); and towards technologisation (an effect of the new technologies used for identification). This three-sided evolution is changing supervisory/monitoring activity. It is reviving tension between the demands of integrity and those of quality and brand authenticity. Thirdly, the monitoring of circulation is linked to the construction of forms of authority and of sovereignty. In her ethnography of the customs administration in Ghana, the anthropologist Brenda Chalfin reminds us, basing her argument on Tilly, that an institution of this sort cannot be separated from the emergence of the authority of the State.[5] She adds that the "neoliberal swing" has brought about a renewal of interest in customs administration, and in collaboration between national governments and international organisations, often in the form of mixed public-private management. Seen from this point of view, customs controls reveal both the exercise of sovereignty and the transformations undergone by government institutions in the process of expanding commercial relationships. The control of the trajectories followed by pharmaceuticals obeys a similar logic. We can observe it in the role of the State and its institutions, in that of international organisations, and in that of private operators who modify the exercise of authority and the nature of "infrastructural power".[6]

In examining these three aspects (the performance of control, the evolution of practices, and the transformations in forms of authority and of sovereignty), we gain a deeper knowledge of relationships between practical notions of security, evolving forms of organisations, and foundations of authority. This involves taking account of methods, approaches, techniques, and knowledge mobilised in operations of control.[7] It leads to a better understanding of the notion of circulation of pharmaceuticals that remains implicit in the course of routine operations. Lastly, it shows that the current concern for public health lies at a confluence of health, commercial and technological interests. According to the proponents of securitisation, the safety of persons is indissociable from that of things, the securitisation of people being ensured by that of the flow of goods (ensured by regulation and technologies); the well-being of international markets is also the well-being of society.

Control tests

According to the WHO, the quality of medicine consists on the one hand in its efficacy and harmlessness, and on the other on its conformity to specifications (identity, action, purity, and other properties).[8] The authorities and market operators have to ensure that the quality of products is maintained, and ensure this by means of various procedures that constrain the organisation of the market. A medicine has to have market authorisation that has been granted by governmental authority, and it has to be registered; manufacturers and distributors too have to be duly licenced and registered. Products have to meet specifications determined by pharmacopoeia, and the ways in which they are produced, distributed and stored must follow the rules of best practice, either national or international. All of these obligations have to be checked either at particular times, or on a random basis. Quality control focuses mainly on conformity to specifications. More generally, to guarantee the quality of medicines "*a system of organisation and supervision of the entire process*" has to be set up, "*from the acquisition of a pharmaceutical substance to its transformation to a finished product put at the disposal of the consumer*".[9] There are three dimensions to a system of this sort: legal (legislation concerning the medicine), regulatory (framework of action by the governmental body responsible for drug approvals, licencing, and inspection), and technical (standards of quality, testing, and rules of best practice). The parties engaged in these activities are manufacturers, distributors, and regulatory authorities.

There are three main forms of surveillance that can partly overlap: inspection (focused on the conformity to standards set for products and/or professional activity in production and/or distribution), analysis (of documentation and, in the laboratory, of quality), and postmarketing surveillance of the effects of the medicines concerned. Practices of inspection and auto-inspection are numerous. They also concern dossiers, sites and practices of manufacture, distribution, and storage, and the products themselves – in which case inspection can apply to raw materials, articles used in packaging, semi-finished products and finished products. Inspection can be carried out on sites of manufacture, distribution, storage, or sale. Its rules vary according to the market in which the goods are sold. For example, an Indian firm has to follow the regulations prescribed by Schedule M if its medicines are sold in Indian territory, but if sold outside India via international donors, the regulations to be followed are the rules of best practice edited by the WHO. If the medicines are bound for the US market, the rules applicable are those of the Food and Drug Administration (FDA).

Analysis can be carried out on-site or elsewhere. It can consist of an examination of documents, or a test of the quality or quantity of products, their organoleptic properties (appearance, taste, smell, texture, consistency), their stability, purity, sterility, and microbiological cleanliness. In the analysis, control, and securitisation of medicines Regulatory provisions and technical tools are applied in laboratory analyses, exemplifying a second conception of supervision. It consists mainly in measuring the characteristics of the medicine concerned, comparing them with those prescribed by the national or international pharmacopeia. Observation – for example, of a sample of public data in a Gujarati laboratory – can show that most of the problems raised are due to a deficiency of the active ingredient. The analysis, however, can also reveal other irregularities: the presence of particles (glass, unidentified particles), inadequate sterilisation, or disintegration or dissolution that do not conform to specifications. The analysis focuses on the chemical properties of the medicine, with reference to current standards. Conformity to these standards is required for the medicine or the firm producing it to be registered. Registration can also be linked to regular inspections or to inspection as part of postmarketing surveillance, such as that organised in Kenya in the case of anti-tuberculosis drugs.

The third mode of control differs from the other two: it is not upstream from the moment of consumption but downstream. This is the ex-post control carried out in the context of pharmacovigilance studies that begin by examining the effects of drugs on patients, using an information system to track adverse reactions.[10] It is a mode of postmarketing surveillance that relies on a system of feedback to record adverse reactions. It implements a control system based on reports made in the field by patients and healthcare staff, as well as an information system that takes into account adverse events that would otherwise not be properly noticed.

From the point of view of a sociology of science that is attentive to the importance of practices, the monitoring activity (inspection, analysis, postmarketing surveillance) is thus based on a series of operations whose main objective is to ensure the integrity of pharmaceutical circulations, but whose particular forms each carries a specific notion of what exactly constitutes legitimate circulation. Inspection checks up on the conformity of the circulation apparatus (examining sites and practices); analysis verifies the conformity of products; reporting verifies the conformity of the effects obtained. As a result, ex-post inspection, analysis and reporting constitute "tests" in the eyes of pragmatic sociology: they are contingent because they are based on a dynamic equilibrium between the legal, regulatory and technical parameters of trajectories, the trajectories of products and the interventions of operators.[11]

Relationships between the institutions that undertake these tasks are not part of a functionalist plan that has been defined once and for all; they are dynamic, influenced by divergent conceptions of the control process and by competition for access to resources. The Kenyan case is an example. In Kenya, the Pharmacy and Poisons Board competes with the National Quality Control Laboratory (NQCL), which enjoys a certain amount of autonomy in relation to the Board, its hierarchical superior in the administration. The PPB was set up in 1957 under the Pharmacy and Poisons Act, chapter 244. At the time the Act did not specify the way in which testing was to be carried out. The NQCL was set up later, under an amendment passed in 1992. In principle NQCL reports to PPB, but the amendment does not specify how this is to take place. From a strictly legal point of view, NQCL is thus a semi-autonomous government body, but in actual fact it is largely independent. The two institutions thus compete with one another, as their missions overlap. In particular, NQCL is in charge of analysing medical substances and issuing certificates of good manufacturing practice, whereas PPB licenses the firms involved in production and distribution. However in 1981 and 1991, when Good Manufacturing Practices (GMPs) came into being, gazette notices empowered PPB to inspect these GMPs. Competition between the two bodies has arisen in the first place as a result of the lack of precision in the dispositions coordinating their activities. In some other countries the equivalents of PPB and NQCL are one and the same institution. But in Kenya they were made separate, initially to reduce conflicts of interest, but this actually entailed conflict between the two bodies.

As of the years 2011–2012, NQCL applied to the ministry to be able to make joint inspections; PPB refused. NQCL argued that as a result it would be unable to fulfil its performance contract. A legal battle ensued. In 2016 NQCL began to carry out inspections parallel to those of PPB.[12] The stakes were in the first place financial, as inspection carries a cost, which is paid by the firms concerned, the proceeds going to the entity that performs the inspection. But there are also differences as to the conception of the work of supervision and control, and the two bodies accused one another of not having the competencies (human resources, laboratories, technologies) needed to be able to analyse medicines properly. As we have seen in Chapter 3, the stakes were also linked to accusations of corruption. Some agents in these institutions hoped nonetheless to put an end to the conflict by modelling the two institutions on the American FDA, a development that according to a member of NQCL was bound to happen anyway "*in two or three years' time*".[13] The conflict between the two Kenyan bodies shows that the stakes involved in the meshing of the organisational network are more than merely institutional; they are also legal, regulatory and technical, each institution defending its own particular thinking in the matter of control and the methods to be employed. All of this is of course compounded with broader representations of the distinction between legitimate and illegitimate circulation.

This example, taken from the Kenyan situation, displays inter-institutional dynamics that can affect testing. It suggests that pharmaceutical surveillance involves a complex articulation of various parameters (institutions involved, procedures favoured, objects to be examined). Our three next sections will take account of this dynamic aspect of control, and analyse the transformations that can affect it. Carrying out control is influenced by three main developments: the privatisation of organisations, the policing mode of intervention, and the increasingly technological pressure on methods. These evolutions are in turn related to the framing of pharmaceutical regulation in terms of security.

Privatising control

In recent years, the actual performance of control has to a large extent been privatised, in both institutional and organisational terms. National regulatory bodies, national laboratories and customs authorities, however, still play a predominant part. As we have already mentioned, India and Kenya both have national regulatory authorities: the Central Drug Control Standard Organization (CDSCO) and decentralised authorities in the various states in India, and the Pharmacy and Poisons Board in Kenya. These bodies register new medicines and grant licences to producers, retailers, importers, and wholesalers. They also gather information by means of a system of pharmacosurveillance. In India the central authority authorises medicines, but decentralised state authorities (e.g., in Gujarat: the Food and Drug Control Administration – FDCA) can authorise manufacture and carry out inspection, in collaboration with or independently of the national authorities. The question of unifying the various bodies has been discussed ever since the 1970.[14] Besides this, in India as well as in Kenya, certified laboratories are operating. In India, five "central" laboratories and three regional ones test medicines, as do 28 laboratories approved by regional states[15]; in Kenya the only approved public laboratory is the NQCL. These laboratories are in charge of analysing medicines. Customs authorities in both countries control and supervise the circulation of medicines. Their mission and the characteristics that they inspect are not the same as those observed by the pharmaceutical authorities. Their job consists in analysing documentation and inspecting containers; they contribute to surveillance by analysing the conformity of medicines to specifications in the accompanying documentation.

Critics frequently point out that these bodies lack staff and equipment, and that their inspection routines are inadequate.[16] In 2011, the Indian authority had a staff of only 264, which was very low, according to observers, given the number of manufacturers in the country. Moreover the number of vacant posts – especially for inspectors – was very high: a hundred posts were due to be filled.[17] Lack of drug inspectors, both in the central services and in the regional states, has frequently been pointed out: the total quoted is 846, but according to FDA estimates and to the Mashelkar report, between 2500 and 3200 would be needed.[18] In Kenya in 2012 the inspection department of the GMP had 6 inspectors in charge of auditing some 40 manufacturers, with more than 1000 foreign firms registered in the country.[19] The inspection department dealing with Good Distribution Practices (GDP) had a staff of 57, who had to supervise the entire distributions sector (wholesalers, retailers, hospitals).[20]

Many operators in the private sector have taken up this argument, stressing the sheer size of the job to be done, in order to justify the intervention of private firms in the surveillance activity. To take one example: the security officer of a major European pharmaceutical firm in Kenya explains:

> *Nothing comes here that says "pharmaceuticals". It comes in containers that are labelled "furniture, carpets", etc. It's never labelled as pharmaceuticals. And here, out of 16000 containers, they control four! So they say, you know in English "eenie meenie miny mo"... Even in very stringent ports like Amsterdam, they control about 5 to 10% of the containers coming in. [...]. When you have a "cordon sanitaire" and something gets through, then you need a second line in order to deal with the problem. This is where we come in*[21]

Proponents of the privatisation of security are sometimes harshly critical of national authorities, accusing them of not doing their job properly. Blame is laid on national regulatory authorities, seen as lacking both means and efficient organisation, as well as being incompetent and prone to corruption. The interviewee, an industrial operator in Nairobi, had a poor opinion of the Kenyan regulatory authorities, blaming them for the development of counterfeiting:

> *The problem of counterfeit medicines has been growing during the last ten to fifteen years. Driven by a poorly regulated environment ... when I talk about poorly regulated, the regulator is the PPB. The way this PPB is constituted, the governance structure is so weak, so linked to the government ... The chairman of this board is the director of medical services, the CEO of this board is the chief pharmacist, so he's playing a double role and his boss is the chairman and then the whole issue of corruption ... The importation of medicines into this country, there's a very clear policy guideline. How you can put a product in the Kenyan market, you have to go through a very rigorous process. If you want to import you'll have to apply for an import authorization through the PPB, etc. Now that process has been abused and through that, the fact that the regulator has not done his job well, that's were the issue of counterfeit comes.*[22]

In a context of this sort, control and surveillance are far from being a State monopoly; they are part of a series of public-private and private-private sector partnerships – an aspect already mentioned and studied in the case of customs authorities.[23] Manufacturers, wholesalers and distributors carry out self-inspection of the quality of the materials they use and the goods they produce and distribute. These activities can be subcontracted to yet other private operators, for example, Kenyan production firms can pay Indian private players to check the quality of the raw materials they import from India. In addition to these interventions by governmental and private agencies, there are those of international agencies such as the American FDA, which has had an office in India since 2009; in December 2015 three full-time employees were carrying out inspections (in addition to the visiting inspectors who came in regularly).[24] More and more international organisations (WHO), developmental agencies (United States Agency for International Development [USAID], Gesellschaft für Internationale Zusammenarbeit [GIZ]), standardisation authorities (US Pharmacopeia), and private firms and organisations contribute to monitoring either by taking part in building up the capacities of the State or by performing self-inspection of their own distribution networks.

Privatisation of the exercise of surveillance and control has been gaining ground with the emergence of private operators and public-private partnerships, all of them increasingly active in capacity-building, detection and seizure operations. An example of this development is the IRACM (Institute for Research Against Counterfeit Medicines), an anti-counterfeiting research body. In June 2015, this organisation took part in the first Indo-French workshop on the struggle against counterfeit medicines, organised for the benefit of police forces, pharmaceutical regulators, and the Indian customs authorities.[25] In September 2016 IRACM took part, with the World Customs Organization (WCO) and the Kenya Revenue Authority in a training course held over several days in Mombasa for the benefit of the customs authorities of 16 African countries.[26] IRACM is a private body set up in 2010 with financial support from Sanofi. It operates in partnership with international organisations (WCO, Interpol), public bodies (the University of Paris 1, the French Ministry of Foreign Affairs), and organisations representing private interests (the International Federation of Pharmaceutical Manufacturers and Associations). It has worked with the world customs organisation on policing operations (Vice GRIPS 2 in 2012, Biyela in 2013), with the University of Paris 1 in setting up a course on pharmaceutical crime, and with IFPMA on the "Fight the Fakes" communication campaign. Its main orientations aim at enforcing intellectual property rights, carrying out policing operations, and training customs and police personnel to combat counterfeiting.

At the governmental level, this trend towards privatisation can be seen in public-private partnerships and in institutions in which market operators play a part. An example is the Kenyan Anti-Counterfeit Agency, set up under the anti-counterfeit law in 2008. This law created an agency dedicated to the anti-counterfeit struggle, its function being to apply the content of the law, to provide information to the public on counterfeiting issues, and to combat counterfeiting. The law redistributed competencies, giving the agency the power to intervene in the control of medicines, hitherto the exclusive prerogative of the Pharmacy and Poisons Board. The agency's inspectors were empowered to seize goods and to arrest persons on suspicion of counterfeiting. Furthermore, the law set penalties – prison sentences and fines – for violations. The executive committee of the agency had 16 members, two of them from the private sector, appointed by the Minister of Industry by virtue of their competence in matters of intellectual property and the protection of consumers.

Opponents of the privatising trend interpret it in terms of transfer. The intrusion of private firms and the development of public–private partnerships (PPP) stem less, in their opinion, from a weakness of the competent authorities than from a desire to have the State carry the cost of the struggle to protect the interests of the owners of brand names. According to a lawyer who took part in the case brought against the Kenyan law,

> *There is a global trend to strengthen IPR and to minimize the cost of enforcement, even by transferring the cost of enforcement to governments. I mean, the anti-counterfeit law is an example of one trying to enforce private rights through public means. ACTA is another example of that.*[27]

The transfer mechanism works in two ways. On the one hand, it enables private firms to shift to the State the costs induced by the defence of their commercial interests. The Kenyan agency makes civil servants available in order to trace violations of copyright that in the main affect only the interests of a few firms that dominate the market. But the development of public-private partnerships also has another effect: it enables firms to move into the field of surveillance, gaining the power to propose initiatives in collaborating with the authorities. This enables firms to influence in their own favour not merely thinking but also practice. This transfer is first and foremost one of tasks and interests, as the State takes over the defence of the interests of private enterprises, on the pretext of protecting the general interests of society as a whole. Secondly, it is also a transfer of authority, the private sector using the authority of the State when acting within the framework of the partnerships. Privatisation of control procedures, as a result of the double transfer, thus entails an evolution of practices that can be described as a policing approach to the surveillance function. A nuance should however be noted here: this evolution does not affect all governments in the same way: the Indian government, for example, does not have an institution such as the Kenyan Anti-Counterfeit agency.

Policing control

Organisational changes in the struggle against illicit medicines are converging with a general evolution in the practice of surveillance and inspection. Quite naturally, for example, the pharmaceutical security provided by multinational firms is motivated more by the protection of copyright and brand rights than by a concern for access to quality medicines – despite the fact that this concern is often voiced by the multinationals in question, as we have seen in the previous chapter. The security officer of a multinational based in Kenya explains:

> *They are speaking of numbers between 30 and above percent either counterfeit or substandard medicines. I am not interested in substandard drugs myself, because it is not in my mandate, which is to look at those medicines that come in that deliberately mislead and copy people's brands in a way to indicate that it is our product.*[28]

Brand holders, as could be expected, see pharmaceutical security as a defence of their interests rather than as the pursuit of an overall objective of medicinal quality. This being their approach, the protective methods multinationals use are similar to those of pharmaceutical inspection; however, they are distinguished from them in several ways. This can be illustrated by a story told by a private detective who worked for a major European brand.[29] His account reveals the commercial nature of the interests he is protecting:

> *We maintain surveillance along the ports so that we are able to tell when to goods are delivered at our ports and where they are heading. Then we are able to design our way of catching the goods. Because at the end of the day, we are paid to catch the counterfeit goods.*

He continues, showing the imbrication of private and public interests that is entailed in inter-personal relationships, and the forms of collaboration that this develops:

> Question: And are you entitled to seize the goods? Answer: No, we seize in the presence of the police. We facilitate the seizure. At the port, we look for friendly custom officers to work with. They will pass us information, then we can make a formal request for the container to be stopped. All we do at that point is to assist the custom officers to say "yes, this is genuine or this is counterfeit". Then from this there is a possibility to make the seizure.

His account highlights the close relationship between public and private forces in the practice of sampling and analysis:

> *After the goods have been seized, there is a procedure which is defined by the anti-counterfeit act: if there is a suspect consignment at a port, then the brand owner files a formal complaint at the anti-counterfeit agency, which gives you authority to participate in the verification of that consignment. So that the brand owner or its representative is present on the day of verification of that consignment. After that, that is now casual observation, we are able to tell that this product has several indicators of counterfeit product. From there we ask for sample, we have to pay for the sample (to*

> *the agency). Then we send it to the client for technical analysis and technical report.*

Lastly, it brings out the policing approach to inspection, as its primary aim is to put an end to "unfair competition" from counterfeit products:

> *This report will be used by the agency to prosecute. The law says that if the agency doesn't prosecute within 90 days, then the importer is able to get their goods back. So from there there are two ways. Either the culprit will be found and jailed and the goods destroyed, or he or she will just be fined and the goods will be destroyed. Prosecution takes ages in Kenya so we always push for destruction.*

Most inspections are not carried out in a private framework, as is the case here, where inspection is carried out by a detective agency. But the above conversation nonetheless takes place within an overall trend in the treatment of the issue of illicit medicines: that towards a policing approach, seen in the multiplication of police operations and a concomitant tendency to put these interventions well in the public eye and make them "news". The example given at the beginning of this chapter – seizures of Indian medicines by European customs authorities – is particularly revealing; but there are many others that should also be mentioned. The policing approach is particularly visible in operations carried out by Interpol in collaboration with the WCO and other operators in several regions: Pangea 1–9, targeting online sales between 2008 and 2016 (coordination by Interpol); Mamba 1–3 in East Africa between 2008 and 2010 (Interpol, with IMPACT support); Cobra, and subsequently Porcupine, in West Africa between 2011 and 2014 (Interpol); Vice GRIPS 2, and subsequently Biyela 1 and 2, in Africa south of the Sahara between 2012 and 2014 (WCO in partnership with IRACM and the Chirac Foundation); Storm 1–6 in South and East Asia between 2008 and 2015 (Interpol, with WHO support in the case of Storm 2); and Giboia, mainly in Southern Africa in 2013 and 2015 (Interpol). These operations show the growing importance of the policing approach to the issue, in the form of public-private collaboration (involvement of IRACM in the Biyela operations) and of collaboration between health and policing institutions (WHO and IMPACT in Mamba and Storm 2).

Governments themselves have engaged directly in similar operations. In Kenya, the PPB regularly organises crackdowns in which inspection forces target a zone or a neighbourhood and carry out checking. As a result, there are bans on pharmacists who do not have licences or proper qualifications; medicines that have expired are impounded, and so forth. In August 2016 Kenyan newspapers announced, for example, that more than 60 traders had been arrested for selling medicines without being properly licensed to do so.[30] During these operations police officers accompanied medicinal inspectors – displaying a very coercive understanding of the regulation of the pharmaceutical profession. Furthermore, a special unit was set up to deal with criminal cases; composed of police officers, it collaborates with the industry in tracking illegal activities:

> *This unit has been created three years back, with three officers, now four, trained on advanced investigation by the police – criminal investigation. We really collaborate with the private sector, we have informants who give us information throughout the country, we have intelligence gathering and some other companies. So we do private linkage*[31]

These operations set up a periodical rhythm and enable what could be termed advertisement or announcement effects. In a surprising inversion, it sometimes even happens that the authorities make a show of destroying bogus "fake medicines" to indicate that the problem is being dealt with energetically. When I interviewed the deputy director of the anti-counterfeit agency, he told me that counterfeit medicines had been burned on the occasion of the world day of struggle against counterfeiting:

> *Question: You had them burned just like that? In the open air? – No, obviously we couldn't do that, for reasons of hygiene and security. The real counterfeits were impounded in standard conditions. Here it was more of a symbol; so we just burned the packages of fake medicines, but there weren't medicines inside them.*[32]

Operations and events of this sort reveal a special concern with surveillance and inspection: staging police action for the benefit of the media is part of their aim, together with ensuring the quality of medicines. They show concern with control of illicit medicines, bringing out their proliferation at the same time as the determination of the authorities to combat it. Put more prosaically, the operations aim at "frightening":

> *These days you have to frighten people, it's the only thing that works. It's amazing, actually, but that's how it is. If you don't frighten people, if you don't have a big communications plan, nothing happens. We can make big seizures, but if we don't communicate, nothing happens. We found some veterinary products once, real crap it was. Well, there was no reaction, nothing … the guys said to them, "You see, the customs people let stuff in that is bad!" and they just say, "Yeah, of course, yeah …" I think that's suicidal.*[33]

The policing approach to surveillance and inspection thus comes together with and corresponds to a development of seizures and prosecution in the courts. It involves a multiplication of collaborative arrangements between regulatory authorities, police forces and private operators. This marks a new development both in the field of healthcare (more frequent recourse to police forces) and a novelty for the police (which had hitherto had little to do with healthcare), as Julia Hornberger has pointed out.[34] This policing trend mobilises a communications apparatus to launch the problem as a theme in the media, showing how the surveillance and inspection agents intervene. While some operators in the field of regulation are critical of this development – they see it above all as an advertising initiative that has a little real impact on the quality of medicines – it has nonetheless been imposed increasingly as a privileged form of action on the circulation of medicines.

Technologising control

The third noteworthy development in surveillance and inspection is the increasing recourse to new technologies, a marked departure from the methods of inspection and analysis hitherto favoured by the regulatory authorities. The need for new technologies is expressed in several different ways and responds to a number of constraints. It can consist in piecemeal arrangements, but also general infrastructural equipment, as illustrated in the case of analysis laboratories. In Gujarat, a new laboratory was being set up when I was doing interviews there in 2015. According to the head of the surveillance authority, as new, stricter standards were introduced and had to be checked, existing apparatus was no longer adequate.[35] In Kenya in 2016, the Pharmacy and Poisons Board set up an internal laboratory to settle its dispute with the national laboratory (see above); in parallel, the national laboratory applied for a new site for its offices as, even though it had been pre-qualified by WHO, its current premises were unsuitable and too small. However, whereas the infrastructural transformations mostly concern the upgrading of analysis laboratories, a vast new field of innovation has emerged that is for instance linked to projects of e-governance, systems of information and identification of pharmacists via text messaging (as in Kenya), or to the digital registration and traceability, as in Gujarat. These innovative dynamics are not limited to the national level as they involve international exchanges. To take an example, in 2014 the Kenyan authorities received through USAID a Laboratory Information Management System (LIMS), two ultra-high-performance chromatography devices, and a dissolution apparatus, enabling the laboratory to increase the number of its sample tests carried out each month and to keep a better organisational record.[36] These changes also apply on a global scale. The IPM (*Interface Public-Members*) system promoted by the World Customs Organization, for example, is being adopted by most countries in the world to manage the traceability of products entering their territory. IPM is a platform ensuring communication in real-time, associated with identification tools that make it possible to trace the circulation of any particular product and to identify any counterfeit products that might enter into the distribution chain.

Acquisitions of this sort are prompted by the burgeoning market for security and technological solutions to problems arising in the course of the movement of pharmaceuticals. Apparatus for testing medicines, holograms, and bar codes are technologies produced by stakeholders and imposed in some cases by governments, or promoted as a part of partnership arrangements. All of this is opening up a new market for security technologies. In June 2014 IRACM recorded on its Internet site 91 different technologies for securitising the circulation of pharmaceuticals.[37] Some of these (e.g., "blisters", bottles) are simple and have been known for a long time; others are based on new, sophisticated techniques and can only be applied in special laboratories, for example, video-spectral analysis and comparison, which combines various techniques to analyse the authenticity of documents; or terahertz spectroscopy that makes it possible to check medicines without opening their packaging.

To give an idea of the stakes involved in this development, I will return to two technologies that failed for a time in Kenya but, after some changes, were adopted by PPB. Each of these technologies applies primarily to a specific type of fraud; each thus defines the concepts of "quality" and "security" in a particular way. Through technologisation, it is the very definition of quality that is at stake, according to analyses already produced by the economics of conventions, applied here to technological choices.[38]

The first technology is one of authentification, which I will call Genverif (Genuine Verification). The Genverif is a hand-held remote-control device about 20 cms in length, used for scanning product packaging, or contents to be inspected without opening the packaging. The technology involved is Raman spectrometry, usually very cumbersome. In Genverif its components have been miniaturised; the remote is a portable tool for checking either pharmaceutical raw materials or medicines by comparing substances that have already been registered in a database. Comparison leads to identification and authentication of the product analysed. Each device costs about $50,000, and (an important detail) is sold mostly to countries that are considered not to have robust surveillance and inspection capacities. In 2014, the Nigerian government had six of the devices; France had only one. A similar tool was donated to Kenya's PPB by the Pfizer company – raising criticism in the civil service and in some specialised media outlets. Could there be a conflict of interests here? Had the device been configured solely to identify Pfizer products? (One of the PPB heads later alleged this when I interviewed him; he had refused to attend the handover ceremony.) Though the general press took a rather positive view of Pfizer's gesture, issues were raised in professional circles.

The main problem with Genverif is that it can use only a database that has already been configured, and in which only a limited number of medicines can be registered. The device enables the inspector to compare, for example, two boxes of an anti-diabetic of the same brand, but not to compare two anti-diabetic generics. Analysis and checking here are based not so much on the proportion of the active substance actually contained in the medicine, as on its mere identity (is it similar to the pre-registered version?) This raises a problem of efficacy. As stakeholders in public health in Kenya pointed out, on a market in which generics play a central part, what exactly is the purpose of the test? This example shows that the technology promoted is inseparably linked to particular conceptions of authentication, quality and security. In this particular case, securitisation of the market is made to depend on authentication based on a particular manufacturer's pre-registered product. As it happens, Pfizer's gift was never put to use. However, sometime later, similar portable Raman spectrometers were acquired by PPB. This tends to show that although the authorities are at times cautious of industrial partners' "gifts", they share their enthusiasm for new technologies of security. PPB proclaimed on Facebook its relatively undiminished faith:

> *Drug analysts have undergone training on how to use the newly acquired Handled Raman Spectrometers. The new technology will enhance surveillance of falsified and substandard drugs, a global health problem particularly in low- and middle-income countries.*[39]

The second example is a "track and trace" procedure that uses a proprietary device; I will call it *AuthentiPhone*. It is used to identify a box or "blister" of medicine, by means of a scratch code that can be entered into a mobile telephone and authentified if the product has been registered in a database. The project was invented mainly by a Ghanaian entrepreneur and was tested in various places, one of them being Kenya. Authentication is based on the packaging, and on the principle of registration. Securitisation thus depends on the registration of a product and the certification of its logistic path. This procedure was not contested in Kenya. Testing it, however, required collaboration between the firm that produced AuthentiPhone, an international telecom operator, a local manufacturer of medicines, and the government of Kenya. This procedure was relatively inconclusive, mainly because of the cost of putting the code on the packaging; the manufacturer of the medicine taking part in the experimentation had to carry this cost, and it was not made obligatory by legislation. Apart from this, the arrangement raised a number of other issues: in a country where medicines are frequently sold without their packaging, how exactly could consumers be expected to play a part? This was not clear. The technology sprang from concern for the integrity of legitimate healthcare products. Once again, the focus of the testing was less on correspondence between the substance of the medicine and its generic chemical properties, than on respecting certified forms of circulation. Despite the lack of success of this first project, in 2016 the PPB worked at a similar system in partnership with Safaricom (the largest telephone operator in Kenya), but with a database that was to be managed entirely by PPB.[40] In this second example, a new technology is set up on the initiative of a private group, unsuccessfully at first; it subsequently reappears in a new firm run by the regulatory authority.

It should be noted that this system of authentication by means of a mobile telephone is part of a far broader technological development, involving larger information systems and database building. In India, for example, similar systems were set up; but the most important change during the period we are examining was the obligation of traceability ensured by imposing bar codes.

This was a staggered process, the obligation being applied gradually – and not without giving rise to criticism and protest from industry, particularly SMEs. Between 2009 and 2016, the three levels of packaging (primary, secondary, and tertiary) each had to carry bar codes. On the primary level (packaging in contact with the medicine), the bar code was two-dimensional; it was still optional, as was the global universal identification number. Secondary packaging (as of 2013) and tertiary packaging (since 2011) of products to be exported had obligatorily to carry bar codes in order to meet international standards – and also to restore the flagging reputation of Indian medicines by distinguishing "good" Indian products from possible copies made, for example, in China. In particular, the various packaging were linked by their bar codes, which were sent to a central registration and logistic management system. Manufacturers protested in particular against the obligation to code the primary packaging, and against "mono-cartons" being classified as secondary packaging. The DAVA project (*Drug authentication and verification application*), its pilot phase launched in June 2015, went further, setting up a data platform for registering different levels of packaging of medicines, and also enabling consumers to check the bar code of a medicine on the relevant internet site to make sure that the medicine concerned was authentic. The aim of this project was to prevent all export of illicit medicines from India. It bears a close resemblance to the Kenyan project.

These technological histories bring out various aspects of the relationship between government and private operators. In the case of Genverif, a donation was involved that was not unanimously approved in the PPB. The device in question was never put to use, mainly because of disagreements linked to a conflict of interest with Pfizer, the donor. In the case of AuthentiPhone, an experimental project was devised together with an East African telecom operator and an IT start-up, with the approval of the Kenyan pharmaceutical regulator. The telecom operator's project manager told me in an interview that the relationship with the regulator was a strained one, as the regulator wanted the operator to set up a hotline as part of the project.[41] The power relations exemplified by these projects vary from project to project, and the involvement of the Kenyan authorities and their regulators also varied. Government representatives sometimes questioned aid coming from outside agents, sometimes submitted to it, and sometimes tried to impose their own views on the operators who were bringing aid. In addition to this, these technologies do not exist in isolation. They take place in an entire field of securitisation, with all its conflicts and controversies over the uses to which technologies can be put. The technologies cohabit with other arrangements that ensure quality control on pharmaceutical markets: WHO pre-qualification, awareness-raising campaigns, other analytical technologies applied in the national laboratory analysing the quality of medicines (chromatography, mass spectroscopy on samples, etc.).

Furthermore these technologies, the arrangements they entail, and the principles of securitisation they deploy are all supposed to strengthen various aspects of the pharmaceutical distribution network. They respond to specific types of fraud and defect that they contribute to define. Genverif shows up discrepancies between the quality of a chemical component or medicine and that on which it is based, enabling the tester to pinpoint alterations in the product due to poor manufacturing (e.g., under-dosing), to faulty transportation and storage (e.g., lapses in refrigeration), or to expiry. AuthentiPhone, like the bar codes in India, makes it possible to verify that transportation conditions have actually met requirements as regards the registration of products with a view to their distribution on the market. Fraud and defects treated in this way range from negligence by the manufacturer to precarious refrigeration and to criminal dishonesty; a broad variety of quality factors are taken into account.

However, these technologies are part of an overall trend towards a technologisation of surveillance and inspection. They were already "in the air" during the interviews I made in Kenya and in India. Agents involved in regulation discussed their advantages and disadvantages, and entrepreneurs were getting involved in setting up technological projects. In 2014, during my interviews in Kenya, for example, despite the failure of the AuthentiPhone experiment, I met several people who were setting up start-ups to compete in using mobile phones to monitor the circulation of pharmaceuticals. These technologies resonated with current trends in securitisation, all the more so as the agents promoting them were also contributing to the discourse on counterfeit (and its current framing) in frequent contributions at meetings on the struggle against illicit medicines.

Furthermore, these technologies, though based on different principles of control and authentification, all converge on an essential point. Authentication, whether based on chemical identity or on packaging, does not deal satisfactorily with the generic quality of medicines. It does not try to find out whether or not the medicine has been manufactured under proper conditions, whether it contains the correct proportion of the active ingredient by generic standards; instead, it simply seeks to find out whether or not medicine has respected an initial standard of authentification, and whether it meets pre-registered specifications for chemical substance and packaging. The securitisation process illustrated here by these technologies is thus entirely determined by identification and authentification, and not by qualification according to a generic standard. From a public health point of view, this techno-political rationale is highly problematic: the market in Kenya is based mainly on generics – 56% in value, corresponding to about 80% in volume.[42] On a market of this sort, might it not be more urgent to check up on generic qualities rather than on brand identity and authenticity? The authorities, however, deplore the expense and complexity of these verifications that do not involve the same strategies of securitisation. It should be pointed out that the current rationale of securitisation processes meets the needs of brands' sales strategies, while dealing with issues of economic cost and the availability of a workforce in the countries concerned.

Visibly, as Julia Hornberger has shown in the case of the "policing" of control,[43] public health has not been a priority for the designers of the technologies, applied to the struggle against counterfeiting; their main aim has mostly been to supply the market for control technologies. It would seem, thus, that this technologisation fulfils several different purposes. Firstly, it constitutes a non-tariff barrier, as firms that have to invest in technologies are not always able to afford this. This aspect should not be overlooked: it shows that intellectual property today is only one of the strategies applied by dominant firms to preserve their market shares, and that it is only one of the obstacles to enabling the major part of the population to gain access to medicines. It is also part of a logic of economic and symbolic enhancement of pharmaceutical products: it displays the highly technical nature of their circulation. This in turn has two aspects to it: non-tariff barriers are added to that constituted by IP, while a logic of enhancement (of the market and the products) is embodied in the technologies used to ensure the circulation of the products, in all its various forms. Lastly, these technologies play a part in shifting the sites of the testing involved in control. It becomes possible to inspect not only the environment in which medicines are produced, but also the production processes, the origins and subsequent trajectories of products, the characteristics (e.g., such as absence of contamination, and proper proportion of the active substance) of the raw materials employed, and the quality of production. This means that the surveillance function is no longer confined to the traditional form of inspection, analysis and reporting; thanks to new arrangements associating inspection and analysis by means of mobile apparatus, or devices that have been integrated into the products themselves, it is now spread out over the entire chain of distribution. Thus technologisation, coming on top of privatisation and policing, also plays a part in transforming the monitoring and securitisation of the circulation of pharmaceuticals.

At the end of this second part, the multiple shapes taken by the problem of illicit medicines in developing countries seems to get clearer. On one hand, a global and hyper-competitive market in which coexist highly heterogeneous industries. The market actors resort to diverse strategies in order to master access to distribution networks that would allow them to move the goods to the market. The resulting tensions are manifested by the multiplicity of issues related to liceity. On the other hand, a powerful enterprise of markets' securitisation. This enterprise first owes to the strategies of the dominant firms, in particular in terms of intellectual property; but in no way it could be reduced to this. It is indeed part of a wider array of media discourse, scientific knowledge or organisational transformations and practices. In that sense, the securitisation of markets expresses a more general evolution of the "public health concern" through which international public health, more often termed today as "global health", is being managed.[44]

But what is left of health when security gets hold on it? And what do societies become when power bears first on flows of objects – such as medicines?

The security dynamics let us catch a glimpse of a very peculiar form of government – where the desire to control trade flows prevail any other consideration. One question – and not the least – remains: what kind of power expresses the shift to the security framework, based upon the fight against counterfeiting, through legal principle, regulatory texts, private organisations, police forces and technologies? What government rationale – for medicines, but for public health and populations as well – is at play in these transformations? And also: how one could escape it?

Notes

1 Abbott, F. M. (2009). Worst fears realised: The Dutch confiscation of medicines bound from India to Brazil, *Bridges*, 13/1, International Center for Trade and Sustainable Development, 30 March http://ictsd.org/i/news/bridges/44192/.
2 Health Action International (2009). *Another Seizure of Generic Medicines Destined for a Developing Country, this Time in Frankfurt*, Press Release, 5 June, en ligne: http://haieurope.org/wp-content/uploads/2010/11/5-Jun-2009-Press-release-Seizure-of-generic-medicines-in-Frankfurt.pdf.
3 Jacob, F. (1995). Les douaniers français aux frontières de la sécurité intérieure, *Déviance et Société,* 19(4), 339–354; Chalfin B. (2010). *Neoliberal Frontiers: An Ethnography of Sovereignty in West Africa*, Chicago: University of Chicago Press.
4 Hauray, B. (2006). *L'Europe du médicament. Politique, expertise, intérêts privés*, Paris: Presses de Sciences Po.
5 Chalfin, B. (2010). *Neoliberal Frontiers: An Ethnography of Sovereignty in West Africa*, Chicago: University of Chicago Press, p. 25.
6 Mann, M. (1984). The autonomous power of the state: Its origins, mechanisms and results, *European Journal of Sociology/Archives Européennes De Sociologie / Europäisches Archiv Für Soziologie*, 25/2, 185–213.
7 For an overall view of the broad market for security, see Klein, N. (2008). *La stratégie du choc. La montée d'un capitalisme du désastre*, Arles Actes Sud [2007].
8 Organisation Mondiale de la Santé (1995). *Rapport du Comité OMS d'experts sur les politiques pharmaceutiques nationales, Genève, 19–23 juin 1995: Contribution à la mise à jour des directives de l'OMS pour l'élaboration des politiques pharmaceutiques nationales*.
9 Organisation Mondiale de la Santé (1995). *Rapport du Comité OMS d'experts sur les politiques pharmaceutiques nationales, Genève, 19–23 juin 1995: Contribution à la mise à jour des directives de l'OMS pour l'élaboration des politiques pharmaceutiques nationales*.
10 Demortain, D. (2015). Les heurts de la transnationalisation, 109–122 In S. Boudia, E. Henry (dir.) *La mondialisation des risques*, Rennes: Presses Universitaires de Rennes.
11 For a pragmatic approach to authentification testing, see the foundational work of Bessy, C., & Chateauraynaud, F. (2014). *Experts et faussaires*, *Pour une sociologie de la perception*, Paris, Pétra [1995]; see also Barthe, Y. et al. (2013). Sociologie pragmatique: mode d'emploi, *Politix*, 3, 103, 175–20; Martuccelli, D. (2015). Les deux voies de la notion d'épreuve en sociologie, *Sociologie*, 6/1, 43–60.
12 Interview of the Senior Deputy Chief Pharmacist, National Quality Control Laboratory, Nairobi, 15 September 2016.

13 Interview of the Deputy Chief Pharmacist, National Quality Control Laboratory, Nairobi, 15 September 2016.

14 Jeffery, R. (2009). *Regulation without implementation: India in a global pharmaceutical world*, Working Paper.

15 Information obtained from CDSCO, online: www.cdsco.nic.in/forms/contentpage1.aspx?lid=1425.

16 Department-Related Parliamentary Standing Committee on Health and Family Welfare (2012). *Fifty-Ninth Report on The Functioning of the Central Drugs Standard Control Organization (CDSCO)*, Presented on the 8th of May, Rajya Sabha Secretariat; Kadam, A. B. et al. (2016). Correcting India's Chronic Shortage of Drug Inspectors to Ensure the Production and Distribution of Safe, High-Quality Medicines, *International Journal of Health Policy and Management*, 5/9, 535–542; Thakur, D. S., & Reddy, P. T. (2016). *A report on fixing India's broken drug regulatory framework*, 4 June.

17 Department-Related Parliamentary Standing Committee on Health and Family Welfare (2012). *Fifty-Ninth Report on The Functioning of the Central Drugs Standard Control Organization (CDSCO)*, Presented on the 8th of May, Rajya Sabha Secretariat.

18 Kadam A. B. et al. (2016). Correcting India's chronic shortage of drug inspectors to ensure the production and distribution of safe, high-quality medicines, *International Journal of Health Policy and Management*, 5/9, 535–542. In Gujarat, FDCA personnel in 2016 totalled 1403; the authority operated three laboratories (interview of the Commissioner, Food and Drug Control Authority, Gandhinagar, 7 October 2016). According to other research, however, there were 168 inspectors in 2015. In view of the number of pharmaceutical sites to be inspected, this seems highly inadequate (Chokshi, M., Mongia, & R., Wattal, V. (2015). *Drug Quality and Safety Issues in India*, Policy Brief, Indian Council for Research on International Economic Relations, September).

19 UNIDO (2012). *Kenya Pharmaceutical Sector Development Strategy.*

20 UNIDO (2012). *Kenya Pharmaceutical Sector Development Strategy.*

21 Interview of the Regional Director of a large European pharmaceutical company, Nairobi, 8 May 2012.

22 Interview of the Regional Director of a large European pharmaceutical company, Nairobi, 8 May 2012.

23 Chalfin, B. (2010). *Neoliberal Frontiers: An Ethnography of Sovereignty in West Africa*, Chicago: University of Chicago Press.

24 Silverman, E. (2016). FDA warns another Indian drug maker for a laundry, *Statnews.com*, 10 February, online: www.statnews.com/pharmalot/2016/02/10/fda-india-drug-maker/.

25 Central Bureau of Investigation (2015). *Director CBI inaugurates 1st Indo-French Workshop on Combating counterfeit medicine at New Delhi*, Press release, 24 June.

26 Beja, P. (2016). War against fake drugs intensified in Kenya, *Standard Digital*, 5 September.

27 Interview of a lawyer involved in the court case against the Kenyan anticounterfeit law, Nairobi, 9 May 2012.

28 Interview of the Regional Director for Economic Security of a large European pharmaceutical company, Nairobi, 8 May 2012.

29 Interview of the Managing Director, and the Head of Operations, Anti-Illicit Trade Agency, Nairobi, 3 February 2016.

30 Ndunda, J. (2016). Poisons board arrests 60 quacks three days into Nairobi crackdown, *The Star*, 24 August.
31 Phone interview of an investigator at the PPB Crime, Investigations and Enforcement Unit, 17 September 2016.
32 Interview of the Deputy Director, Research, Awareness & Preventive Services, Anti-Counterfeit Agency, Nairobi, 14 May 2012.
33 Interview of a representative of IRACM, Paris, 26 June 2014.
34 Hornberger, J. (2016). Policing counterfeit medication, In L. Manderson, E. Cartwright, A. Hardon (Eds.) *The Routledge Handbook of Medical Anthropology*, London: Routledge.
35 Interview of Commissioner, Food and Drug Control Authority, Gandhinagar, 20 November 2015.
36 Mutegi, L. (2014). Kenya: Meds' new laboratory information management system to enhance war against counterfeit drugs, 12 September, *AllAfrica*, online: http://allafrica.com/stories/201409150169.html.
37 Online: www.iracm.com/en/table/.
38 Eymard-Duvernay, F. (1989). Convention de qualité et forme de coordination, *Revue économique*, 2, 329–359; Gomez, P.-Y. (1994). *Qualité et théorie des conventions*, Paris, Economica; Callon, M. et al. (2002). La qualité. Dossier-débat, *Sociologie du travail*, 44, 2, 255–287.
39 Pharmacy and Poisons Board (2017). Public post on Facebook, 2 June.
40 Interview of the Deputy Registrar, Pharmacy and Poisons Board, Nairobi, 29 January 2016.
41 Interview of the Authentiphone project manager for a large European telecom operator, Nairobi, 10 May 2012.
42 International Finance Corporation (2008). *The Business of Health in Africa. Partnering with the Private Sector to Improve People's Lives*, Washington, Annexe 3, p.76.
43 Hornberger, J. (2016). Policing counterfeit medication, In L. Manderson, E. Cartwright, A. Hardon (Eds.) *The Routledge Handbook of Medical Anthropology*, London: Routledge.
44 Some crucial transformations brought up but the "global health" paradigm have been analysed by the project supervised by historian Jean-Paul Gaudillière, "From international public health to global health". Presentation available online: http://globhealth.vjf.cnrs.fr/.

Part 3

Pharmaceutical logistics

Commodities circulation and lifeforms

To the dominant account of the illicit medicines problem, I have opposed two counter-narratives. In the first part of this study, I have shown that the problem of illicit medicines is linked to the geographical re-composition of markets and the growing importance of intermediate activities in the circulation and valorisation of medicines. In the second part, the problem of illicit drugs was explained by a "securitisation" dynamic through which the protection of public health is increasingly defined in the light of policing, technological, and commercial understanding. In this section, I am presenting a third counter-narrative, as a complement to the others. Pursuing thinking in terms of "drug circuits",[1] I will focus on the way in which drug trajectories are defined, and on the role of logistics. According to this counter-narrative, the problem of illicit medicines can be explained by a system that assigns trajectories to pharmaceutical products; it is the intensification of – and diversions from – these trajectories that lead to the appearance of illicit objects. The challenges to this regime reveal the general importance of the "pharmaceutical logistics regime" to society; by assigning trajectories to things, this regime sets up a socio-political order that governs relationships between people.

Two aspects of this pharmaceutical logistics regime are particularly interesting. The first concerns the conceptualisation of drug flows. The second concerns the material organisation of trajectories, their insertion into geographical space and the tools that are used to define them. To deal with these two aspects, I am taking two complementary approaches. I approach the material and infrastructural dimension using critical geography and cultural studies on logistics, which identify the technical and political stakes involved.[2] Additionally, to analyse the conceptual dimension of trajectories and flows I propose to use the work of Gilles Deleuze and Félix Guattari to help understand what is at play in the control and assignment of trajectories.[3] These two series of works will lead me to treat the system of trajectories assignment as a "logistical regime" in which debates on illicit medicines take shape. Recourse to work of Deleuze and Guattari (D&G) on the notion of *flow* will also help me to delineate the vanishing points of the system. Vanishing points are important, as the main problem that remains to be addressed is the relationship between the coercive dimension of the system and the unaccounted

DOI: 10.4324/9781003194767-9

residues that escape from it: the leaks, the overflows, the diversions and "hijackings" or misappropriations of flows.

A first set of works will help me to see the illicit as part of a system of trajectory assignment. In the social sciences – ranging from geography to cultural studies – several authors have recently examined logistics and come up with tools that enable us to grasp a situation in which capitalist strategies focus on designing circulation processes that maximise profits. The consequences of this strategic practice have also been put into perspective. Marazzi, though mainly interested in financial flows, mentions the "capitalist colonisation of the circulation sphere".[4] Tsing, following Massey and Meegan, shows that the contemporary specificity of capitalism is, so to speak, a "supply chain capitalism", though she deals mainly with the delocalisation and outsourcing of production, and is less interested in the effects produced by the circulation of consumer goods.[5] Other authors have shown the interaction of financialisation, movement of goods, and logistics. Mezzadra and Neilson have analysed the current articulation of financialisation, the extraction of raw materials, and logistical operations.[6] This highlights a crucial evolution of capital as a social relationship mediated by things: "*What Marx called the mediation of social relations 'by things' is nowadays the object of the flourishing management science of logistics*".[7] These two authors have also stressed the importance of understanding and producing an analytical framework so that I can see that this flow-management is actually a management of relationships between people. They explain:

> *In our use of the term, an operation refers primarily to this fabrication of the world, to the production of the connections, chains and networks that materially envelop the planet enabling and framing the labour and action of subjects well beyond those directly involved in the execution of the operation itself*[8]

On the one hand, the interest of such research lies in its analysis of the interactions between the circulation of objects, modes of organising work, and forms of life in the context of rapidly expanding logistical activity. On the other hand, these works also help us understanding the importance of the material dimension of the control of flows and of the operations shaping them: for example, the role of instruments such as containers or distribution algorithms.[9] Academic work on logistics provides us with the means of analysing a major aspect of the organisation and development of flows of trade goods: the legal, technical, and political complex known as logistics. This work will help us gain a grasp of the mechanisms to be described in the next section.

The conceptual constructions of Deleuze and Guattari based on the notion of flow are also important to my approach; I would like to outline some of their features here. The notion of flow (*flux*) plays a central role in their *Anti-Oedipus*, where it is inseparable from life, at once the object of control and that which thwarts control. Although D&G do not actually define flows, they evoke an inexhaustible variety of flows.[10] To put this another way, flows are "that which flows on the socius",[11] that is, movements that affect the social body and are cut off by machines or poles that are connected in their turn by flows. These flows can be, for example, corporeal (breast milk leaving the "breast pole" to flow to the opposite pole: "the mouth of the infant"), transnational flows of goods, psychic flows, or geopolitical flows. By treating all movement as flow, D&G bring out an essential homogeneity of all types of movement. Thus it is less important to understand the singular nature of a particular flow than the ways in which all flows are organised or "coded" by forces (e.g. the State), and the ways in which they are "decoded", by means of phenomena such as capitalism or schizophrenia. D&G then provide elements to help us understand the "social inscription" of flows, or their "legibility", to borrow James Scott's term.[12]

The basic control operation in any society is thus the "coding" of flows. The core problem for society (the socius) is not to prevent flows but to "code" them, to make them legible, irrespectively of whether one is *explaining* them, for example, the flows of desire for the mother (the Oedipus complex), or simply *registering* them, for example, different food flows appropriate to caste affiliations. From this point of view, the *fact* that circulations take place is only secondary as far as society is concerned; what matters primarily is the *meaning* that the circulations acquire through operations of a semiotic and organisational nature. With this in view, D&G identify three historical sequences of the organisation (or tagging) of flows. The first sequence takes place in the "primitive" societies in which flows are initially coded; the second sequence in State societies, with their despotic machines, in which the primary coding is replaced by over-coding: a sovereign appropriation of the coded flows, or a specific code linking the flows to a central figure in the State, the despot; and lastly, capitalist society, which replaces the coding and over-coding operations with something radically different: the generalised decoding of flows. For D&G, capitalism is actually a conjunction of multiple "decoded flows"; this leads them to characterise it in part as a movement for the liberation of energies.

Capitalism is a particular social formation that differs from both primitive societies and despotic machines in the way it organises flows: these are no longer coded or overcoded, but totally *decoded*. The main reason for this configuration is that it maximises the extraction of added value. In fact, general decoding is accompanied by the liberation of both capital and labour (decoded flows of production freeing money, which becomes capital; decoded flows of labour freeing work from social constraints), as well as producing a general abstract equivalence: money.[13] This does not mean, however, that capitalism does not interfere with flows: D&G show that capitalism is not conceivable without the intervention of forces to carry out operations of re-encoding and control. The tools of this control are re-territorialisation and axiomatisatisation. In re-territorialisation are mainly involved the repressive bureaucratic apparatus inherited from the sovereign State (the remains of which persistently recode flows); axiomatisation, on the other hand, is specific to capitalism: instead of codifying flows, as events unfold that affect the system, it produces axioms. Thus, it is only in a "relative" sense that capitalism carries out "absolute" decoding. Where capitalism decodes any flow only in a limited way, schizophrenia would decode them in an absolute way – hence the conjunction and opposition born in the subtitle of their book – capitalism and schizophrenia.

D&G's thinking on flows provides some tools for my study of the situation of illicit pharmaceuticals. Firstly, it encourages us to think about pharmaceutical flows as entangled with other types of flow such as geopolitical, economic, physical, and psychic ones, and to analyse the general principles that organise these flows – instead of isolating pharmaceuticals flows from the others. Pharmaceutical flows raise issues involving manufacturing and the international division of labour, conflicts between international and national regulatory standards, and practices of individual consumption that are supervised by both governments and industries. The notion of flow thus leads us to shift our attention to the general principles of organisation that articulate and organise the different types of flow on different scales. Secondly, D&G's notions of coding/decoding and of the "conjunction of decoded flows", emphasise upon a contradiction within capitalism – between the ever-increasing liberation of concomitant flows and the increasingly forceful effort needed to control them. Such contradiction is particularly revealing in our case. On the one hand, capitalism is releasing more and more drug flows and equating treatment with market valuation; on the other hand, drug flows are being constrained more and more strictly by standardisation and trajectory identification. Finally, D&G envisage, if not actual exit gates or forms of emancipation, at least modes of intervention that cannot simply be reduced to mere facets of the capitalist regime, and that are in fact modelled by the contradictions of the regime. Schizophrenia – "absolute decoding" – is a way of looking at overflows from the system, its limitations and ways of questioning them, as it disconnects and reconnects flows, disconnecting and deriving circuitry. This imaginary of diversion can be used to identify the resources with which individuals and social groups can protest against the current pharmaceutical trajectory assignment regime.

Social research on logistics as well as D&G's works upon capitalism and its flows both provide support for an attempt to reformulate the problem of illicit pharmaceuticals as a manifestation of pharmaceutical capitalism, seen as a liberation of the flow of goods which would be at the same time and effort to control them. I propose to further the analysis of this phenomenon by using the notion of "logistic regime", which focuses on the political role played today by logistics. This will lead me to define the different stakes involved in the organisation of object trajectories designed as a form of organisation of social relations. It will also lead me to speculate on possible loopholes in this regime. Chapter 6 will discuss the particular form of control to which the logistic regime corresponds and define in detail what is covered by the notion. It will describe the principles underlying the pharmaceutical logistic regime and show how its main power is that of assigning trajectories. Chapter 7 will show how the trajectories – of individuals and of objects – can escape from the grid of this regime, and will consider possible forms of emancipation implicit in a political system that is defined by the movement of objects. For this reason, it will develop several scenarios based on the diversion of trajectories.

Notes

1 Peterson, K. (2014). *Speculative markets. Drug circuits and derivative life in Nigeria*, Durham and London: Duke University Press.

2 See e.g., Neilson, B. (2012). Five theses on understanding logistics as power, *Distinktion: Journal of Social Theory*, 13/3, 322–339; Harney, S., & Moten, F. (2013). *The undercommons: Fugitive planning and black study*, Wivenhoe, New-York, Port Watson: Minor Compositions; Cowen, D. (2014). *The deadly life of logistics: Mapping violence in global trade*, Minneapolis: University of Minnesota Press; Samaddar, R. (2016). *Neoliberal strategies of governing India*, London: Routledge, chapter 8: "Logistical governance".

3 Deleuze, G., & Guattari, F. (1972). *L'Anti-Œdipe. Capitalisme et schizophrénie*, Paris: Ed. de Minuit.

4 Marazzi, C. (2010). The violence of financial markets, 17–59 In A. Fumagalli, & S. Mezzadra (Eds.), *Crisis in the global economy. Financial markets, social struggles, and new political scenarios*, Los Angeles: Semiotext(e) and Ombre Corte, 44.

5 Tsing, A. (2009). Supply chains and the human condition, *Rethinking Marxism*, 21/2, 148–176; Massey, D., & Meegan, R. (1982). *The anatomy of job loss. The how, why and where of employment decline*, London: Methuen.

6 Mezzadra, S., & Neilson, B. (2013). Extraction, logistics, finance. Global crisis and the politics of operations, *Radical Philosophy*, 178, 8–18.

7 Mezzadra, S., & Neilson, B. (2013). Extraction, logistics, finance. Global crisis and the politics of operations, *Radical Philosophy*, 178, 10.

8 Mezzadra, S., & Neilson, B. (2013). Extraction, logistics, finance. Global crisis and the politics of operations, *Radical Philosophy*, 178, 15.

9 Levinson, M. (2006). *The box. How the shipping container made the world smaller and the world economy bigger*, Princeton: Princeton University Press; Altenried, M. (2016). "Le container et l'algorithme: la logistique dans le capitalisme global", *Revue Période*, http://revueperiode.net/le-container-et-lalgorithme-la-logistique-dans-le-capitalisme-global/logistique dans le capitalisme global.

10 In the *Anti-Œdipe* one finds flows of desire, bodily flows (of milk blood, sperm, excrement, menses), flows of wealth, flows of work and of workers, flows of energy (in the physical system), flows of consumer goods, of prestige articles, of women and children (described by Bohannan in Tiv society), flows of alliances, family flows, of hair, of writing (a deterritorialised flow – even the "first deterritorialised flow"), flows of stupidity, of production, financial flows, flows of herds, or grain, etc.

11 Deleuze, G. (1971). "Nature des flux", Lecture on 14 December 1971, University of Vincennes, online: www.le-terrier.net/deleuze/anti-oedipe1000plateaux/0214-12-71.htm.

12 Scott, J. C. (1998). *Seeing like a state. How certain schemes to improve the human condition have failed*, New Haven: Yale University Press.

13 Admittedly commercial trade does exist in pre-capitalist societies, but the trade relationships are always framed in coding operations that prevent money-relationships from abstracting themselves from the nexus. In that regard, in pre-capitalist societies money is simply a particular flow that is coded, while in capitalist societies it becomes an "abstract quantity".

6 Logistic regimes and the exercise of power

The salt march

One of the most famous acts of nonviolent resistance undertaken by M. K. Gandhi in the struggle for India's independence was the famous "salt march". On 12 March 1930, Gandhi left his ashram of Sabarmati in Ahmedabad (Gujarat), accompanied by a few dozen followers, to go to Dandi, about 300 km further south on the Gujarati coast. He decided to make a gesture there that in its simplicity would rock the empire: collect a little seawater to preserve its salt. On arrival, thousands of people were following him and the demonstration, relayed by the media, was repeated throughout the occupied territory: the Indians decided to disregard the monopoly established by the British Empire and to collect salt without paying taxes anymore. The Dandi march, or salt march, has become one of the most significant events in the struggle for independence – a symbol of the end of Indian allegiance to the Crown – and an essential part of satyagraha, the civil disobedience or non-violent resistance advocated by Gandhi. But although this resounding political action is well known, its concrete objective is rarely evoked: what exactly was this salt tax that Gandhi opposed? After several unsuccessful attempts in the 1760s and 1770s, Warren Hastings, Governor-General of Bengal, achieved his goal in 1780: the salt trade was brought under government control. The salt production areas were placed under the responsibility of a Controller and divided into agencies, each headed by an appointed agent. Salt workers had to sell their production to the agents, who in turn resold it to wholesalers and levied a tax that was equivalent to more than half the initial price. Salt became a very important source of income for the British East India Company. The system of collection and taxation, modified only marginally until it was abolished on Independence, was established as one of the proofs of England's economic exploitation in India. The government did everything it could to maintain its monopoly and did not hesitate to combat fraudulent producers by putting up barriers around salt marshes to block their access. Gandhi's action thus corresponded to economic, social and political criticism – and his denunciation of the salt tax was aimed not only at

DOI: 10.4324/9781003194767-10

economic injustice but also at a whole system of political subservience whose infrastructure was the movement of an essential commodity, salt.

This story reminds us that the circulation of a commodity as common as salt can catalyse legal, economic, social, political, and geopolitical issues. Part of the Indian nation's history has been built on salt and its movement. Gandhi's nonviolent revolt is only one of the developments in this history, together with the lives of salt workers, the legal and administrative infrastructure set up to collect and resell salt, the economic power conferred on the Company by the tax, the production bans and the accompanying convictions for fraud, and the routes followed by the goods to consumers in India, Britain, and elsewhere. The history of the salt tax exemplifies the importance of the logistical regimes developed to control the circulation of economic goods: a combination of forms of labour, of laws, of modes of transport, of administrative devices, and of control practices – but also of the protest movements and revolts that contributed to the construction of Indian society during the colonial period. It even suggests that such regimes have certain properties that are generally attributed to political regimes: they are based on fundamental values that organise conceptions of social justice, inducing particular forms of representation and decision-making.

Conflicts caused by anti-counterfeiting policies also highlight the logistical regime under which the circulation of medicines is organised. When they demonstrate in favour of access and against the greed of multinational corporations, the activists campaigning for access to medicines denounce a phenomenon broader than that of simply securing pharmaceutical markets. Their denunciations of anti-counterfeiting policies call into question not only police control strategies, but also a legal system that is based on intellectual property, on the maintenance of inequalities in technical skills, on the primacy of certain transport routes over others, on fragmentation of the system that produces and distributes medicines, and on pricing policies that make certain treatments inaccessible to part of the population. These demands and denunciations converge in questioning what we propose to call the current pharmaceutical logistic regime, which mobilises transport infrastructures as well as regulatory texts, standards and pricing strategies. This shows that a logistical regime is not merely an organisation of circulation, but also a political regime: it entails a certain conception of the distribution of powers, of the constitution of a public and of political subjects, and a conception of what is justice and what is public good.

In the rest of this chapter, I will define more precisely both the general notion of a logistical regime and the particularity of the regime of contemporary pharmaceutical logistics. The purpose of the logistics-regime concept used here is threefold. Firstly, it enables one to grasp in one set of eyes the logic structuring circulation patterns that are usually treated separately: as geopolitics and economics, norms and standards, transport infrastructures, and so forth. A logistical regime should be thought of not as a juxtaposition of products with segmented trajectories, but as a form of organisation of the movement of goods, the elements of which depend on an overall architecture that has to be identified. Markets are hierarchical, as Fernand Braudel has shown in his studies of capitalism,[1] but the examination of a logistic regime allows to show how these markets are connected and articulated. Secondly, the notion of a logistical regime suggests that controversies over anti-counterfeiting concern not merely a series of laws and seizures of medicines, but a global regime of circulation involving a transport infrastructure, a conception of law, and economic power relations. What is "political" in anti-counterfeiting conflicts is not so much to be found in single events as in the overall organisation that they denounce – an organisation bearing on circulations. In that regard logistic regimes are political regimes, and the conflicts and controversies they raise point at their limitations and contradictions. Thirdly, and as a consequence of the two previous points, if the concept of logistics designates an architecture of circulation and if this architecture provides space for a policy to be applied, then we should attempt to define what are today the politics of logistics: of which politics exactly could logistics be the aegis?

In other words, my demonstration will aim to show how the current regime of pharmaceutical logistics, such as it appears in conflicts over medicines, organises the movement of goods. It will seek to determine the reasons why, and how, this organisation produces politics. It will also explain why logistical regimes should be viewed as political forms: the circulation of objects constitutes an all-important site – a site on which social relations, orders of equality, needs, and conceptions of justice are all negotiated, thrashed out. Finally, I will question the specificity of politics of this sort: what conceptions of community and justice do they promote, and what social operations do they favour? What inconsistencies and contradictions do these politics contain? The chapter will define a notion of a logistical regime that is analogous to a political regime. This will make it possible to show the extent to which logistics can structure society – an extent usually attributed to traditional politics rather than to a technical activity such as logistics. It will also show (at least in an analogical mode) the essentially political nature of an activity that is generally seen as merely technical and commercial. The growing importance of the movement of goods in our lives, and the type of framework in which these movements are carried out, make the concept of a logistics system indispensable for any study of the kind of politics proper to the world of today. To grasp this, we must turn first and foremost to the multiplication of commercial circulations that characterise today's societies.

The chaos of circulations

The contemporary era has seen an exponential increase in commercial exchanges. This phenomenon is both massive – bringing about changes in the environment and society – and chaotic – it seems difficult to grasp at any single time the innumerable rules that determine the multiplicity of movements. More and more things are circulating, coming and going from all quarters. For a start, to judge by the statistics, between 1950 and 2005, the volume of world trade increased 27-fold, according to World Trade Organization estimates.[2] This expansion was particularly pronounced in the case of manufactured goods: trade in manufactures grew more than twice as fast as trade in agricultural produce (7.5% and 3.6% of annual growth, respectively). This is unprecedented. During the first wave of globalisation between 1870 and 1914, for example, the growth rate in world trade was only half that recorded since 1950. The historian Frank Trentmann recalls some of the figures that illustrate this phenomenal growth: in the United Kingdom, in the year 2006, women bought twice as much clothing as in the whole of the previous decade; in the United States, the amount of furniture found in municipal garbage doubled between 1960 and 2009 to about 10 million tons; in 2004, an American kitchen contained an average of 1019 objects.[3] Increasingly, it is in a world of objects that society is evolving today.

However, the figures do not adequately reflect the chaotic and unpredictable nature of these developments. It cannot be denied that the movement works in all directions. First of all, because over and above the growth in the volume of trade, the objects that circulate are increasingly diverse and heterogeneous. In the statistics manufactures (e.g., refrigerators, cars, television sets) are mingled with cultural goods (books, disks, cassettes and DVDs); agricultural products processed by the food industry (food, drink) are combined with products derived from the human body and processed by biomedicine (blood derivatives, gametes); objects incorporating expensive technologies and requiring extensive processing are mixed with common objects that can be produced with little technical skill. Secondly, because consumer goods that cross the planet in various directions (from North to South, South to South, South to North) often follow complex trajectories. Products that are part of a certain "value regime" subsequently at some point in time can change direction. Goods take shape in chains of production, processing and distribution on sites where their value and significance as objects can change.[4] Lastly, because the socio-economic rules governing the movement of objects are neither clear nor obvious. Yann-Philippe Tastevin, in his survey of the globalisation of the rickshaw, for example, shows how the marketing of an object, its maintenance and spare parts, are all based on human networks, on contingent and uncoordinated (or discrete) commercial aims (or willed actions).[5] If one wants to understand the logic of economic globalisation, then it is high time to stop looking only at multi-national companies. It is also required to pay attention to the trajectories of individuals who model it on a day to day basis, through their multiple moves. Janet Roitman, writing on forms of regulation in Central Africa, shows how rules (whether national or transnational) concerning certain goods do not in any way prevent the circulation of particular and illicit categories of goods, and can sometimes even foster it.[6] Anna Tsing, in her wonderful study of the matsutake, explores the entanglements which connect the histories of Oregon pickers – Vietnam war veterans and

South-East Asian migrants – to those of Japanese consumers of this luxury food product.[7]

Circulations are heterogeneous and take place on multiple levels. They involve a growing and increasingly diversified number of objects; poles catalyse them, with new poles constantly emerging; they obey rules so numerous and contradictory that it is very difficult indeed to extract dominant principles. Thus, at first glance, it seems impossible to find an overall sense or meaning in these circulations: stacked, multidirectional, there are simply too many of them.

To add to the chaotic nature of the movement of consumer goods, we can note that the movement of an object never takes place in isolation. Admittedly, transport activity does, first of all, make it possible, and this means that the multiplication of object movements must be accompanied by a growth of transport activity. For example, sea freight increased in volume from 2600 tonnes per year in 1970 to 9800 tonnes per year in 2014,[8] a multiplication by 3.8. But the movements of objects are themselves dependent on other movements: those of persons, of texts, of know-how and of yet other objects. The consumption of a drug in Kenya, for example, requires, if the drug is produced in Kenya, the importation of machines manufactured in Germany, of active ingredients developed in China, of expatriate personnel brought from India, of the implementation of standards developed in England, and so forth. In 1994 the Ford Escort was assembled from components manufactured in 15 different countries[9]; this means that when this car as a finished consumer product eventually became part of the flow of traffic, it had entailed movement of components between 15 different countries. In 1997, the World Resources Institute showed that a consumer in one of the wealthy countries would have had to carry three hundred extra shopping bags a week if he or she had to supply the materials needed to produce the goods he or she usually bought.[10]

This interdependence of circulations is linked to a basic principle of the market economy. This principle is defined in classical economics through the notions of "comparative advantage" and of the division of labour between individuals, enterprises, or nations. It is being pushed to a new extremity by the very nature of the objects that circulate today: techno-products, as historian Dominique Pestre[11] has called them, or "technological goods and commodities" – underscoring the commercial and technical nature of circulating objects – of which medicines are a characteristic example. An essential feature of the current period is the technical nature of the things that circulate: technological objects, that are the result of R&D work, and "technologised" goods, such as agricultural products, which are increasingly subject to technical expertise. These objects, insofar as they are technological, integrate formalised knowledge and are the result of a specialisation of tasks: research work in "lab" form, and segmented practices of industrial production, implying links between intellectual property rights as a method of valorisation and a standardisation of the modes of supervision. They are transported from one continent to another, and from a workspace to consumer space. Their circulation is affected by different categories of institutions: producers, distributors, competing market operators, institutions that promulgate standards, and others that draw up the rules governing trade. They are part of a system for the circulation of regulated, secured objects, because the objects present new dangers due to our knowledge of them, or lack of it.

This global growth, both structured and chaotic, of the trade-in technological commodities, raises at least two questions. The first is this: what are the rules and forces that organise these ever-expanding movements? What can the meaning be of this simultaneous continuous expansion and branching of the circulation on the one hand, and the organisation of this complex movement on the other? For example, in the case of medicinal products, how can we articulate in a single explanation the explosion of the use of pharmaceuticals, on the one hand, and on the other the multiplication of forms of control that are being brought to bear on medicines? The second question concerns the mixed effects, both on people's lives and on the production of a comprehensible world, of the increasing circulation of objects and the rules that govern them. What are the effects of humanity's entry into the "phagocene"[12] – the era when consumption became the driving force of social and environmental change – on the making of the contemporary world? The densification of the circulation of consumer objects upon the planet calls for an explanation that accounts for the ways in which objects transform the world; it should also take into account the effects of circulation itself, as well as the effects of the rules that organise it. Beyond the overall impression of a market chaos that emanates from our world, what are the principles of organisation that analysis can describe?

From logistics to logistical regimes

The phenomenon that provides an answer to the joint question of the liberation of commercial traffic and its tightening control is the development of logistics after World War II. Logistics is an age-old discipline, initially linked to the art of war; it was focused on organising the transport of troops and their supplies of food, weapons and ammunition. In the aftermath of World War II, rising economic activity and growth in trade led to the development of profit strategies based on the movement of goods, and to the introduction of tools to implement these strategies. Logistics became a science of market expansion, covering a set of activities: the various means and methods involved in the physical organisation of companies, and in particular that of the input and output flows of materials before, during and after production.[13] According to the geographer Deborah Cowen, the "logistical revolution" dates back to the 1960s in the United States, a period during which the issue of supply and distribution became crucial to business management. It was at about this time that the management guru, Peter Drucker wrote: "*Physical distribution is today's frontier in business. It is one area where managerial results of great magnitude can be achieved. And it is still largely unexplored*".[14] This interest was spurred by the creation of new institutions: the American Management Association dealt with it at a seminar in the late 1950s, and the National Council of Physical Distribution Management was created in 1963 (and renamed the Council for Logistics Management in the 1980s), accompanied by its introduction into university curricula in the 1960s. These developments sometimes materialised at a point where the military and commercial sectors intersected; the Logistics Management Institute, created in 1961 at the instigation of Defence Minister Robert McNamara, who hoped that this new institution – in thinking out a new field and in innovating – would play the same role in logistics as the RAND corporation in the operational aspect of military activities.[15]

This revolution was based on knowledge production: in the early 1960s, the science of systems made it possible to move on from thinking in terms of minimising the costs of transport to thinking in terms of added value produced by transportation. This was accompanied by a new way of calculating the costs of producing and transporting goods: total-cost analysis. Firms could now identify, by analysing the increasing amount of data provided by computerisation, the total cost of producing goods and putting them into circulation – including, for example, the costs of warehousing, transport, obsolescence of equipment and communication. This new type of calculation led, for example, certain authors of a seminal article on total-cost analysis, to point out that it might be more interesting financially for an American company targeting consumers in Dakota to manufacture in Ohio rather than in Illinois – even though the latter was closer.[16] The revolution was also based on new technical devices, the best-known of these being the container.[17] Containers were first used by the US military during World War II and then during the Vietnam War; after World War II, their non-military use became more widespread. Containers shortened significantly the time needed to load and unload goods, increasing "turnaround time" and the speed of transport. More recently, other technologies have been playing an expanding role in the organisation of traffic, such as algorithms and computer technologies that continue to transform logistics.[18]

All these innovations became central to firms as of the 1970s and 1980s, following the oil crisis. Deborah Cowen recalls that it was also during this period that the strongest wave of deregulation in the American transport sector took place, providing room for other developments such as intermodalism – moving goods by combining different means of transport – involving the imposition of standard units such as pallets or containers. These transformations have led to a far-reaching recomposition of the time-space relationship. They have also shown that the upsurge of commercial circulation, the liberation of international trade and the deregulation that makes it possible are all concomitant with the introduction of very high levels of knowledge, technology, standards and regulation. In this sense, logistical activity provides us with an initial answer to our question on the structuring of flows of commercial goods: these flows are increasingly driven by a process of cost rationalisation calculated at the stakeholder level, that is, that of companies – and not of States, individuals or populations.

One should not overlook the link between logistical activity and the social production of illicit forms of circulation; it highlights a fundamental aim of logistics within the capitalist system. Stefano Harney and Fred Moten show that in "logistical" capitalism, as profit stems from the way things, signs and people move and intersect, the object of appropriation has become movement itself and access.[19] The value generated by offshoring, distribution chain management and license agreements plays an essential role in the strategies of multinational companies. As a result, movement itself is subject to renewed forms of control and discrimination in order to maximise the profit potential that displacement models can generate. It also implies that "to move wrong or not to move is sabotage": the law of profit is based on the constant increase of organised movement.[20] In the same vein, Deborah Cowen explains that in mobilising dreams of absolute control of movement, logistics is always already threatened by implosion. She argues that logistics cannot exist without a downside: interventions that can jeopardise the integrity of the supply chain. She pays particular attention to the figure of the *pirate*, one of whose essential traits is that of having been constructed in the process of governing spaces of circulation:

> *The exceptional legal status of the pirate as marked by his "location" beyond the reach of the law was not simply a matter of metaphor; rather, it exposes the legal geographies that are centrally at play.*
>
> *(Cowen 2014, p. 137)*

Seizures of goods by pirates matter less by their subtractions than by their challenge to the legal structure of territories and trajectories. What makes piracy unbearable for organisers of commodity networks is that it reveals both the institutional architecture of circulations and the multiplicity of other possible trajectories – beyond the reach of the State and institutional markets. There are always alternative ways of accessing goods. In the pharmaceutical context, such issues of illegality (sabotage, piracy) directly question control mechanisms: what rules are likely to be flouted? What knowledge is being challenged or reformulated? In this perspective, logistics accounts not only for the multiplication of trade exchanges, but also for the forms of control that weigh on them and for the practices of contestation and diversion that respond to this control. It fuels capitalist development in a crucial manner. Focusing its power upon movement itself, as Harney and Moten recall, it aims at fostering trade and commodity circulations. But it does it *through* control, management, and the discrimination between "good" and "bad", attributing directions, segmenting flows. It does not confront the expansion of circulations to their control; on the contrary, these two phenomena become two sides of a single coin.

The empire of logistics is thus not limited to the organised movement of objects. Logistics, as a discipline of knowledge, an organisational practice and a major trend in contemporary capitalism spreads a much more general logic, which is not limited to the rationalisation of firms' inputs and outputs: it propagates nothing less than a new social order. "Logistical power is political power", as Brett Neilson has argued.[21] To recognise this, one has to refuse, as Cowen does, to reduce logistics to the particular logistical arrangements of firms, and admit that the concept involves a broader series of transformations, ranging from the definition of traffic standards to the integration of regional economic zones. To a certain extent, logistics is inseparable from the other transformations of capitalism that aim to facilitate the physical movement of consumer goods. In India, for example, "Export Processing Zones" appeared in 1965 with the creation of the Kandla zone as a seaport of Gujarat.[22] Areas like this are intended to boost export policies and integrate developing countries into international trade by attracting foreign companies thanks to a "relaxation" of labour legislation, offers of tax rebates and provision of an infrastructure to facilitate exports, shortening or even eliminating customs delays. This type of export zone is set upon the initiative of a government and fulfils a broader objective than the mere management of business inputs and outputs. In order to attract foreign companies, it mobilises at least in part a strategy similar to that on which logistics is based, making infrastructures available, simplifying procedures and shortening the time taken to put consumer goods into circulation. The restrictive conception of logistics gives way to a broader understanding in which all market players, and in particular firms and States, jointly pursue the objective of putting more products into circulation on international markets, and doing so faster and faster.

Logistics manuals clearly identify this issue: "*in improving logistics and supply chain management in developing countries, some essential infrastructures are required, including: legal infrastructure, hardware infrastructure, software infrastructure*", among which are listed 18 items including "appropriate" import-export policies and customs practices, "reasonable" bank interest rates, nationwide definitions of quality standards, road networks, communication infrastructures, a "reasonable" competition policy, etc.[23] Logistics is therefore by no means merely an activity that processes the trajectories of raw materials and finished products. It deals at local, regional, national and transnational levels with the entire material and immaterial context in which objects circulate for the purpose of consumption.

The circulation of objects, however, is not specific to the modern period, or even to capitalism, let alone in the latter's neoliberal form. Circulations obey different logics at different times. Logistics (understood in a general sense) is therefore embodied in a variety of temporally and geographically situated logistical regimes. This dilated movement of logistics as a principle structuring market circulation, but specific to particular periods of time in each regime, enables us to understand the contemporary implications of market circulation in general, and of pharmaceuticals in particular. One can even argue that although the history of logistics might not coincide with that of capitalism, contemporary capitalism, with its permanent rationalisation of the art of movement and the transportation of goods is a particularly efficient engine of production of logistic regimes.[24]

A logistic regime can thus be defined as a set of rules, technical means and arguments determining the trajectories of consumer goods. It structures the movement of objects in a particular way. The logistical regime defines the goods that are allowed to circulate, those that are prohibited, the norms and standards that govern their validity, and the forms (operators, places, trajectories, means of transport) that their movements have to take. As a concept, the notion of logistical regime relies on an analogy with the notion of political regime, to underline their proximity. It has been borrowed from several other "regimes": in particular from the regimes of knowledge production defined by the historian of sciences Dominique Pestre, and the global health regimes described by the sociologist Andrew Lakoff, both of which stem from the work of Michel Foucault. According to Pestre, a system of knowledge production is the result of multiple conjunctions: of places, forms of work organisation, regulatory standards, rules of appropriation, ways of managing living things and populations, and of producing subjectivities.[25] According to Lakoff, a global health regime combines normative and technical components that provide a rationale – in the sense of Foucault's governmentality – for managing an object (in the case of global health regimes: infectious diseases). Both components formulate a vision of social life that requires the achievement of an innovative technological project.[26] They have a vision of social order and of the technical means to establish that order. Conceptually, a logistical regime has more than a merely analogical resemblance to a political regime. Both regimes are based on fundamental conceptions of what has to be governed, and of the procedures to be implemented in order to do so; both regimes also establish institutions and forms of organisation needed to carry out the governing. Last but not least, both political and logistical regimes produce spaces for – and objects of – contestation, defining the objects to be targeted in the competition for power.

The concept of a logistical regime takes from Lakoff's and Pestre's definitions the idea that social objects (health, knowledge, the circulation of objects) are part of a general political project that is not limited to the technical management of production and trade, but that shapes a social order, affecting the individuals who live in it. Logistical regimes, by means of the management of the movements of goods that they stipulate, encourage the emergence of particular types of society, the rules of which they help define. Between the 15th and 19th centuries, for example, the "triangular trade" was a system in which "goods", values and exchange orders, means of transport and trajectories were all stipulated. The type of commerce organised in order to trade slaves was, in its extreme – and horrendous – form, the paradigm of a market order that was also an order of the world. In short, logistical regimes not only determine the circulation of consumer goods and the materials of which they are composed, but also make the circulation itself the central phenomenon around which societies take shape. From logistics to logistical regimes, traffic flows become the focal point of government efforts, the central phenomenon from which all other societal construction issues are derived, as far as order and justice are concerned. This means that understanding the logistical principles underlying the movement of a given set of goods enable us to understand an entire section of the overall social order – that is, the corresponding regime. In order to continue this analysis, we must now specify the nature and characteristics of the particular regime we are interested in: the pharmaceutical logistic regime.

The pharmaceutical logistic regime

Some public relations specialists have tried to promote the fight against illicit medicines as a definitive solution to a topical problem. Going at war against pharmaceutical terrorists and other goons would be enough to clear the pharmaceutical trade. The first two parts of this book have shown exactly the opposite. Illicit medicines express tensions which cannot be that easily suppressed from pharmaceutical markets. The globalised and heterogeneous production activity, the international competition for distribution channels in relation to harmonisation requirements, the politics of securitisation lie at the heart of the problem – a problem that is only pointed at by "fake", "counterfeit", "falsified" medicines. But if illicit medicines are not the problem – what is it then? Are social sciences only here to dissolve public authorities' and populations' concerns in a bath of relativism?

To answer these questions, I suggest looking at things from a different angle, based on the discussion of logistical regimes. Instead of seeing the fight against illicit medicines as a way to protect markets and their organisation rules, I consider this fight itself as the organisation principle of markets. The fact that securitisation dynamics are a product of a general public health concern that goes beyond the strategies of industrial actors hints at the legitimacy of such an approach. Furthermore, securitisation dynamics mobilise tools, processes, organisational forms in the name of a conception of justice and common good, whose realisation depends on the markets order. At last, securitisation dynamics, designing medicines as the objects of government, legitimising trajectories and commodities and excluding others, edict principles for the circulation of commodities, which is coherent with my definition of logistical regimes. Put differently, securitisation dynamics displace the exercise of politics on the distribution terrain, in the realm of organisation of flows of commodities and access to these commodities. These dynamics materialise a logistical regime.

This pharmaceutical logistic regime is characterised first and foremost by the kind of control it exerts, or rather: by the object which is supposed to be controlled. At first sight, as any logistical regime, it bears upon trajectories – that of medicines. What it is monitoring is where a medicine (or a group of medicines) can go, where it cannot go, under which conditions it can be used. Such control differs from usual forms of power and political regimes: individuals and populations are not anymore the object of power – objects are. In a traditional political regime, be it a democratic or authoritarian one, power aims at individuals: their freedom of movement, of expression, the means provided to fight against the inequalities that divide them. Objects, commodities, non-humans are also controlled, but individuals and populations attract most of the attention of power. The pharmaceutical logistic regime proceeds differently, since most of its attention is dedicated to commodities and their trajectories, while the control of individuals is only a secondary goal. Remember that, according to Harney and Moten, the main purpose of logistical capitalism is the expansion of surplus-value, which implies to put into circulation more and more commodities. Reaching such a goal calls for attention to the "human factor" and to influence individual and collective behaviours. But *in fine*, the regime's attention is focused upon flows of commodities – an attention that affects human lives only collaterally. This particularity is the essential feature of the pharmaceutical logistic regime: how could one account otherwise for the tension between the application of the securitisation programme and the moral requirement to make medicines accessible for the largest population? The primacy of trajectory control, of discrimination between good and bad medicines, to the detriment of considerations on needs and access conditions in developing countries, illustrates very clearly this feature of pharmaceutical capitalism – let's manage commodities first, patients second.

However, pharmaceutical logistics exceeds securitisation dynamics. The pharmaceutical logistics regime works primarily through an infrastructure. The main elements of this infrastructure are the following: the establishment of a form of research based on appropriation and financial valuation by application of patent and copyright; a geographical fragmentation of the manufacturing sector; policies of harmonisation of standards that accompany an integration of the world market; a part played by State and health coverage in terms of access in the countries of the North, and a progressive emergence of this same trend in the countries of the South; the importance of donors and private operators in structuring markets in the South; and the segmentation and interconnection of markets. The logistic regime determines the movement of goods, using tools such as intellectual property, licensing, pricing, forms of payment and reimbursement, solutions to transportation problems, and monitoring. Many tools are involved in this overall plan. Some are specifically designed to structure the regime, for example, the International Conference on Harmonization, while others, such as the TRIPS Agreement, serve several different regimes simultaneously.

But as this list suggests, securitisation dynamics resort to many elements of the regime and manifest a particularly coherent expression of its rationale. They highlight the relationship between trade structure, actors' strategies and power relations. They illustrate the schizophrenic logic through which "ever increasing" quantities of medicines ask for "ever increasing" forms of control and exclusion, both being fundamental to capital expansion.

One needs to resist the temptation to explain any pharmaceutical phenomenon through securitisation dynamics though. The pharmaceutical logistic regime manifests itself in multiple ways, circulation processes, monitoring activities, growing or diminishing flows. Sociologist Joseph Dumit has analysed, for instance, some of the consequences of the pharmaceutical regime – understood as a regime of pharmaceutical consumption – for consumers.[27] His work upon preventive treatment against cholesterol in the US society has shown that, in order to sell increasing quantities of medicines, a growing population has been redefined "at risk" – meaning at risk of a cardiovascular accident. Even though he does not speak in terms of logistical regime, one could see it at play here: a regime that pursues the aim of expanding consumption through a form of control over trajectories of medicines. This aim results in considerable collateral damage: a huge part of the American population becomes at risk, and the identity of millions of individuals is transformed – from healthy, they become "threatened". This example shows that the pharmaceutical regime, by promoting growing consumption, influence individual becomings, subjective formations – what Dumit called the "pharmaceutical self". Furthermore, Dumit's work underlines one of the regime's features that my own investigation left aside. Whereas anti-counterfeiting politics illustrate the restrictive dimension of the regime – that is how it excludes medicines – Dumit shows, on the contrary, its role in the ever-increasing consumption patterns.

Other investigations have shown that the pharmaceutical logistic regime both manifests and feeds social order – which legitimates certain circulations (or breaks) and renews them. Sociologist Johanna Crane has shown, for example, that the inaccessibility of anti-retroviral drugs in Africa in the late 1990s was justified by epidemiological arguments on the risk of increasing resistance to treatment – arguments based on the alleged "fact" that African patients tended to be lax in following the treatments prescribed.[28] Her work shows that the organisation of the logistical regime, by foreclosing access to antiretrovirals, has been supported by the production of representations about ways of living and behaviours of people. Crane recalls that such representations have been swept away when the logistical regime changed and that medicines became more widely accessible. It appeared then that Sub-Saharan African patients followed medical representations in the same way as any other patients, as long as their infrastructural and socio-economic conditions of access were similar. The pharmaceutical logistic regime is then supported by behavioural representations and knowledge about how to manage them.

Similarly, in her work on cancer in Africa, Julie Livingston has shown that the limited availability of cancer care in African countries was justified by an epidemiological discourse on the low prevalence of cancer in those countries, cancer being seen as a disease proper to the more affluent countries.[29] As a result, the availability and unavailability of treatments, against HIV or cancer – but these are only two of the many examples – have materialised at a point of confluence: that of political options (to maintain robust intellectual property rights and high prices), that of representations of the individuals concerned (Africans who are not observant, or are not severely affected by "non-communicable diseases"), and that of the order to which objects have been assigned. It eventually becomes impossible to separate the order of things from the order of people and of the world.

A third phenomena left aside in my own investigation is the fact that social actors offer variable understandings of the logistical regime. They acknowledge its political nature in different ways and therefore engage in various manners. The most visible divide is that between patient groups claiming consumer rights and groups engaging as political actors. Sociologist Janine Barbot has shown such a divide between patient groups involved in the fight against HIV in France during the 1990s: Some groups advocated health consumption principles (e.g., Actions Traitements), emphasising access to treatments before anything else, while some other groups denounced inequalities and domination forms at play in the construction of the epidemy (e.g., Act-Up Paris).[30] Barbot's work reminds us that engagement and protest facing a logistical regime are rarely unified.

These works shed lights upon some crucial characteristics of the logistical regime. Much more would be needed – revealing the contradictions and the elements of convergence between regimes. These investigations remind us first that understanding a logistical regime requires empirical research. They also give another opportunity to insist on the fact that a pharmaceutical logistic regime defines a problem space which is analogous to that of a political regime. It shapes the bio-social life of individuals; it reflects social orders; it generates political subjectivities and causes conflict. It is based on a particular relationship between the public and private spheres, between the geopolitical architecture that governs State/corporate relations and the production of therapeutic individualities.

This political nature is particularly visible in the controversies raised by anti-counterfeiting policies. In challenging the line between licit and illicit drugs, access activists reveal the political significance of what is presented as a mere series of management operations. Opponents of these "operations" have constantly shown that they are in fact part of a much larger set of strategies aimed at assigning, for example, to intellectual property a disproportionate importance in conflict resolution, or at exploiting the fragmented geopolitical localisation of pharmaceutical production. The activists draw attention in this way to the power relations "built into" the political sphere. Last but not least, the issues raised in the controversies tend to lead on to a broader debate on issues of law, equality and domination. Seen in this perspective, the controversies on anti-counterfeiting sketch out a vast strategic space that goes far beyond anti-counterfeiting laws and the seizure of medicines: an ethical space where the right of individuals to life and health can be debated – as can issues such as the balance of power between firms and States in the North and the South, and the limits placed on social projects by contemporary forms of capitalism. As anti-counterfeiting legislation is a tool of the pharmaceutical logistics regime, the controversies that challenge it show up the political dimension of this regime; they lead the regime at the edge of disruption and reveal its nature. They bring to light the broader politics implicated by the movement of goods, and reveal the movement of goods as a *site* of politics. But what about these politics and how to qualify them?

The colonisation of trajectories

An unexpected category of the exercise of domination transpires from securitisation dynamics. It seems first that the promoters of such strategies do not take any particular stance on the political economy of production and distribution. But the fight they lead has broader consequences for everyone: patients, governments, manufacturers, distributors. From a geopolitical perspective, securitisation contributes to power relationships between nations – power relationships whose stake is the organisation of international trade and how firms benefit from it, with the risk of maintaining least developed States in a subaltern role with the imposition of regulations which would slow down their development. From the perspective of subjects, securitisation threatens access to treatments and therefore endangers the existence of specific populations. The profit-maximising strategies they materialise result in new risks and news subjectivities. Such a situation, especially if we think about the salt march that opens this chapter, shares some elements with former colonial policies. When greediness leads private firms and States to maintain their power upon others by any means, without any regards for the consequences to be supported by governed populations … can we still talk about free trade competition? Would not it be more appropriate to discuss in terms of the execution of an imperial logic? In that sense the domination of the powerful nations over the others is characterised by its continuity: maintaining least developed States into dependency, attributing them a peripherical role is by no means new for the most industrialised states, even though unequal exchange is today supported by harmonisation plans, standardisation policies or intellectual property promotion.[31]

However, if one can talk about the pharmaceutical regime in terms of an imperial or neo-colonial rationale, it is also important to acknowledge that the rules followed by such a form of imperialism differ from those of classical imperial strategies. In particular, what is at stake here is neither direct territorial domination nor source materials exploitation. On the contrary, in some way, the pharmaceutical logistic regime fosters the emergence of new economic and industrial developments and the proliferation of producers in developing localities. The exercise of power lies therefore somewhere else: in defining the channels through which medicines can be sold, in establishing prices, sanitary regulation barriers, intellectual property rights, free zones and privileged routes. The episode of the seizures illustrates this argument.

Goods seized by European customs came from India and were being shipped to Vanuatu. One might be surprised at the sheer strangeness of the journey that the drugs were taking: Vanuatu is about 10,000 km east of India; why send the drugs 7000 km in the opposite direction? In terms of fuel economy, it seems absurd, not to speak of other aspects. But this bizarre route takes on another meaning when we take account of the way trajectories are set. Numerous logistic studies have shown that distance is only one of the economic parameters taken into account, and not necessarily the main one. The logistic poles that catalyse trajectories are also poles of economic and political control. It is the stakeholders in this polar system who define, legitimise and assign the routes to be followed by goods in the logistics regime of the world economy.

In this system of circulation, though points of origin are multiple, trajectories are fixed. They are set by the agreements on patents and licensing by which firms and States assign trajectories to medicines. For the dominant players in the game, the main challenge is not so much to maintain control over production and distribution (increasingly unthinkable, despite the coercive power of laws protecting intellectual property) as to manage trajectories and organise mobility. Actors operate in a world where there is no absolute control over who produces, who distributes and who consumes. On the other hand, however, it is possible – and this is precisely the purpose of the logistical regime – to organise the possible trajectories, prohibiting some and authorising others. The dominant players can thus open roads and feed flows, even though they are no longer the producers of the goods they put into circulation.

Seen in this light, trajectory-setting has become today a form of imperialism. It works a lot like neo-colonial strategy, even though the domination it exerts is less a matter of territorial control, of resource extraction, and of cultural hegemony than one of regulations, standards, transportation techniques, facilities offered by export zones, that together form a system. Under this new type of imperialism, countries of the South are allowed to trade, but their ability to actually do so is conditional: it is governed by the legal practices, technical standards and transport infrastructures that regulate the trajectories of goods. The setting of trajectories thus changes the stakes in the neo-colonial game, which is now less about territories than about interstices, less about spaces than ways of occupying and moving in them – and, of course, moving things. In other words: anyone can sell, but not sell anywhere. For example, because of standards, it is difficult for Kenyan firms to sell outside the regional market; it is impossible for Indian firms to sell certain medicines outside the territories for which they are licensed. As flows are now manipulable, the logistical regime assigns them and thus controls them by means of a special type of imperialism: the colonisation of trajectories.

For long the pharmaceutical industry has shown great capacity to anticipate trade and capitalist trends.[32] As suggested by the former analyses, it seems that once more, the transformations at play on pharmaceutical markets are at the forefront of contemporary capitalist profit and control models. The pharmaceutical logistic regime glances at a form of capitalism in which wealth lies upon the continual densification of market exchanges through the infinite diversification of supply and demand poles. But it also let us see a form of capitalism in which power *and* profit would depend upon "what links" – that is to say the unending commodity flows that unite consumers.

However, as any power mechanism, the pharmaceutical logistic regime opens as many emancipatory futures as it seems to close them. In order to understand and seize these emancipatory processes, it is therefore needed to turn towards those who seem to occupy only a subsidiary role in the regime: the pharmaceutical users. Through their day to day acts, they create multiple detours, diversion, substractions – isn't it the way in which we can understand the regime's subversion?

Notes

1 Braudel, F. (1985). *La dynamique du capitalisme*, Paris: Flammarion.
2 World Trade Report (2007). *Six decades of multilateral trade cooperation: What have we learnt?*, 243.
3 Trentmann, F. (2016). *Empire of things: How we became a world of consumers, from the fifteenth century to the twenty-first*, London: Allen Lane.
4 Appadurai, A. (Ed.) (1988). *The social life of things. Commodities in cultural perspective*, Cambridge: Cambridge University Press; Hughes, A., & Reimer, S. (2004). *Geographies of commodity chains*, London: Routledge.
5 Tastevin, Y. P., & Pliez, O. (2015). « La discrète filière de l'autorickshaw. Une ethnographie de la mondialisation », *Revue Française de Socio-Économie*, 2 (Hors-série), 121–137.
6 Roitman, J. (2005). *Fiscal disobedience. An anthropology of economic regulation in central Africa*, Princeton: Princeton University Press.
7 Tsing, A. L. (2015) *The mushroom at the end of the world: on the possibility of life in capitalist ruins*, Princeton: Princeton University Press.
8 CNUCED, *Etude sur les transports maritimes*, 2015, p. 7.
9 Gereffi, G., Korzeniewicz, M., & Korzeniewicz, R. P. (1994). "Global commodity chains",. In G. Gereffi, & M. Korzeniewicz (Eds.), *Commodity Chains and Global Capitalism*, Westport, London: Praeger, pp. 1–14.
10 Quoted by Trentmann, F. (2016). *Empire of things: How we became a world of consumers, from the fifteenth century to the twenty-first*, London: Allen Lane.
11 Pestre, D. (dir.) (2014). *Le gouvernement des technosciences. Gouverner le progrès et ses dégâts depuis 1945*, Paris: La Découverte.
12 Bonneuil, C., & Fressoz, J.-B. (2013). *L'événement anthropocène. La terre, l'histoire et nous*, Paris: Seuil.
13 Langevin, A., & Riopel, D. (Eds.) (2005). *Logistics systems: definition and optimization*, New York: Springer.
14 Drucker, P. (1962). The economy's dark continent, *Fortune*, 72, avril.
15 Cowen, D. (2014). *The deadly life of logistics: Mapping violence in global trade*, Minneapolis: University of Minnesota Press.

16 LeKashman, R., & Stolle, J. F. (1965). The total cost approach to distribution, *Business Horizons*, Winter, 33–46, cited in Deborah Cowen (2014) p. 38.

17 Levinson, M. (2006). *The Box. How the shipping container made the world smaller and the world economy bigger*, Princeton: Princeton University Press.

18 Altenried, M. (2016). « Le container et l'algorithme: la logistique dans le capitalisme global », *Revue Période*, http://revueperiode.net/le-container-et-lalgorithme-la-logistique-dans-le-capitalisme-global/.

19 Harney, S., & Moten, F. (2013). *The undercommons: Fugitive planning and black study*, Wivenhoe, New-York, Port Watson: Minor Compositions; Harney, S., & Moten, F. (2015). Mikey the rebelator, *Performance Research*, 20/4, 141–145.

20 Harney, S., & Moten, F. (2015). Mikey the rebelator, *Performance Research*, 20/4, 141–145, 142.

21 Neilson, B. (2012). Five theses on understanding logistics as power, *Distinktion: Journal of Social Theory*, 13/3, 322–339, 328.

22 Neveling, P. (2014). Structural contingencies and untimely coincidences in the making of neoliberal India: The Kandla Free Trade Zone, 1965–91, *Contributions to Indian Sociology*, 48/1, 17–43; Jenkins, R., Kennedy, L., & Mukhopadhyay, P. (2014). *Power, policy and protest. The politics of India's Special Economic Zones*, Oxford: Oxford University Press.

23 Farahani, R. Z. , Asgari, N., & Davarzani, H. (2009). *Supply chain and logistics in national, international and governmental environment. Concepts and models*, Berlin: Springer-Verlag.

24 In a way logistic regimes are close to the notion of « economic circuit », that indicates both the materiality and the heterogeneity of the organisation of circulations. Cholez, C., & Trompette, P. (2016). Economic circuits in Madagascar: "Agencing" the circulation of goods, accounts and money", *Consumption Markets & Culture*, 19/1, 148–166.

25 Pestre, D. (2006). *Penser les régimes de science en société. Production des savoirs, appropriation, régulation dans l'histoire et aujourd'hui*, Séminaire transversal « Nouvelles frontières, nouveaux objets », 28 September 2006.

26 Lakoff, A. (2010). Two regimes of global health, *Humanity: An International Journal of Human Rights, Humanitarianism, and Development*, 1(1), 59–79.

27 Dumit, J. (2012). *Drugs for life*, Durham, NC: Duke University Press.

28 Crane, J. (2013). *Scrambling for Africa: AIDS, expertise, and the rise of American global health science*, Ithaca, NY: Cornell University Press.

29 Livingston, J. (2012). *Improvising medicine: An African oncology ward in an emerging cancer epidemic*, Durham: Duke University Press.

30 Barbot, J. (2002). *Les malades en mouvements. La médecine et la science à l'épreuve du sida*, Paris: Editions Balland. See also Epstein, S. (1996). *Impure science: AIDS, activism, and the politics of knowledge*, Berkeley: University of California Press.

31 Frank, A.-G. (1969). *Le développement du sous-développement. L'Amérique latine*, Paris: Maspéro; Amin, S. (1973). *Le développement inégal, Essai sur les formations sociales du capitalisme périphérique*, Paris: Ed. de Minuit; Wallerstein, I (2006). *Comprendre le monde. Introduction à l'analyse des systèmes-monde*, Paris: La Découverte.

32 Van der Hoogte, A. R., Pieters, T. (2015). Quinine, malaria, and the cinchona bureau: Marketing practices and knowledge circulation in a Dutch transoceanic Cinchona–Quinine Enterprise (1920s–30s), *Journal of the History of Medicine and Allied Sciences*, 71/2, 197–225.

7 Diverting flows, contesting power

Subjection: citizen-consumers

If the pharmaceutical logistic regime imposes its politics on the commodity flows that unite consumers, what exactly is the relationship between citizen-consumers and these drug flows? What exactly means citizenship for people living in the world described by Deborah Cowen: that of the "citizenship of stuff"?[1] What is the role of individuals in the configuration? What space is opened up for them in the circulation, the decoding and diversion of flows? Dealing with these questions is one way of responding to the call by the anthropologists João Biehl and Adriana Petryna to

> *also engage crucial questions about the role of the state and the market in global health design and delivery, and investigate what happens to citizenship when politics is reduced to survival – all while maintaining a deep and dynamic sense of people in local worlds.*[2]

Faced with the standardisation of methods imposed by global health institutions and the imposition of powerful and constraining forms of organisation, the social sciences, if they are to remain critical, must necessarily link the global dynamics to the lives and trajectories of people. This chapter will therefore adopt a more ethnographic approach to patients. It will consider a number of stories.

Biehl and Petryna use ethnography to counter the sweeping discourse of global health institutions; I will use it here in another way. My aim is not to undo the discourse of anti-counterfeiting policies – we have seen from the beginning of this book that health activists are succeeding in this without the help of sociologists and anthropologists. What I am trying to do is somewhat different: I will take some narratives of experiences as a basis for categorising the relationships between individuals and logistic regimes, particularly when these relationships result in a deviation – a deviation from drug trajectories and from the norms imposed by the regimes. If the flow of drugs has a political significance, and if the status of drugs is unstable because they are the object of argument and conflict, then we must try to understand what switching

DOI: 10.4324/9781003194767-11

mechanisms make it possible for drugs to abandon, or deviate from, their pre-set trajectories. If, as shown in the last chapter, flows have become a matter of politics and attempts are being made to impose trajectories on them, then any "deviation" of medicines from the pathways assigned to them becomes a form of political resistance or contestation. This is the case no matter whether it is formulated as such or whether it is simply the result of some sort of necessity, sometimes even without people having the impression that they are infringing on any regulation. This means that the *substance* of this resistance has still to be defined.

We have seen that the focus of the logistics regime is primarily on flow. But this has led us to defer examination of the ways in which people fit into the regime. What is the place of the human subject in the logistics regime? What form does this subject take? What are its characteristics? In the logistical regime, the government does not show itself controlling individual behaviour and human bodies; it is first and foremost a technological protection of flows of goods that link citizen–consumers on a global scale. Our right to consume things – that is, to access them and to benefit from them – entails an organisation of flows, a logistics of the movement of goods. In this way, the logistical regime reveals another dimension of our current experience of citizenship and politics, the citizen being not only an actor in a public space but also a consumer in a world of trade. In this particular world, the regime does not define or guarantee the civil rights of citizens or even their socio-economic entitlements; it simply defines and guarantees their access to goods, their connection to commercial flows. The basic substance of the community is made of these flows of goods that the regime supervises and organises.

This image of the citizen–consumer is not particular to pharmaceutical markets. It is the outcome of a historical construction process that has accompanied the growing importance of trade. Protests against the organisation of commercial life, like the formulation of access demands, for example, are old themes. They reveal the porosity of the categories involved and the circulation that takes place between the figures of the consumer and the citizen.[3] At the same time, the citizen-consumer of logistical regimes is a particular historical figure linking citizenship and consumption. It is shaped in the era of generalised logistics and of the colonisation of trajectories: a world in which the overriding purpose is to optimise and integrate flows of goods and to protect the integrity of both goods and flows. The consumer–citizen in logistic regimes is thus confronted with a coding of flows that streamlines and rigidifies their trajectories and excludes stocks that do not correspond to the flows coded. The citizen–consumer's demands, whether as to availability, prices, or circuits take the form of action on the coding and directionality of flows. These demands constitute a form of resistance that draws its strength from the constant connection/disconnection of flows and that manifests itself in the diversion of goods.

Three stories about this divertive activity will help developing this argument. The first is the story of a criminal – or at least that is what it would appear to be in newspaper reports. The second is the story of a hero. The third is the story of ordinary people, the man and woman in the street (or in the fields). These stereotypes should not mislead the reader; I am using them to merely illustrate the construction of trajectory control in logistic regimes. The rules of dominant logistic regimes are put into question by the production of alternative trajectories, meanings and modes of administration. As the status of medicines is contingent and as they can easily get from licit to illicit, it matters to identify the tipping points and the switches where changing conditions happen. Life stories give such tipping points greater visibility; they also show that deviation or diversion do not manifest moral deviance, but instead, they manifest ways of actually contesting logistical regimes.

Black market and flow connections

An important challenge to the pharmaceutical flow system is the black market for medicines. The existence of this market is intrinsically linked to the formal market; each of them feeds the other. In Nairobi, I met Francis, formerly an illicit drug user who had been addicted to both prescription and illegal drugs, but who now was "off" them. In the late 1990s, he had worked as a sales representative for a company that imported and distributed medicines in Kenya, mainly non-prescription drugs, but also some on prescription. In the course of this activity, Francis had developed an addiction to diazepam, fenolbarbitol, barbiturates, rohypnol, and codeine, which he often consumed mixing them. He told me that he had financed his own consumption by selling drugs on the black market to individuals and also directly to pharmacies. After selling his own company's medicines on the black market for some time, he had come into contact with other dealers:

> *After a while, I found myself tied to people who were selling drugs. I was only selling a few drugs here and there. They would get one or two cartons directly from the port and would then have to dispose of them. Importers brought drugs into the market legally, but dealers stole them and sold them on the black market. Big thieves would steal directly from the port.*[4]

After this addiction to pharmaceuticals, Francis moved on to heroin. For some time, he switched between heroin addiction and very heavy pharmaceutical treatment and eventually left his job after stealing more drugs than usual. It was to take him years to put an end to these addictions and overcome the problems that they had generated.

Francis' story brings together three issues. First of all, of course, the story of his addiction or addictions and how he developed them, switching from one addiction to another. Then there is the connection between the markets – the informal market and the official one. Thirdly, there is an issue without which Francis' story would not take on its full meaning: the order of markets, their organisation, and the interpretation Francis puts on the order of the

Kenyan pharmaceutical market. These three issues form a nexus, knotting together two types of connection (addiction hook-ups, market connections) and the encompassing order that allows these connections to be made.

To start with the history of his addictions: Francis had become addicted to heroin after being addicted to medicines. His dependence on prescription drugs can only be understood as a series of "trips" between the *illicit consumption of illegal* products and the *illegal* consumption of legal products. These trips constitute a series of connections between different addictions:

> *For example, people will start with heroin, and then they'll switch to analgesics. Then they come back to heroin…A problem is that when you are addicted to prescription drugs, you can't always get access to them, so you move between drugs according to what happens to be available. Sometimes it's easier to get an illegal medicine than a legal one!*

Studies of drug use in Kenya often give measurements of this type of circulation, highlighting the frequent use of prescription drugs for recreational purposes, combining them with other drugs or with prescription medicines.[5] The use of prescription medicines to satisfy addictions is less frequent in Kenya than the use of alcohol, cannabis, *khat*, glue, heroin, or cocaine. However, when prescription drugs are used, it is almost always in combination with one or more other addictions. Diazepam (also known as *tap-tap*) and rohypnol are regarded as emerging consumptions, increasingly widespread thanks to their availability in upscale social environments, though not only in these.[6]

Linking prescription drugs to other addictions leads to specific problems in treating the addiction:

> *Prescription drug addiction is really the worst thing. It's almost easier to treat heroin addiction. Because [in the case of medication] you change all the time, you switch between very different medications. The other problem is that the medicines, whether you combine them or not, aren't like the heroin, where you tell yourself… whoa… it's heroin, it's hyper dangerous…With prescription medicines you don't have the same way of thinking at all…I had two suicides close to me with prescription drugs, people die because of the addictions to prescription medicines, it really gets them high. You become a zombie. And besides, it takes a really long time to get out of it. Anyway, you can't just replace drugs with other drugs or more drugs […] I used about five different medicines all the time. I really started to like this. I'd go home, get ready, start sleeping, and then I'd get this huge high. The next day I went to work, people saw that I wasn't OK, too medicated, they'd send me home. One day I figured it out and thought, "That's enough of this, I'm going to do heroin." Then I went to work the next day and they said, "Wow, you look so much better!" (laughs). Of course I went on, until I stole and ran away […].*

Connecting addictions to one another also entail another type of connection: that between legal and illegal markets. Though in Francis's mind there is no continuity between these two markets, in fact, as he sees it, they are simply constantly interconnected by a reorientation of flows: this makes it possible in particular to finance an addiction by means of diversion operations: *"My first job was a pharma rep. I was working for a company. For a while, as I was an addict, I 'd sell a little bit of my stock on the black market*". Connections such as these are not limited to individuals however; in general, they show that the illegal market and the legal one never cease interacting: illegal vendors are in contact with legal sellers, as legal storage and distribution sites such as retail pharmacies constantly supply the illegal market, and the same medicines find their way onto the market for either legal or illegal use. As Francis explains, "*Drug dealers have got their connections with pharmacists*". This type of connection shows that registered medicines provided by the formal sector, whether private or public, can easily find their way into the illegal circuit:

> *"Medicines found on the black market are medicines that have been stolen from the private circuit, either from hospital shelves or just directly, when they arrive in port". And "sleeping pills are easy to find on the black market".*

Connections are not made in an obvious way, however; circulation between the domains is not completely fluid; there is some friction. According to Francis, the paucity of resources allocated to the enforcement of compliance with regulations facilitates the flow of medicines from the legal to the illegal sector considerably. All that it needs is a modicum of "facilitation" such as financial gain or a little pressure:

> *It's going on all over the place. The drugs I was reselling, selling them directly to people or to other pharmacists.*
>
> *Question: But why to pharmacists, who could get the drugs legally?*
>
> *Answer: Because of course I was selling them much more cheaply than anyone else. I had the drugs at my disposal free of charge, all I had to do was sell them for cheap, for example, at half the wholesale price.*

Or:

> *Yes, today it may be a bit harder to get the medicine without a prescription at the pharmacy, but if you just pretend to phone a doctor, people give you whatever you want....*

In Francis's story, two different forms of oscillation between the licit and the illicit are intertwined. On the one hand, there is his addiction that alternates between licit and other drugs; on the other hand, there is the circulation of medicines between the legal and illegal markets, in which he himself was a participant, selling on the side in order to finance his personal consumption medicines of which he was in charge. But this dual oscillation makes sense only in the light of Francis' ongoing interpretation of his own case, which involves a broader understanding of the pharmaceutical market. In the interview Francis repeatedly says about pharmaceuticals, "*It's an industry worth billions of dollars*"! This makes it particularly hard to combat the addictions it generates. In fact, from Francis's point of view, the black market is not an aberration; it merely follows a logic that should be exposed:

> *Every market has an order. Even the black market has its own implicit order. It sounds messy at first glance, but it may well be that unscrupulous people order directly on the black market.*

However, this order exists only in relation to a larger market that encompasses it: the official market for prescription and non-prescription medicines. The first reason for this is the "lack" of regulation:

> *Here, we are just beginning to straighten up the sale of medicines. Otherwise, as before, anyone could go in anywhere, ask for any treatment and get it. Now we have to pay a bit of attention, because there are beginning to be measures – but we are still a long way from [real] regulation.*

This "lack of regulation" does not consist solely in the ease with which one can obtain products; it is also linked to other lacks: the lack of qualified pharmacists, the lack of supervision in authorising pharmacies to operate, and the drug vendors' lack of knowledge of the goods they distribute:

> *There are not enough pharmacists across the country to staff the pharmacies. Most pharmacies are run only by "pharm. Techs" …sometimes just a cousin of the owner's…a guy who doesn't have any idea what he's selling.*

Furthermore, this lack of regulation is sustained by competition among retailers, who have increased and multiplied to meet the growing consumption of medicines and the increasing penetration of biomedicine into Kenyan consumers' habits: "*Everyone is competing on the same market…prices are so absurdly different…And so it's also leaving an opening for a lot of drugs on the black market…*".

Another reason is the ratio – altogether unreasonable – between the value of pharmaceutical goods and the wages of the staff whose job, like Francis's, is to transport these goods:

> *The problem is also that people like me have relatively low wages, but they're carrying a very high value in terms of products, so we sell, we bring the black market to life this way.*

A final reason is the lack of awareness among doctors. Pushed by industry, they sometimes prescribe as many drugs as the industry prompts them to do:

> *Before, doctors used to prescribe valium just like that, like biscuits. They prescribed it for example in cases of alcohol addiction, and like that they went and produced other addictions…*

According to Francis, the *raison d' être* of the black market is linked to the relationship between the very low salaries of the people who sell medicines, the competition between retail pharmacies, which were increasing in number at the time, and the high – though very variable – value of medicines, all of which encourage recourse to the black market. Also involved were the responsibility of doctors and of the industry that, in order to generate more profits, continued to put more and more "legal drugs" on the market, even if they ended up on the black market. In Francis' story, the existence of the black market is due in practice to flow connections: flows of drugs re-routed, away from the official market. But these flow connections are themselves determined by the conditions (wage levels, the number of retailers, competition, instability, and price variability) under which the official market operates. The existence of the black market is also based on the connection between the legal consumption favoured by suppliers of medicines and the illegal consumption that results from oversupply in distribution on a growing market. Thus Francis' story illustrates the way in which the dominant logistical regime, because of its inherent contradictions, opens up new flow connections that lead to the emergence and supply of alternative markets, such as the black market. On the one hand, it decodes and frees, multiplying the consumption of pharmaceuticals; on the other hand, it rejects addictive consumption and parallel selling practices, declaring them illegal. Individuals who disobey this injunction become illicit – but in doing so, take up the liberation of flows by making new connections.

Buyers clubs and flow diversions

Another way of contesting the logistical regime by promoting alternative connections is described in Greg Jefferys' journal of his trip to India (published on the Internet). Jefferys, an Australian, in August 2014, discovered at the age of sixty that he was infected with the hepatitis C virus. The infection had probably been contracted many years before and had been dormant until then. In the second half of 2014, Jefferys began to find out about the different ways of getting rid of the virus. The most common treatment had a lot of side effects and its success rate was only 60%. He also found out, in the course of his research, mainly on the Internet, that there was another, more effective treatment: sofosbuvir. However, this very recent treatment was still under review for market approval. The Australian regulatory authorities were considering it but had not yet arrived at a conclusion. He decided to wait for it to be approved. Meanwhile, he completely changed his diet to relieve his liver as much as possible. Quite soon after taking this decision, he heard that sofosbuvir was now undergoing clinical trials. Not yet available in Australia, it could be purchased in the United States – though at a prohibitive price: $84,000 for a 3-month course of treatment. When the drug was being tested in trials in Melbourne and Sidney, Jefferys tried to enlist as a participant, but he was not considered ill enough to take part. The doctor in charge of the trial explained that the medicine would probably be put on sale in Australia in a few months' time, but that, given its high price, access to it would certainly be difficult. It was unlikely that the Australian government would fund treatment for all patients. By this time, Jefferys was beginning to despair of getting treatment before his condition became much worse. It was then that he learned from a friend that the treatment would soon be available in India for a fraction of the price of the original branded drug.

From that moment on, Jefferys entered the distribution labyrinth in search of a way to receive the Indian treatment. First of all, he discovered that "Australian law allows an Australian to bring in a three month supply of a drug from India"[7] – provided that a prescription is produced together with the consignment; but Australian doctors were not allowed to prescribe the medicine, as it had not yet been authorised in Australia. Jefferys then thought about buying the drug online, but he did not have much confidence in this way of going about it. So he decided rather to go to India himself. He commented on the price factor as follows:

> *Now here I will be totally honest. The trip will end up costing me around $3,000+. I have paid for that with my credit card because I do not have that kind of money hanging around. A couple of friends also helped me out a bit (thanks again). But what are the alternative options??? Like most people, I could not afford the $90,000 for the treatment. I now knew I was not going to get onto a trial and I was not going to get the treatment through the government health system. So what do I do? Do I wait around until I develop liver cancer or severe cirrhosis and get sick enough to get treatment? Or do I go to India and (hopefully) get it sorted that way? It seemed like a no-brainer to me?*[8]

Even so, the decision to buy a flight ticket was by no means simple. Jefferys would use his savings to pay for the flight and the treatment – but he still had no idea of exactly how he would actually get the treatment.

When his symptoms worsened, Jefferys finally went to India. A few days before he left, his general practitioner told him about the role of Indian drug manufacturers in the HIV epidemic, pointing out a certain historical continuity between situations. The experience of Jefferys resonated with another era.

> *My GP worked in an AIDS clinic in Africa during the early 1990's and he told me how, because of the high cost of the HIV drugs then, getting HIV*

> *was basically a death sentence for most of his patients. Then the Indian government had decided to ignore the patents on HIV drugs and started manufacturing and supplying cheap HIV drugs for India and also its African neighbors. My doctor said that all of a sudden his clinic was able to help people with HIV.*[9]

For Jefferys, the decision was nonetheless difficult as India was a largely unknown healthcare territory. While on the plane, Jefferys wondered what would happen once he reached Chennai:

> *As I drift into that aeroplane half sleep I find myself wondering/worrying what will happen when I wake up tomorrow and go out to find a doctor in Chennai ??? Is there going to be some kind [of] red tape nightmare getting the prescription? What if I have to see a specialist and cannot get an appointment within the time I have? What if they do not accept the Australian test results and want to do their own? There are so many things that might stall things. I'm only in India for seven days. Maybe I should have given myself more time?*

When Jefferys arrived in India, his experience of medical tourism began. There were complications due to the novelty of the treatment and a complete lack of guidelines and formal procedures. Everything happened in a relatively unexpected way. When he landed in Chennai, Jefferys was put in contact with another patient, who advised him to see a gastroenterologist who worked at one of the most important local hospitals. However, he had to go there the very same day: the doctor was about to leave for two weeks, and Jefferys was staying in India for only ten days. This doctor would give him a prescription, and after that, it would be easy to get the medication. When he saw the doctor, it turned out that he did not have all the documents he needed – the Fibroscan results were missing. The doctor was about to leave, but they agreed on an arrangement: the doctor gave him the prescription on condition that he promised to produce the fibroscan examination the next day.

After this first step, Jefferys discovered a little more about the complexity of Indian drug distribution networks in treatments for a disease like hepatitis C. Once the tests were completed, he tried to get in touch with the drug distributors and obtained the phone number of one of them, S., who

> *... explained again to me, in greater detail, how different the distribution of pharmaceuticals is in India. He explained that the Indian pharmacies rarely carry stock of the very expensive drugs such as Sofosbuvir and that it is common for the Companies to have a local distributor who one can buy direct from.*

He found himself in contact with two firms distributing the medicine (Mylan and Cipla) and, realising that telephone communication was complicated by language differences, he tried to meet people face-to-face; this took him a few more days. Eventually, he was able to place his order. He chose to buy sofosbuvir under the brand name Sovaldi, paying a little more than for the generic version, but as his prescription indicated Sovaldi, he wanted to avoid possible problems with Australian customs on his return. When his order arrived, it was not delivered by the distributor's agent but by a wholesaler. Above all, however, it turned out that it was not possible to obtain three bottles of Sovaldi (the complete treatment) because of the anti-diversion practices set up by the manufacturers. After some moments of intense anxiety, Jefferys managed to obtain not the two extra bottles, not under Sovaldi's brand, but under MyHep, the generic version of the drug marketed by Mylan, all paid for in cash. As he wrote in his blog, Jefferys had to take into account the complexity and specificity of distribution practices, especially as he was unfamiliar with the formal process, discovering it only day by day.

> *The tricky thing with India is that things are done very differently here. It is not simply a case of taking your script down to the local pharmacy, handing it over the counter, waiting ten minutes and walking out. It's a different system, not a worse system or less reliable system, just different, and, like learning a new language, at first it is difficult but once understood and mastered it's not a problem.*[10]

Greg Jefferys flew home with the treatment, started it, and was cured in three months. The success of his experience was widely publicised, thanks to his blog and some local press articles published after his return. He became the "medical tourist" for hepatitis C. His story recalls similar HIV situations[11] involving imports, reported elsewhere; in Jefferys' case, however, it involves a patient from a wealthy country who travels to India for treatment that would be financially unavailable to him at home. Above all, this story shows how a patient can enter the supply chain to get a drug in an unconventional way: how individuals find their way into the logistics regime and how their initiative is based on a concrete intervention in the distribution system.

This is not, however, the end of the story. When Jefferys got back to Australia, he began to receive messages from people in different parts of the world who wanted to obtain the medicine. His experience took on a collective significance. It suggests that we view engagement with the logistics regime not only as an individual action but also as an example of a broader collective practice that challenges certain forms of organisation. One extension of Jefferys' action is of particular interest: the buyers club.

In the film *The Dallas Buyers Club*, Matthew McConaughey plays Ron Woodroof, a real-life character who in the late 1980s set up a buying group, the Dallas Buyers Club that imported many HIV drugs into the United States, including some that were not registered in the USA, leading to conflict with the Food and Drugs Administration. In his history of the fight against HIV,

Steven Epstein recalls that in 1987 there were about ten similar groups (also known as "guerrilla clinics") in the United States, as well as some in Canada and in London.[12] The basic idea of a buyers club is to organise illegal imports of medicines because (for reasons involving registration or pricing) treatment is unavailable in the importing country. The activity of these groups is based on access to health activism and generates little or no commercial profit. However, each treatment imported in this way can represent a financial loss for the patent holder. Naturally, pharmaceutical companies are well aware of the financial risk to which they are exposed by differentiated pricing policies and the geographical restrictions that accompany them. As a result, they tolerate some leaks as an integral part of their strategy. The boundary between "some leaks" and "major leaks", however, is not always easy to determine. As Gilead's Executive Vice President of Corporate and Medical Affairs has said, "*Some leakage is a given, our goal isn't to stop it 100 per cent; if we wanted that, we'd do it the draconian way and not be in the country at all. But we do want to stop large leaks*".[13] A few months later, however, a report from the firm warned against the possibility of obtaining counterfeit goods through purchasing clubs; this shows that its managers were increasingly worried about the loss of revenue resulting from this practice.[14] Interestingly, buyers clubs have not been restricted to Northern countries. They also emerged in other countries during the 1990s and early 2000s providing HIV treatments that, for reasons of cost and availability,[15] were otherwise unavailable. This practice spread in several directions: from Brazil and India to sub-Saharan Africa, but mainly to the latter from Europe. It has also become common in HIV groups, as illustrated by the remark of an Indian activist: "*Since hepatitis C came up, this thing [buyers clubs] comes up. But I have been doing this for the last ten-fifteen years*"*!*[16]

In several respects, however, the case of hepatitis C drugs indicates that to a certain extent, the practice has been reviving. Firstly, the use of the Internet makes it much easier to set up networks of buyers and distributors. As another activist involved in an Indian buyers club explained to me: "*This is the beauty of Internet. We are people from different continents, taking part in the same project. We have met only once but we managed to set up a very efficient organisation*".[17] The Internet makes it possible to connect as many people as possible to the buyers club without having to plan travel. Greg Jefferys, for example, offers on his blog to put interested patients in touch with his contacts in India to order inexpensive medicines. He also points out that many people contact him from different countries around the world.

The second aspect of this renewal is the pressure that anti-Hepatitis C groups have put on governments by threatening to resort to buyers clubs because of the enormous price differences and the selection procedures set up by health insurance systems. In France, for example, the *SOS Hépatites* group has published an open letter to the Ministry of Health, threatening to resort to parallel imports if nothing is organised soon:

> *We have conducted tests showing that there are no difficulties involved in importing generic drugs on an individual basis. We have therefore imported generic treatments. SOS Hépatites is always at the disposal of health authorities to facilitate further investigations. We are well aware that the import of medicines is regulated by law, and we are also well aware of potential counterfeiting issues. You bear the responsibility. At present, there is no response to these patients who are unfairly being denied access to care.*[18]

The third aspect of this revival was explained to me by another activist in an interview that showed that the fight for access to medicines also depends on the dynamic development of new strategies:

> *I think a lot of activists who are part of anti-HIV movements got institutionalized. They get so stuck on "quality issues" that they cannot move. But new people are coming who have no idea about all these rules, and they say: "OK the medicines are available let's go and get them". And that's what I really like about Hep C because a lot of us in the HIV movement are always waiting for the drugs to be prequalified by MSF or WHO before even offering to try to get it for persons who are dying. With Hep C these questions, the fear of quality and rules have disappeared and the new activists don't conform to rules, because we have no time and we have to make choices now.*[19]

Finally, it is important to stress that the work of buyer clubs can go so far as to promote certain ways of composing medicines, in particular by importing only the active ingredients (and not the finished products) so as to compose the medicine once it is on site. Jefferys explains:

> *Up until December 2015 [before availability of Indian generics] a lot of people did take the Hep C API treatment option and imported APIs from China, mostly from Mesochem, a large company that specialises in making the APIs for all kinds of drugs, including Hep C medicines. Mesochem made the pure active ingredients; 99.9% pure Sofosbuvir and Ledipasvir and Daclatasvir.*[20]

For these reasons, in the case of hepatitis C, organising buyers clubs provides "diversion" – meaning significant political commitment – within the logistics regime governing the circulation of medicines.

A central issue for buyers clubs is this: just how does one create a diversion in a logistical system? One activist told me that in September 2015, he had begun sending generic Indian sofosbuvir abroad. By the time of our interview in May 2016, he was sending about 100 treatments per month to patients around the world: in European countries, South America, Central Asia, and elsewhere. He lost no time in stressing the importance of logistics know-how in this type of activity.

> *What helped me in running the buyers club is the work I have been doing in my former organization on the logistics of medicines, the knowledge I got there. And that helped me to go up and assist other patients too.*[21]

Most of the time spent was devoted to finding out: (1) how to organise transfers and deposit the money; and (2) how to get treatment across a country's borders.

> *For instance if you are asking from Serbia it can be difficult. But if you have a friend in Romania it's easier: I can send the medicines there. Many Serbian people have friends in Romania, then they can come to Romania and go back. Because the customs officers will not allow the medicines alone to get in Serbia, even with a prescription. So I see with the Serbian patients if they have friends that can help them in Romania and then I send the packages.*

Furthermore, if the medicine is being imported, this probably means that it has to be exported from India and that the consignments have to be organised in such a way as not to arouse suspicion in customs authorities:

> *From where I am based now, we are getting from three ports. It goes through different customs officers and that is a very good point. I also segregated my parcels via different transporters in order to make them less visible.*

More importantly, this logistics activity is seen as a way of circumventing the restrictions imposed by both pharmaceutical companies and governments:

> *I told my family: "Bear very clear in mind that I am not dealing with narcotics. These are completely legal drugs. What we are fighting is the geographical restrictions which have been laid down by the Big Pharma". […] I know there are grey areas through which I'm working but it has to be done. Someone has to take the sword in his hands. It's not possible to sit back and relax and to let the companies or the capitalists make the rules and regulations on who survives and who doesn't.*

Patients in foreign countries also take part in these logistics arrangements, becoming part of a collective movement. Our interviewee explained:

> *My contacts are some persons. For instance, in the UK, one hepatitis C patient came to know me via another friend and now he is arranging with other people from his country. It is similar in other countries.*

One example is the case of Carine, a French patient who received treatment before the French government declared universal coverage for the medicine.[22] Carine was 15 years old, in 2013, when she was diagnosed with hepatitis

C. She waited for two and a half years, became weaker and depressive. But she followed the activity of hepatitis C groups on several online forums. She learned about Greg Jefferys' initiative and decided to get the drugs the same way. Initially, her parents were not convinced; they did not want to break the law and were also concerned about the quality of drugs that had not been obtained legally. But Carine managed to convince them. Through a forum, she contacted someone who obtained the first part of the treatment through a contact in England. Only two-thirds of the treatment was available in this way, however. A few weeks later, she went to Paris with her father and boyfriend to obtain the rest of the treatment – this time through another internet contact: a French person who was returning from a trip to India had agreed to bring the rest of the treatment in her luggage.[23] In this story, diversion from the logistics regime is far from straightforward: as drugs tend to move segment by segment, following different routes or circuits, individuals have to catch them at certain nodal points. At the same time, however, in the context of over-coded markets, the very irregularity of the trajectories makes it possible to recombine the conditions of access.

The Jefferys story and buyers clubs are both examples of a way of engaging logistic regimes critically. Both bring out the importance of situating contestation in supply chains and distribution channels if one is to overcome the flow dividers introduced by the logistic regime. Seen in this perspective, it is the trajectories of medicines that determine access to them. The trajectories are formed in this way by IP laws, production capacities, and territorial licensing agreements. Individuals, however, can engage critically with this assemblage by creating their own circuits from the rules and tools available for other logistic regimes (postal and transport organisations, international flights, etc.). Their intervention constitutes a second challenge to the pharmaceutical logistics regimes whose specificity is to "divert" or "maintain" different flows and not to connect them. Whereas Francis connects the flows of the legal market with those of the illegal market and legal consumption practices with illegal consumption practices, Jefferys and buyers clubs divert flows designed for certain geographical areas to different geographical areas. Their action consists not in connecting flows but in diverting them.

Self-medication and flow disruptions

Asha has tuberculosis. She lives in Bihar, India, in a village whose inhabitants belong to a low caste. It is far from the road and there is no electricity. When I meet Asha, she begins by explaining that she has health problems and tells me about the difficulties she is up against. Then she shows me a box of drugs with the DOTS (*Directly Observed Therapy*) stamp on it, the official mark of treatment for tuberculosis.[24] Because of the development of strong resistances to TB treatment in India – which is attributed in part to bad observance – the treatment has to be given in the presence of healthcare personnel – or to be monitored regularly by the latter. When Asha opens her box of drugs, it is obvious that the treatment has not been properly followed: the aluminium packaging is only half-opened, some tablets have been taken and others not. Asha explains, however, that from time to time, a community health worker visits the village, but that it is too far from the road for the worker to come as regularly as she should; when she does come, she does not take the time to talk to Asha as much as she should.

Bihar is the third most populous state in India, with 104 million inhabitants. It is the second most rural state: less than 11% of the population live in cities. It is also by far the least literate state in India, with a literacy rate of 61.8% (56.7% of married women aged 15–49 are illiterate). Only 10.7 per cent of women work (i.e., are paid for their work), compared to 27 per cent in India as a whole; per capita income in Bihar is less than half the Indian average.[25] In this context, access to health care is particularly problematic and the quality of the care is often very poor, especially in terms of access to medicines in the public system.

It is *gaon ka* (village) doctors, often called "quacks" by both formal health workers and patients, who provide healthcare and medicine in villages; most of those I met had neither a license nor a diploma. They had not been trained to prescribe drugs or even to sell them. Yet, they administered everything from vitamins to antibiotics, acted as first-aid providers, and referred patients to the public or private system when they were unable to cure them. They did recognise a division of labour (for example, between themselves and public hospitals); but their main concern was simply to be able to continue practising:

> *We do not accept patients who we cannot cure. We refer such patients. We are very social people and are connected to the society. Cannot take risk, we are also afraid. If the patient is not getting cured for 4–5 days, it comes upon us. So there is risk.*[26]

The situation of village doctors, as providers of healthcare and medicines gives them a special position in the pharmaceutical regulation system; they can use this to circumvent restrictive regulations:

> *Question: Do you need a license even in villages to run a medical shop? Answer: Of course, if you run a medical store even in a village, you need license for it. If you sell higher antibiotics, you need a refrigerator and a concrete building with proper store facility. Q: Do you have a refrigerator? A: Yes. Q: Do you have a license? A: No, this is not even a shop. We are rural medical practitioners. This is being done as a social work. Q: Is there some certificate for RMPs? A: Yes, for RMPs a rural medicine certificate is given. It is given from Patna. You have to complete a six months course for that. We haven't done any such course.*[27]

Most of them obtain their medicines from local retail stores, but some of them are in contact with wholesalers in the district capital. Many of the village doctors I met had direct links with retail drug vendors. In some cases, one family member worked as a doctor while another worked in the adjoining pharmacy.

The village doctors are far from being the only actors in the health system working outside the regulatory framework. In particular, the role of retail drug vendors is important. With neither diplomas nor licenses, they have no legal right to sell drugs. There are also the retail vendors who do not have qualifications, and are therefore not registered as pharmacists, but who have nonetheless been licensed as pharmacists. This is quite common and many of the retail vendors we interviewed said that they had been able to obtain a license through friends or family members who were properly registered. In case of this sort, interpretation of the Drugs and Cosmetics Act is very loose indeed: under the Act, prescription drugs must be sold "under the direct supervision of a registered pharmacist". One wonders just how "direct" this supervision can actually be when the official licensee lives hundreds of kilometres from the shop of the actual seller. Next comes the category of duly registered and licensed pharmacists. Only one of the drug vendors we met during our survey was in this category. Yet for all categories, the sale of prescription medicines can only take place "*on prescription of registered medical practitioners*" and "*[t]he supply, otherwise than by way of wholesale dealing, [...] of any drug supplied on the prescription of a Registered Medical Practitioner shall be effected only by or under the personal supervision of a 3 [registered Pharmacist].*" (Drugs and Cosmetics Act, 65, 2). Yet all the persons we questioned in the shops admitted that they sold medicines such as antibiotics without asking to see a prescription. In their answers, sellers would combine terms such as "sell", "give", and "prescribe":

> *There are many patients who I know that certain medicines would suit to them. So, I give medicines to them. If I give them medicines and they are not cured, it will be a problem. With God's Grace, most of the times, whatever medicines I prescribe they work on patients. And obviously, if certain medicine is meant for specific symptoms, they will work.*[28]

This multiplicity of categories of sales shows in the first place that the pharmaceutical logistics regime, intended to maximise the value generated by the circulation of medicines, does not entail ensuring access under proper conditions by the poorest population groups. These groups enjoy the lowest degree of State protection; they are not treated in the same way as groups that are better off or better integrated into distribution channels. In certain situations, there is no access to medicines except under conditions that are illegal: doctors and pharmacists without diplomas or licences are sometimes the only professionals available to certain patients seeking medication. In this context, entry into the illicit market is neither the result of deviant social behaviour (such as drug abuse) nor of a form of access activism (as in purchasing clubs). It is a reaction, generally accepted by everyone – government officials, pharmaceutical companies, and patients – to the loopholes in the logistics system. In a sense, what we find here is not so much a matter of illicit "connection" or "diversion" as simply a rupture in the logistics regime. This is also why practices such as self-medication should not be analysed as a breaching practice or as an offence to medical norms. It is sometimes the simple result of the holes in the structure and rather than manifesting deviance, it can manifest conformity with the rules of the regime.[29]

Rupture can be observed here in different ways. On the one hand, Asha follows her treatment discontinuously in a process that ends in complete cessation. The break is in observance. On the other hand, actors who are supposed to carry out the assemblage of the logistics regime – for example, public drug supply institutions, doctors, retail pharmacists – have in some cases simply disappeared and are being replaced by people without proper qualifications. This makes it difficult for us to establish whether the disruption should be attributed to the patients involved, or whether to people who enter the distribution system illegally, or whether it is due to the regime which confines itself to a limited space and leaves it to individuals to manage compliance, prescription, and provisioning as best as they can. This last example thus highlights another facet of the criticism and challenges that emerges within the logistics regime. It is neither the deviant figure of the drug user nor the heroic figure of the activist that is causing diversions of flow. Rather, it is the figure of the patient who has been abandoned by the State, whom the free medicines in the public system cannot reach, the patient of whom the institutions have never fully taken charge, and who is being supplied on a private market by ersatz doctors and pharmacists who, according to Sarah Pinto,[30] are trying, so to speak, to connect the logistical points and cobble together an *ersatz* practice of medicine. This last example illustrates an ambiguous mode of critical engagement with regard to the logistical regime: the rupture of flows.

Electric lives and technopolitical circuitry

These different situations call into question the contemporary logistic regime – or at least the fantasies entertained by firms and international public health institutions seeking absolute control of the trajectories followed by pharmaceuticals. Consumers and users deviate from the norm by committing financially motivated offences, by militant acts, by acts of self-medication, and by recourse to unqualified prescribers and unlicensed retailers; these actions call into question the prescribed pathways. From a normative point of view, however, it is impossible to treat these diversions as a single bloc. A priori, the situations of a drug user, an access activist, or a Bihari farm worker's wife who breaks off her treatment are not comparable. On the other hand, however, from an analytical point of view – that taken up by a critique of the pharmaceutical logistics regime – all of these "irregularities" participate in the same movement, challenging the logic of coding and the set trajectories that are specific to the logistic regime. Each in his or her own way, these subversives reveal the impossibility of assigning definitive trajectories, the inevitable persistence of leaks, overflows and lapses in the logistic regime.

This takes us back once again to the question of flows in Deleuze and Guattari's work. In the conflict between customary practices, the State, and a market controlled by the logistics regime, what exactly is at stake? State and the market "decode" (i.e., release from customary and legal limitations) the flow of medicines, loosening on to the market more and more products in order to provide a universal response to disease. These products are nonetheless manufactured on various production sites under standardised, controlled conditions. The flows are constantly "recoded" or "over-coded": flows remain subject to the regulatory powers of the State and international organisations. This regulatory power takes over from the axiomatic commercial power of multinational firms, a power enforced by laws on intellectual property. But besides these decoding/ recoding/ over-coding operations carried out by State and market, running parallel to them, there is another development: individuals are prompted by restrictions to decode the flows in order to redirect them. Modifying the standard connections and connecting them to different flows, this has outcomes that are incompatible with the logistics regime: overflowing channels (leading to intoxication); flows pent up by moral imperatives; and flows stemming from unplanned or unexpected assemblages and operations. This unforeseen decoding activity is possibly linked to forms of desire that are considered deviant by State authorities; in such cases, the flows are not only diverted but also connected to other flows. This process can be linked to the need for access: flows have to be decoded and diverted to meet needs that cannot be met within the official system of flows mapped out by the State-and-market industrial complex. In other words, we can link this new decoding to failures in the logistical regime, or at least to its inability to implement fully its project of maximising flows and of covering the entire population. What is revealed here is a primary decoding operation – the release of flows – that has broken down. In all of these cases, individuals who question the intense decoding and recoding activity of States and markets under the logistics regime carry out the subsequent diversion.

This interpretation can be pushed further with the notion of the "drug circuit" that the anthropologist Kristin Peterson uses in her thinking drug flows in Nigeria. This term can describe two different levels of drug circulation. Firstly, the drug circuit is that followed by the drug as an object of logistical organisation in a health system. Here "drug circuit" can simply mean "supply chain".[31] But "drug circuit" can also mean the circulation of the drug in the user's body once it has been taken and absorbed. The term "circuit", however, also brings to mind another idea: that of an electrical circuit. The drug circuit can be subject to a number of modifications and derivations; in the course of circulation, neither the object transported by the logistics system nor the molecule circulating in the animal organism keeps its initial properties and effects. Connections, "hijackings", and other diversions carried out by individuals or institutions constantly change the organisation of flows on both geographical and physiological levels. Faced with drastic control of the trajectories of flows, society is inventive enough to decode, branch, disconnect, and condense, inventing new channels, and generating new flows. Under the logistic regime, illicit medicine expresses, at least in part, an "electrical" aspect of people's lives.

The description of the "politics of life" implicit in the logistics regime I have been describing should take into account the reactions of individuals confronted with a systematic way of managing, distributing, and dispensing medicines.[32] Mostly, drug users are thought of merely as one end of the drug chain. Usually, they are not fully aware of the prescriptions, the rules governing dispensing, and the observance that pertain to the medicines they take, any more than they are aware of their composition or the paths they have followed: the logistics and the pharmacokinetics. Both of these fields lie to a large extent beyond the reach of their attention, remaining foreign to them. Yet consumers, by simply getting on with their own lives, constantly disturb the prevailing patterns. The dream inherent in the logistics regime is that of citizen-consumers mechanically linked to the treatment production system; yet reality constantly interrupts the dream by waking the circuitry up. There is not a single coding that is definitive; nothing remains stable, not a circuit that can be maintained unaltered: the intervention of individuals within the logistics regime results in an incessant redirection and redefinition of its flows. Consumers' behaviour patterns challenge a particular form of imperialism – an imperialism that no longer aims primarily at extracting wealth from nature or disposing of excess reserves, but rather at keeping control of movements, their volume, density, value, and significance, imposing its patterns on people's lives and on life itself. This "colonisation of trajectories", as I have called it, makes a show of a certain liberalism: everything must circulate, must move! However, if it circulates a little too much, if it flutters or stutters a little too noticeably, the underlying system reveals its real purpose, resuming its overt control of the flux. "In the interests of public health" of course, it stands to reason! But achieving this turns out to be an interminable task. Streams escape because they are constantly being decoded, diverted, connected to unauthorised channels. Diversionary initiatives of all sorts spring up, challenging the overall logistics regime, and its colonisation of trajectories. What shows up in the world of flows governed by logistics is the electrical dimension of life, indissolubly a world of flows that escape from logistics. It is this life that underlies the conflicts between different conceptions of flows, and between competing practices of flow orientation and management. It is the life that emerges in the loopholes in the complex intertwining of the movements of merchandise.

Notes

1 Cowen, D. (2014). *The deadly life of logistics: Mapping violence in global trade*. Minneapolis: University of Minnesota Press.

2 J. Biehl & A. Petryna (Eds.) (2013). *When people come first. Critical studies in global health*. Princeton, Princeton University Press. pp. 15–16.

3 F. Trentmann (Ed.) (2006). *The making of the consumer. Knowledge, power and identity in the modern world*. Berg; Trespeuch, M., & Steiner, P. (dir.) *Marchés contestés: Quand le marché rencontre la morale*. Toulouse: Presses Universitaires du Mirail.

4 Interview of Francis, Nairobi, 15 September 2016.

5 Kahuthia-Gathu, R., *et al.* (2013). Trends and emerging drugs in Kenya: A case study in Mombasa and Nairobi County. *Journal of Applied Biosciences*, 67, pp. 5308–5325.

6 Kahuthia-Gathu, R., *et al.* (2013) Trends and emerging drugs in Kenya: A case study in Mombasa and Nairobi County. *Journal of Applied Biosciences*, 67, pp. 5308–5325.

7 Jefferys, G. India to the rescue (again). Retrieved from www.hepmag.com/blog/india-to-the-rescue (originally published upon My HepC Diary).

8 Jefferys, G. "India to the rescue (again)", www.hepmag.com/blog/india-to-the-rescue (originally published upon My HepC Diary)

9 Jefferys, G. Countdown to leaving for India. Retrieved from www.hepmag.com/blog/countdown-to-leaving-for-india (originally published upon My HepC Diary).

10 Jefferys, G. The medicine is out there but I can't afford it. Retrieved from www.hepmag.com/blog/cant-afford-hepatitis-c-medicine (originally published on My HepC Diary).

11 Nguyen, V.-K. (2010). *The republic of therapy: Triage and sovereignty in West Africa's time of AIDS*. Durham: Duke University Press.

12 Epstein, S. (1996). *Impure science: AIDS, activism, and the politics of knowledge*. Berkeley: University of California Press.

13 McNeil, D. G. (2015). Curing Hepatitis C, in an experiment the size of Egypt. *New York Times*, 15 December 2015, Retrieved from www.nytimes.com/2015/12/16/health/hepatitis-c-treatment-egypt.html.

14 Dandekar, V. (2017). Gilead warns against Hep C drugs from buyers clubs, says patients may be at risk. *MoneyControl.com*, 22 May, Retrieved from www.moneycontrol.com/news/business/gilead-warns-against-hep-c-drugs-from-buyers-cVinh-Kim; Nguyen. (2010). *The republic of therapy: Triage and sovereignty in West Africa's time of AIDS*. Durham: Duke University Press; Egrot, M. (2014). Donner des médicaments: L'esprit du don en marge des logiques du soin. In A. Desclaux, & M. Egrot (dir.), *Anthropologie du médicament au Sud. La pharmaceuticalisation à ses marges*. Paris: L'Harmattan. pp. 63–77; Taverne, B., & Egrot, M. (2014). Enjeux locaux et globaux d'un "trafic" de médicaments antirétroviraux entre le Sénégal et l'Europe. In A. Desclaux, M. Egrot (dir.), *Anthropologie du médicament au Sud. La pharmaceuticalisation à ses marges*. Paris: L'Harmattan. pp. 113–128. Retrieved from www.moneycontrol.com/news/business/gilead-warns-against-hep-c-drugs-from-buyers-clubs-says-patients-may-be-at-risk-2285193.html.

15 Nguyen, V.-K. (2010). *The republic of therapy: Triage and sovereignty in West Africa's time of AIDS*. Durham: Duke University Press; Egrot, M. (2014). Donner des médicaments: L'esprit du don en marge des logiques du soin. In A. Desclaux, M. Egrot (dir.), *Anthropologie du médicament au Sud. La pharmaceuticalisation à ses marges*. Paris: L'Harmattan. pp. 63–77; Taverne, B., & Egrot, M. (2014). Enjeux locaux et globaux d'un "trafic" de médicaments antirétroviraux entre le

Sénégal et l'Europe. In A. Desclaux, M. Egrot (dir.), *Anthropologie du médicament au Sud. La pharmaceuticalisation à ses marges*. Paris: L'Harmattan. pp. 113–128.

16 Interview of an access to medicines activist, New Delhi, 22 March 2016.

17 Interview of an access to medicines activist, New Delhi, 26 April 2016.

18 SOS Hépatites, lettre ouverte à Marisol Touraine, 1 April 2016. Retrieved from www.soshepatites.org/wp-content/uploads/2016/04/Lettre-ouverte-au-ministre-de-la-sante.pdf.

19 Interview of an access to medicines activist, New Delhi, 26 April 2016.

20 Jefferys, G. Treating Hep C with Chinese APIs: An early solution revisited. 19 April 2016. Retrieved from http://hepatitisctreatment.homestead.com/Treating-Hep-C-with-APIs.html.

21 Interview of an access to medicines activist, Pune, 19 May 2016.

22 This declaration, however, did not change the situation very much. Chabrol, F., David, P.-M., & Krikorian, G. (2017). Rationing hepatitis C treatment in the context of austerity policies in France and Cameroon: A transnational perspective on the pharmaceuticalization of healthcare systems, *Social Science and Medicine*, 187, pp. 243–250.

23 Interview of Carine, Paris, 1 July 2016.

24 Interview of Asha, Bihar, 24 December 2016. The interviews cited in this section were carried out in the course of fieldwork in Bihar with Marine Al Dahdah and Aalok Kashyap in December 2016.

25 Data taken from the article: Al Dahdah, M., Kumar, A., & Quet, M. Empty stocks and loose papers. Governing medicines through informality in rural Bihar, *International Sociology*, 33/6, 2018, pp. 778–795.

26 Interview of a village doctor, 19 December 2016.

27 Interview of a village doctor, 19 December 2016.

28 Interview of a pharmaceuticals retailer, Bihar, 21 December 2016.

29 Das, V., & Das, R. K. (2006). Pharmaceuticals in urban ecologies: The register of the local. In A. Petryna, A. Lakoff, & A. Kleinman (Eds.), *Global pharmaceuticals: Ethics, markets, practices*. Durham: Duke University Press. pp. 171–205.

30 Pinto, S. (2004). Development without Institutions: Ersatz medicine and the politics of everyday life in rural north India. *Cultural Anthropology*, 19/3, pp. 337–364.

31 Ouzayd, F., *et al.* (2012). Medicine drugs circuit: Analyze performance with simulation models. *International Journal of Computer Applications* (0975 – 8887), 53/14, September; Narayanan, L., & Guennif, S. (2008). A status report on the health care sector in France. *Journal of Health Management*, September.

32 On the "politics of life", see in particular: Rose, N. (2001). *The politics of life itself, theory, culture & society.* 18/6, pp. 1–30; Fassin, D. (2009). Another politics of life is possible. *Theory, Culture and Society*, 26/5, pp. 44–60.

Conclusion

Illicit medicines, expelled medicines

In her book *Expulsions*, the sociologist Saskia Sassen examines a phenomenon that she describes as "complex". This phenomenon emerges out of the convergence of heterogeneous logics that she intends to grasp in a single analytical step.[1] Expulsions of persons, land grabbing, and extraction of resources are all part of a single dynamic that constantly deepens inequality and social exclusion. Expulsions, despite the fact that they take place in an increasingly regulated and technologically sophisticated world, are, in fact, a savage sorting, bearing witness to the persistent brutality of the contemporary world. Sassen highlights several characteristics of today's expulsions. They are produced – or rather, manufactured – by means of technical tools, such as financial instruments. They are characterised by their diversity, by their serious consequences for the people and spaces concerned, and by their sheer scope and scale – a result of the globalisation of markets. According to Sassen, the development of eviction as a principle of government is inseparable from the political and economic turn of the 1980s, which led to the emergence of powerful "predatory formations" that increasingly produce and capture ever-larger shares of economic wealth. Central to her argument is that these expulsions are in no way incompatible with "growth" as the privileged indicators of capitalist development define it.

In Sassen's book, there is no reference to pharmaceutical markets, but her approach to the "systemic logic" that underlies the market suggests a parallel to the specific case with which we are dealing here. In the first place, illicit medicines are constantly presented as those that have to be "excluded" from distribution chains. Sassen's remarks on the construction of expulsion lead us to reiterate a point that I have discussed here at length – that the public health argument for combating "fake medicines" may not be as simple as it seems. The issues involved can possibly be better understood by linking them to the systemic logic of expulsion that has dominated recent decades. Second, expulsions share a common logic and as a corollary to drug expulsions, people are also being expelled. In the fight against illicit medicines, the line between banning smugglers and banning patients can be very fine indeed. The

DOI: 10.4324/9781003194767-12

same can be said of the line between punishing dishonest manufacturers and hampering local industries, and also of the line between seizing the bad drugs and breaking off treatment.

Sassen's remarks are also valuable here because they reaffirm that there is a deep-seated link between exclusionary practices and market growth. According to her, the revival of eviction practices has come hand in hand with new strategies designed to produce and monopolise wealth. The notion of "illicit medicine" was reformulated by applying the notion of "counterfeiting" in the course of the period described by Sassen when pharmaceutical profits recorded continuous growth. Medications, whether illicit, "fake", or "counterfeit" are apparently not so much a brake on growth as a driving force: they are part of a dynamic process that renews forms of ownership, of circulation, and of promotion in the pharmaceutical industry, boosting profits. At last, what Sassen proposes is to broaden the attention we pay to phenomena such as inequality and exclusion; they play an important part in mechanisms often perceived first and foremost as "neutral", that is, technical, complex, intricate, and interdependent. In much the same way, my investigation of illicit drugs helped me to show that vital issues such as consumer citizenship are now being linked to a knotted nexus of regulatory standards, monitoring technologies, appropriation norms, and means of transport. In the spirit of Sassen's proposal, this has led me to hypothesise a "logistic regime" as the form of organisation of the flow of objects.

The illicit as an indicator of the dynamics of capital

Taking a stand at the crossroads between various disciplines (science and technology studies [STS], sociology of development, sociology of industry, sociology of public problems, critical geography, and philosophy), this book has made several proposals. The first proposal concerns the public problem of illicit medicines. Hopefully, I have clarified this problem, keeping well away from the mainstream discourse on "criminals", "pharmaceutical terrorists", and other common denunciations. Rowing against the current of this moralising view that is often steered by the industry of the Northern hemisphere, I have tried to go into the problem in greater depth. I have drawn attention to the influence of industrial transformations that are taking place on a worldwide scale, to the evolution of the modes of control and regulation of the quality of pharmaceuticals, and to the predominance of an overall logistics regime that has given rise to several forms of opposition. This has also given me the opportunity to think again about the contribution of the social sciences to health activists' discourse. Advocates of access to medicines have continually separated problems that are usually linked: discourse on counterfeiting link counterfeiting both to intellectual property on the one hand and to the quality of medicines on the other. Disconnecting these different issues seem, in many ways, to be both important and urgent. But there is a complement that seems to be just as important: understanding how these problems have been rendered, if not entirely unsolvable, at least so thoroughly interlocked, so intractable as to discourage investigation. Exactly why it is so difficult to separate the issue of intellectual property from public health, police surveillance, technologies, and standards – and even from the representations in one country in another country's media? Can the social sciences help us understand? Meanwhile, complicating matters even further, all these issues are based on historical narratives that stem from the colonial and postcolonial past. The issue of illicit medicine has also made it possible to investigate the construction of market regulation "in real time", as it has actually been taking place. It shows, with markets becoming international and public health becoming global, the tensions that actors are facing and the ways in which they are trying to resolve them.

A second interest of this book is methodological. It is based on the in-depth study, within STS, of multi-sited approaches involving the observation of South–South circulations, particularly that between India and Kenya. One contribution is the postcolonial analysis of contemporary science and technology. But although the approach is focused on links between two countries, it is not a "biographical" style of narrative that seeks to follow, for example, the path taken by such-and-such a drug. On the contrary, my project has been to identify transit zones in which institutional forces make themselves felt and exercise control. Many authors have focused their work on "following" objects, sometimes running the risk of underestimating the forces (assemblages and operations) that govern their trajectories. This is why I opted in favour of a multi-sited approach rather than simply trying to "follow" movements. From a methodological point of view, I have banked on the discipline of controversy analysis in going into the criticisms made by actors, drawing crucial inspiration from Luc Boltanski's critique of sociology. This has entailed expanding the critique by making additional investigations in order to go beyond the controversy in question – for example, going into the sociology of industrial practices, regulatory and control practices.

Last but not least, this book proposes several ways to approach the question of the exercise of power in a global world. These consist in reversing the status of the illicit medicine. Usually seen as an object to be analysed, the illicit medicine can be used differently, as a 'developer' – an agent that reveals a latent photograph: in this case, the image of technological capitalism in the act of organising flows of technical commodities. My study suggests that we consider the situation in which the flow of objects is brought under control and the hybrid forms of hegemony involved in this – a hegemony linking discourse, practices, and the material forms that organise them. I describe these using notions such as "security dynamics", "logistic regimes", and "colonisation of trajectories". Finally, this implies reintroducing objects (or "techno-products"[2]) into discussions of science and government, seeing them not so much as tools of government (there is already a plethora of literature on this), but rather as objects to be governed, that is, as things to be controlled by means of routines. In other words, we should reflect on the contribution of science and technology to market organisation. Seen from this viewpoint, one of the main contributions of the book is that to an understanding of the world of objects, of the techno-scientific amenities that surround us and among which we live; and of the ways in which this world is organised and the tensions that stem from this organisation. I have tried to point out not only how this regime affects our lives but also how our deviations from it indicate contradictions that sometimes suggest loopholes, ways out of a situation that can seem completely blocked. Our lives are electric, canalised by the multiple circuits of merchant flows.

But if a spark?

Notes

1 Sassen, S. (2014). *Expulsions, brutality and complexity in the global economy*. Harvard: Harvard University Press.
2 Pestre, D. (dir.) (2014). *Le gouvernement des technosciences. Gouverner le progrès et ses dégâts depuis 1945*. Paris: La Découverte.

Post-scriptum

The great takeover

When the French version of this book got published in 2018, I was far from imagining the crisis which was ahead. In early 2020 though, as soon as the COVID-19 pandemic started, I received emails and phone calls from a few journalists asking my opinion upon the impact it would have on the global circulation of medicines. People and organisations were already observing and denouncing the resurgence of fake masks, fake alcoholic gels, fake chloroquine. What was going to happen when fake vaccines would reach the market – which they did a few months later? I was struck, during some of these discussions, by the power of the narrative according to which *mafias* and criminal groups are the only ones to be held responsible for such dysfunctions. One day, after an hour-long discussion with a journalist from a large French newspaper, trying to explain that the circulation of illicit health commodities also had to do with how markets are locked by intellectual property and with how the wealthy countries are protecting their industry's interests, I was struck to find that my explanation had been summed up in one line. The paper's main focus was the role of criminal groups in the globalisation processes; not a thing was said about the responsibility of multinational pharmaceutical groups and the wealthy states regarding how medicines can be accessed. Accusing gangsters was definitely more exciting than trying to explain capital accumulation dynamics.

For this reason, I think it matters today more than ever to reset our understanding of illicit medicines and to locate it within the general picture of global pharmaceutical markets. For one thing, I know is that the dominant explanations cannot account for current injustices. Early 2021, how could we explain the scandal of the distribution of vaccine doses in the world? How could we explain the fact that 10 countries have appropriated 75% of the available vaccines? The laboratories are fully accountable in this situation: in February 2021, Moderna, which had received nearly a billion dollars from CEPI, a collective financing fund, still had no distribution agreement with countries classified among the poorest. This is in direct contradiction with CEPI's requirements, whose funding commits companies to distribute vaccines equitably and not to the highest bidder. But companies are not the only ones to blame. Rich countries are also at the forefront of this scandal, systematically accommodating collective efforts to their own interests. Canada, one of the ten richest countries in the world, is to receive 1.9 million doses through Covax (a scheme supposed to benefit the poorest countries). The other G7 countries haven't even bothered, too busy buying and pre-empting doses and bypassing Covax – Trump's USA, for example, simply withdrawn from the scheme. The World Health Organisation called this a catastrophic moral failure in January 2021, but that didn't seem to change much, given the determination of the corporations and the richest countries to corner the world's vaccine production. The indignity of the situation at least clarifies what is deeply corrupt about globalised health capitalism – a regime obsessed with capturing flows when it should be in charge of the equitable distribution of care.

Let's take a closer look. Despite President Macron's soppy statements about the importance for rich countries to give a share of their vaccine stocks to the poorest, the facts speak for themselves: the economies dominating the global market have simply grabbed the available doses with the help of the industry. Yet, it is clear that the fight against the virus requires widespread vaccination and the increased risk of contagion as the virus mutates makes this all the more urgent. Is this situation an effect of "vaccine nationalism" as we read here or there? Is it the inevitable consequence of the management of health commodities through market rules? Is it a combination of national egoisms and private interests? The reasons for this aberrant situation are highlighted by the main barriers to equitable access to vaccines on a global scale. At the heart of this system, many voices denounce the centrality of intellectual property. It is primarily because the companies that own the vaccine formulas refuse to share them that current production remains so small. But suspending patents would not be enough to change the situation as it is accompanied by a series of problems. This is evidenced by the difficulties in the very countries where the patent-holding companies operate to obtain doses.

A deeper analysis of the profound injustice of the situation shows that only some of the reasons are directly linked to patents, such as the lack of transparency in price negotiations. Prices are rising at the expense of countries with less room to negotiate. Several developing countries (South Africa, Uganda) end up paying much more for the vaccine than richer countries, which means access to fewer doses or even no access at all. Yet another series of problems are more indirectly linked to intellectual property: this is the case of production capacities that rely on technology transfer. Indeed, the suspension of a patent does not automatically lead to the manufacture of a drug. It is necessary to transfer the know-how and techniques and in the current situation, the slightest delay can become months. Countries with production capacities are clearly given an advantage, as many governments reserve the right to control or even ban exports in the interests of their population, again to the detriment of countries that do not have such resources. It is also the case of regulatory work: better-resourced authorities in rich countries have enabled them to access the vaccine more quickly. Finally, it is the case of distribution, transport, and storage capacities. The current situation thus reveals the importance of underestimated aspects of pharmaceutical capitalism, as "supply chain" capitalism, in ensuring equitable access.[1]

Circulability versus capture

In particular, the current crisis highlights a contradictory dynamic of pharmaceutical markets, which is based on the articulation between the "circulability" of goods and the "capture" of flows. This contradiction is at the heart of the book you are holding. On the one hand, the aim is to put the greatest number of products on the market in order to accumulate the maximum value. As a result, the architecture of pharmaceutical markets aims to accelerate innovation, marketing, production, and distribution of pharmaceuticals as much as possible. This is evident in the role played by regulatory authorities: their role is not to restrict the release of products but to facilitate market access for candidate goods, maintaining as much confidence as possible in their quality and efficacy. The advantage of rich countries in this respect is obvious, as their infrastructure of circulability is much more powerful than that of poor countries. But on the other hand, a key issue in the pharmaceutical regime is to capture the flows once they are released. Production activity has been massively delocalised, and the energy of the firms that dominate the market is devoted to maintaining control over the flow of goods and the value they represent. This exercise in capture is carried out by controlling production sites (who has the right to produce?), transport channels (who can distribute? who can store?), and more generally, the rules of circulation (which medicines are authorised to circulate and to which destination?). It is not insignificant that the first vaccines put on the market required expensive and complicated storage facilities: the means of circulation must be mastered in order to capture the flows and the richest countries benefit from this.

In normal times, the contradiction between circulability and capture is not, or hardly, problematic: the control of firms and rich states overflows seems "natural" because it is based on "objective" criteria of quality, effectiveness, or health safety. But in times of crisis, the issues raised by this linkage take precedence over the rest: the control exercised for the purpose of capture runs counter to circulability because, on the one hand, it limits the marketing, manufacture, and distribution of a sufficient number of vaccines, and because, on the other hand, the most powerful players divert the flows to their own benefit by ostensibly excluding the others. As a result, populations, public health institutions, and governments no longer know which authority to rely on to reintroduce circulability and counter the effects of capture. This can result in the formation of new alliances and the recognition of new forms of legitimisation of goods. For example, in a cacophonous European context, some governments have chosen to look elsewhere and to create alliances with manufacturers that are not acknowledged by the European authorities. This can also involve the resurgence of uncontrolled products or products of dubious quality: in a number of countries, we have seen the proliferation of fake treatments (chloroquine, remdesivir), fake hydroalcoholic gels, and fake vaccines. Once again, fake products are simply a manifestation of a conflicting order. And this order is conflictual because it is deeply unequal.

From this point of view, the current crisis in the pharmaceutical markets has everything to do with the crisis of a *logistical regime* in which the problems of accessibility, law, and industrial capacity (innovation, production, and distribution) should be posed together and on an international scale. In many respects, it is the same problems and contradictions as the recent shortages of masks, reagents, and respirators, which have also resulted in inequalities of access and injustice. By extension, the trials currently being experienced by the health goods sector are simply an expression of the more general failure of a logistical organisation of the world that has made the production of surplus value through the management of flows – and not a reflection on the contribution of goods to global well-being – its central concern. The drama of pharmaceutical logistics thus re-enacts in miniature that of logistical power as a contemporary mode of government.[2]

Reclaiming logistics capitalism

There are several possible courses of action to deal with this situation, some of which are already underway, such as the current request for a suspension of patents to meet the needs of the pandemic. There is also an urgent need to strengthen patent pooling processes, such as the C-TAP mechanism, which has not been mobilised as I write these words and purchasing pooling funds such as Covax. To do this, it would be naive to rely on the goodwill of rights holders, who are currently struggling to keep the intellectual property as they have defined it, that is, in their interests, untouched.

But again, intellectual property is not the only obstacle to more equitable access. Indeed, the countries that have been most protected from vaccine shortages have been those with pharmaceutical production or distribution capacity. We must, therefore, not stop at knocking down intellectual property but encourage the building of regional production, innovation, and regulatory capacities. This work is both urgent to respond to the pandemic and necessary to meet the future challenges of international public health. If health has indeed become global, then the means of care must be better distributed to avoid future disasters.

More generally, we must therefore collectively regain power over the operations of circulability and the capture of flows to ensure that they are no longer systematically implemented by the same actors and in the service of the same interests. We need to build new production poles, new instances of circulation, which will correspond to new directions of flows. The rich countries and the large multinationals will certainly be reluctant to contribute to such a programme, but this is such an international of flows that must be shaped: it would prevent our societies to concomitantly manufacture "essential medicines" and superfluous populations.

Notes

1 Tsing, A. L., Supply chains and the human condition. *Rethinking Marxism*, 2009, 21/2, pp. 148–176.

2 Cowen, D. (2014). *The deadly life of logistics: Mapping violence in global trade*. Minneapolis: University of Minnesota Press.

Index